NORTH AMERICA

SCALE
One mile

TETOBE PASS

REEFS

$16

MAHANATOA

ANATONU

RA'IRUA

VAIURU

Ra'ivavae

EFS

OCEAN

EQUATOR

Galapagos

SOUTH
AMERIC

A4

S I A

Marquesas

Tuamotu

Tahiti

Ra'ivavae

Tubua'i
Rurutu

Austral

Pitcairn

Easter

ISLANDS of the PACIFIC

Island of Passion
RA'IVAVAE

Drawings by James Scott

Photographs by the Author

Island of Passion

RA'IVAVAE

BY DONALD MARSHALL

London

GEORGE ALLEN & UNWIN LTD

RUSKIN HOUSE, MUSEUM STREET

PRINTED IN GREAT BRITAIN
BY BRADFORD AND DICKENS

To

JAMES McCONNAUGHEY

AROFA

PROJECT TAHITI, a long-term study of human behavior based upon the Polynesian research archives of J. Frank Stimson, was initiated by the American Museum of Natural History and sponsored by the Peabody Museum of Salem, Massachusetts. This book reports on a segment of that project. The field research was made possible through the continued interest of James and Susanne McConnaughey and Cornelius Crane, and by a grant from the Committee for Research in Problems of Sex, Medical Division of the National Academy of Sciences, National Research Council. A John Simon Guggenheim fellowship, awarded to aid my subsequent studies of Polynesian leadership and social structure on the island of Mangaia, was of crucial assistance in enabling me to carry out the Ra'ivavae expedition.

My presentation of the ways of life on Ra'ivavae owes much to the creative editing of Kermit Lansner, as well as to the advice of James Perkins. The book itself stems from the interest of Lebaron Barker and Hamilton Basso. I have used brief sections of Stimson's translations of Polynesian literature[1] to better illustrate cultural patterns than could my own prose.

The analyses of sexual behavior stem from attitudes inspired by the late Professor Alfred Kinsey and by Paul Gebhard

[1] *Songs and Tales of the Sea Kings* by J. Frank Stimson, edited by Donald Stanley Marshall, Ph.D., with contributions by Van Wyck Brooks and Susanne McConnaughey (Salem, Mass.: The Peabody Museum, 1957).

7

and his associates at the Institute for Sex Research at Indiana University.

Shirley Morrow Marshall provided immeasurable personal and material support and encouragement.

To those individuals and organizations who made it possible for me to work with J. Frank Stimson, that master of Polynesian language, and especially to my good companions on the expedition to Ra'ivavae—Virginie Bjarnne Richmond, James Scott, F. Alan Seabrook, and Tioti—I am profoundly grateful.

DONALD MARSHALL
Tahiti, French Polynesia, SOUTH PACIFIC

CONTENTS

9

CONTENTS

ILLUSTRATIONS

11

ILLUSTRATIONS

Island of Passion
RA'IVAVAE

PROLOGUE

I WILL never forget the strange, offhand way the whole thing began, this task which has filled my life for the past ten years.

The inner office of Dr. Harry L. Shapiro, Curator of Anthropology at the American Museum of Natural History, is a round room which looks like one of those watchtowers which crown the old captains' houses up and down Cape Cod. It is the office of a working scientist, filled with all the material of his subject: pieces of whitened bone, artifacts from the far corners of the earth, bulky manuscripts describing the customs of primitive peoples, books, instruments, the debris of a hundred different civilizations. When I came to see him for the first time, my mission was a simple one. I was a general anthropologist who had never been out in the field; and I had come to speak to Shapiro about areas where I might begin work and get the firsthand training which is indispensable to our science. We talked about one place or another. We talked about the perennial problem which anthropologists always face: how to get money to finance an expedition. We talked about unsolved problems and unexplored lands.

Suddenly Shapiro reached into an old-fashioned, black leather bag and took out a bulky manuscript. It was in four bound volumes, a massive document of thousands of words typed on an ancient varitype machine. "Here, take a look at this," he said. "See if it interests you. If it does, take it home and read it. You may be the man I've been looking for."

And so I was hooked.

The manuscript was by J. Frank Stimson, a legendary figure in the world of Polynesian ethnology whom Shapiro had joined in an expedition some years before. Its subject—all four volumes of it—was the island of Ra'ivavae, or High Island, a spot of land in the South Pacific, four hundred miles from Tahiti. As I pored over the manuscript during the next few days I realized that an entirely new insight into Polynesia was opening before me. Stimson had looked deep into the past of Ra'ivavae and he had put together a picture of such grandeur, of such dark and vital magnificence, as had never been painted in all the literature on the South Seas.

I learned that two centuries ago the island of Ra'ivavae had been a land of extraordinary beauty. The weathered slopes of her mountains were covered with groves of handsome breadfruit, chestnut, and ironwood trees—the ground beneath free of any undergrowth. In the valleys, held back by an intricate series of terraced dikes, lay sheets of clean, glistening water. Under them grew taro, the food that nourished the thriving island. From the shallow lagoon and from the deep sea farther out came the ever-present fish which gave savor to the taro. Here too was the home of the great sea turtle, hunted by the bravest of the young and eaten only by the nobles and priests.

In its prime Ra'ivavae had been alive with people, proud of themselves and their heritage, of their families and their land; accustomed to sing the praises of their beautiful island in songs which show an intimate love for every familiar place.

> Our bodies are like the tiny-leaved mint in fragrance;
> They have been anointed with the sweet-scented sap of
>   the wild ginger root,
> Gathered on the bold promontory, Hill-of-the-children,
>   jutting into the blue reflection of the lagoon,

From the western flank of the mountain called Life-giving-
*   creator.*
The secluded nook, Land-crab-scuttling-over-the-flowering-
*   dell, is our trysting place,*
Where the plover twitters as it snatches a small fry
*   from the brook, clamoring waters.*

Like most Polynesians, before the blessings of Western civilization arrived, the people of Ra'ivavae were a handsome
group, muscular and graceful. The warriors wore their lengthy
hair in topknots, the women's was close cropped. Both removed all other hair from their bodies. Their bronze skins,
tattooed with the insignia of rank and clan, glistened with
flower-scented oil. Their headdresses were simple turbans. But
for occasions of war or ritual they put on high feather helmets.
Around their loins they wore breech cloths or kilts; from their
shoulders flowed cloaks made of bark cloth. Sometimes these
were pristine white. At other times they were multicolored with
the brilliant dyes of the island. The ears of these men and
women were pierced, and in them they wore feathers or
flowers. On many breasts polished pearl-shell pendants glinted.
Clasped in the hands of the able-bodied males were the insignia of manhood—the ironwood club, spear, or quarterstaff
of the warrior, the symbolic staff of the kings and priests.

Life on Ra'ivavae was filled with a constant round of vivid
experiences. Compared to it the existence of the present-day
Polynesian is a pale thing indeed. From Stimson's account I
could see one aspect as an eternal cycle of pleasure and celebration. Any occasion might be one for delight and rejoicing:
the completion of a temple or a house, the arrival of a bird-
prowed ship from a far-off land, a great catch of fish; birth,
puberty, marriage, death. For these events, great masses of
people gathered from the different parts of the island. In preparation, the dance masters drilled their troupes while warriors

2   17

practiced their re-creations of great battles of the past. Mountains of food were the invariable accompaniment of these festivals, and great care went into the preparation of the meals. When the day of the celebration arrived, the temple drums and trumpets thundered, bands of musicians played on their gongs and clappers, while through the noise came the mournful sound of the nose flute. When the music died away orators would stand up to speak of the reason for the celebration and link it with other great festivals of the past. And then there would be singing and dancing and eating for hours on end—sometimes, even, for days and nights on end.

Yet as I read Stimson's manuscript and learned of the endless pleasures which waited the natives of Ra'ivavae in its great days, I realized that this was only a superficial aspect of their life. Beneath was something deeper and darker which set this strange island apart from the other Polynesian places which have so often figured in tales and travel books. This was an island of passion. There were accounts of terrible battles and of erotic rites. I felt that life in Ra'ivavae was caught between the twin poles of procreation and destruction, between love and death.

From childhood on, the people of the island were steeped in these passions. I read that the most vigorous of the male children were brought up as warriors, their genitals massaged with special unguents to give them courage and virility. As the old chant went, "anointed with the valor-bestowing lotion of the sweet-scented mountain fern." Trained from his earliest years in the use of the spear and club, quarterstaff and sling, the boy could look forward to that day when he would be consecrated as a soldier, honored by the phrase, "mighty warrior, proud defender of the homeland." Those who were not found suitable were trained in other crafts, such as the use of the adze, with which they might spend their days constructing the great ships which set sail to far-off lands. Those who were born into priestly families usually became priests. They would spend years committing to memory the history of their ancestors as well as the prayers to the gods which would insure the virility and continued procreation of the race.

If the men were bred for war and building and religion, the women were brought up for love. The girl children were carefully nurtured and pampered, their skins kept free of blemish and protected from the darkening effects of sunlight. More striking, their sexual organs were the subject of special attention. The clitoris, in particular, was massaged and kneaded by the mother. As the girl child grew older, the organ was tied up with special fibres so that it might be continuously enlarged. The culmination of this practice was the display of the girl's private parts within the sacred confines of a temple. There the clitoris was first inspected and measured by the priest. Then, there was a public ceremony at which the girl and her age mates displayed themselves to the young warriors among whom they would find their husbands.

For the boy, too, there was a "rite of passage" on reaching the age when he was sexually capable. This was a more rapid and less public affair than the one the girls underwent. The male ordeal only involved slitting the upper foreskin and an aftertreatment which would result in a type of scar tissue which left the glans permanently exposed. Then the boy was instructed in the mysteries of sex by a priest; after this came a more practical episode, the removal of the superincision scab by actual intercourse with an experienced partner.

Almost everything on ancient Ra'ivavae was circumscribed by both religious and secular rules. Food-stealing brought public shame and punishment. The disemboweling spear awaited those who tampered with boundary stones or broke the *tapu*. A girl's refusal to sleep with a king might bring a brutal punishment—though one condoned by the customs of Ra'ivavae: she would be raped by a band of the royal followers in public.

And then there were the ties of duty. Woe to the family heir who could not recite his family genealogy in accord with the knotted cord records. Pity the man who could not prove his title to land by reciting in detail his inherited rights and how they came to be.

Looming over everything on Ra'ivavae were the red, stark, stylized images of the gods. Through those forboding stone statues the gods themselves spoke to the people of the island, called down by priestly prayers and sacrifice. But they spoke to the islanders in other ways, too, for all nature was a divine manifestation. The chirp of the crickets signified the presence of the gods as did the peal of thunder. The moan of the wind, the cry of birds, the multicolored arch of a rainbow all spoke of the nearness of the deities. In the subtleties of nature, the Ra'ivavaean could decry the favor or disfavor of the gods who were all around him. He could learn what the outcome of a battle would be, or how the winds would blow on his next voyage, or who would live and who would die.

And since this was so, the natives of Ra'ivavae prayed constantly to their gods, trying to propitiate them at every turn. There were prayers to protect the island from raiders. There were prayers for victory in war and for the completion of any communal enterprise. But most important of all were the prayers and rites in the months of June and November. For it was then that the islander prayed for an abundance of food and an abundance of children. In June the priests paced out the boundaries of the lands, and then prayed for the fertility of the food plants. In November the prayers were for the fecundity of fish.

Most of these prayers were given at the marae, the sacred areas which covered Ra'ivavae. Built from the heavy, volcanic slabs quarried from the mountains of the island, these areas had great paved courts, altars, carved friezes, and lavish furnishings. They were studded with stone phalluses and lined with natural representations of women in various stages of pregnancy. And in these marae, during the prayers for abundance and fertility, actual scenes of copulation took place, often with many couples taking part.

The terrible passion which set man against man, group against group in bouts of brutal warfare was the balance to this celebration of the senses. A constant series of orgiastic rites provided a mechanism which insured the continuity of the race, so often threatened by death in battle. War and sex went hand in hand in ancient Ra'ivavae.

This was the broad outline of the civilization which Stimson had painted. Yet his two thousand-page manuscript, crammed with the most intimate details of life on Ra'ivavae, was only a small part of the vast amount of material he had collected in forty years of work in Polynesia. Stimson was a genius who had gone through a half-dozen other professions before he settled down to his life work of understanding Polynesian culture through the study of its language. But he was an embattled genius, constantly attacked by a more orthodox anthropologist who wondered about his material, suspected his radical conclusions, and was offended by the importance he gave to sex.

Shapiro understood all this. When I returned after reading the manuscript, deeply moved by its extraordinary contents, he told me that he wanted someone to go down to Tahiti, where Stimson lived, to cull the mountain of material which the old man had gathered and decide what was worth preserving and publishing. This treasure included studies of other islands, vast linguistic works, translations of chants and stories, notebooks filled with detailed accounts of the customs of the Polynesian people.

The idea fascinated me. There was a scope to Stimson's work which answered to my own needs. I had been a soldier and seen all the skills and passions of man brought to bear in one great enterprise. Then I became an anthropologist who never settled into a restricted specialty, but wanted to take the full range of human behavior as my subject. Suddenly Polynesia seemed the human laboratory where I could do my work and Stimson the pivot around which my researches could turn.

Moreover, Stimson's manuscript on Ra'ivavae posed problems which were tantalizing in themselves. There was a mystery about his account which seemed worth solving, since there is an intrinsic fascination in the way an anthropologist finds his evidence, pieces it together, and draws his conclusions. A part of Stimson's description of Ra'ivavae was at odds with all we once knew about the life of the Polynesians. It conjured up a dark grandeur which had never emerged in the books of other writers. The islanders of the South Seas had always been known as brave fighters, great travelers, blithe lovers of pleasure; but this awesome side to their existence which Stimson stressed had never been spelled out. As a student I had combed the literature on Polynesia, and although I found occasional intimations that these islands were something less than Paradise, few commentators ventured much farther. Only the great art of Polynesia, often buried in the basements of museums, gave me pause.

Was Stimson exaggerating? Was he projecting his own deepest feelings and wishes on a vanished world? Had he forged a mythical culture out of the odds and ends of information which various men had given him? Had these informants, in fact, lied? Stalking the pages of Stimson's manuscript was that great question: what is truth?

Years later I learned more about the method which Stimson had used to compile his account of life on Ra'ivavae. It is worth mentioning here, for some of the same persons who helped him delve into the past were to do the same for me when I finally visited the island. Stimson had worked with a brilliant man named Alan Seabrook. Together they visited

Ra'ivavae, talked with the people, explored the island, and collected as much data as they could. But most of their voluminous information came from two informants: Tauira'i, who was living on Ra'ivavae, and Hapai, who was then making his home in Tahiti. When Stimson first met Tauira'i, the Polynesian was a man of forty, a young sage who seemed to have an unlimited amount of information about the island's history and culture. He disliked talking about these matters, however, and preferred to write down his answers to a series of questions in blank notebooks, saying that he "wanted to go home, think it over, and then write about things." Everyone said that his knowledge "came from a book," since he was too young to remember much of the island's past, and moreover, he was not bright enough to remember everything that he had been told. But no one had ever seen this book and it was to remain a mystery even to this day.

Hapai was something else again. He was older than Tauira'i and he boasted that he was a "master of the ancient knowledge, the last living student of the school conducted to teach the first-born sons the great learning of the past." According to him, the first Christian pastor of Ra'ivavae, the eminent Ha'uti, had decided that the younger members of the nobility of Ra'ivavae must know the story of the past. Gathering together twenty of the "first sons," he placed them around a table in his house illuminated only by the flickering lights of candlenuts set in stone bowls. For two years they listened intently and learned by ear the chants and the knowledge of ancient days. Their master forced them to repeat their lessons until he knew that they had mastered them word for word, for there was an ancient injunction against changing words brought down from the past.

Hapai stated that of the twenty young noblemen who had started the school, only six had finished, and only he of these six now lived. After each class during the two years in which the school was held, he had gone home and written down all that had been taught. Ha'uti had enjoined him not to reveal this knowledge to others, saying that the people of today had no respect for such knowledge and that they would mock and defame him.

Because he was a Christian pastor, however, Ha'uti had not been willing to reveal his most sacred knowledge—the erotic basis of the ancient religion. He advised Hapai to go to Haramū, an old man living nearby, and have him explain the secret lore. Haramū agreed, but cautioned Hapai not to reveal it to the common people or to the disbelievers of today. Until he confided in Stimson Hapai kept his trust. Stimson felt that he was the greatest sage he had ever met during his long stay in the islands.

I shall have more to say about Tauira'i and Hapai; but it is easy to understand why they intrigued me from the very beginning. The validity of much of Stimson's work rested on the veracity of these two informants.

When I finally accepted Shapiro's suggestion to go down to the South Seas and work with Stimson, I realized that I would have to spend some time on Ra'ivavae before I could know what I was about. There was no way of assessing the truth of Stimson's discoveries without knowing the island as it is today. For even then I thought it unbelievable that such a rich past could vanish without a trace.

But between that moment when I made my decision and the time when I first stepped foot on Ra'ivavae for a prolonged stay, seven long years intervened. Looking back, I realize that I had taken a world on my shoulders when I made that first commitment to look into Stimson's material. To judge his work I had to master all the skills which he had painfully acquired over four decades in Polynesia. Anything else would have been presumptuous. So I went to Tahiti and lived with Stimson on several different occasions, helping him with that massive trove of Polynesian lore he had accumulated. During this period I struck out on field work of my own, adopting the nearby island of Mangaia as my own special laboratory. All the while I tried to raise funds for an extended expedition to Ra'ivavae, but bad luck dogged my efforts—the same bad luck which seems to afflict everyone who takes a serious interest in Ra'ivavae. Plans fell through, backers disappeared, unexpected obstacles blocked my way.

And then finally, in 1957, everything jelled. I found the funds to stage an expedition. Friends loaned me a ship to take a group to Ra'ivavae. I found several colleagues who wanted to go with me and share my work. The long years of preparation were finally over.

The problems I set myself for this expedition were in part the same that occurred to me when I first read Stimson's manuscript. There was first the question as to whether the past of Ra'ivavae was as grand, as erotic, as fierce as Stimson had painted it. To determine this I had to find traces of this old way of life: traces in stone, in words, in behavior, something to corroborate the splendid structure which Stimson had constructed out of his own researches. But even before this I had to understand the island as it is today. For only then could I understand what forces from the past were still alive. Nothing ever dies completely in a society, but it sometimes assumes strange new forms. Had the ways of the West which came to Polynesia long ago completely driven out the ancient customs? Were the basic conditions of life on Ra'ivavae still strong enough to create a link with the past? And what could this island tell me about the ways of man, for this, after all, was my life's work.

All of the facets of human behavior are included within the domain of study of the general anthropologist. But I learned long ago that no matter how broad one's interests may be, no matter how wide an anthropologist's training in theory and technique, to spread his energies too thin when conducting field research may be dangerous. Meaningful answers can be obtained only by concentrating upon the analysis of those factors which relate to a single major facet of human behavior.

It seemed that on ancient Ra'ivavae all of man's aesthetic activities—craftsmanship, art, music, oral literature, and dancing—were directed at war and sex. Despite my avocation as a soldier, I chose sex as the subject of our intensive investigation on Ra'ivavae. This choice stemmed from my personal view of general anthropology, for I believe that the most useful knowledge of human behavior stems from a comparison of past and present activities. Much of man's present behavior is derived from patterns developed in the past, and by comparing past to present, especially when the intervening history is known, we may account for changes in the patterns. Then, by comparing what has happened in several differing cultures throughout the world, we may eventually derive the basic laws of human behavior. In Ra'ivavae warfare no longer existed; therefore, sexual behavior, the eternal basis of human existence, remained as the only major facet for comparison.

The promise that we might learn something of universal significance from a study of sexual behavior on Ra'ivavae stemmed from accidents of both geography and history. Because of its geographic location, Polynesia represents an isolated segment of the Far East which may profitably be contrasted with the West. Through history, until the Europeans arrived in a recent era, there were no outside contacts, no externally inspired changes in the development of Polynesian culture. Thus Ra'ivavaean concepts of sexual behavior were not mingled with the European and Near Eastern religious concepts of sexual morals. The Ra'ivavaean idea of emphasizing the desirability of sexual play by focusing the full force of religious sanction upon copulation—by depiction, precept, and example—was in strong contrast with the narrow, antisexual codes of the first Christian missionaries to Polynesia. Yet during a brief survey trip to Ra'ivavae in 1955, I had seen behavior of such puritanical nature that it reminded me of the rigid atmosphere of my own boyhood in New England. I could see that my major topic of study would be the relationship between sex and religion.

Had the ultimate clash between Christianity and paganism wrought such a change? Or had Stimson's evaluation of early Ra'ivavaean sexual behavior been warped by his own personal interests? It had been charged many times that Stimson was "overly interested in sex." I heard this charge repeated, even by those who most strongly admired his linguistic work, during the period when I had been contacting senior colleagues for their advice as to whether or not to accept the opportunity offered me by Shapiro. To some degree I assured myself that such charges were probably untrue, for when I finally accepted the responsibility of becoming scientific Boswell to Stimson, I began an intensive study of the sexual aspects of human behavior in general and Polynesian behavior in particular. Although there were no university courses given in this subject, through the courtesy of Professor Kinsey and his associates and through years of auxiliary research in archives and museum collections I gradually acquired a substantial background in comparative sexual behavior. Then I was able to say with reasoned conviction that Stimson was not overbalanced in his view on general Polynesian sex life nor did his general data conflict with the mass of evidence I had independently gathered. But whether or not sexual behavior on Ra'ivavae was as dominant in religious practice as Stimson had stated had to be proven by actual field work on the island.

This was the problem I pondered as our ship slipped out of Papeete harbor in Tahiti and set sail for Ra'ivavae.

Chapter One

ECHOES OF GLORY

O ye dying breed!
O dark Goddess of the abyss!
Alas, for your offspring in this World-of-light,
Ever-disappearing in the Twilight-realm,
dimly illumined by the low-hanging Sun.

Now thou hast sunk, O Sun!
Vanished in thy wreath of blood-red streamers
crowning the sunset.

IT WAS early on a stormy September morning that we came into sight of Ra'ivavae—High Island, as it was named by sailors in the last century. Far in the distance the tiny black silhouette stood out against a backdrop of streaming clouds stained as deep a red as the human blood which had once run upon its pagan altars. Even with the black seas raging around, each peak was precisely etched against the early dawn.

An hour later the skies had cleared and the seas were calm. Our ship, the *Mareva*, moved slowly toward the island. *Mareva* is one of those lovely Polynesian names which can only be translated by a handful of English words. It means "she who flits by without visible means of support, is seen for an instant, and then quickly is gone." And as we edged closer to shore I thought of how far this splendid ship had come since the day of her launching. She was built in 1937 by Hodson Brothers of Maine, and her fifty-five-foot wooden hull, rigged as an auxiliary cutter, had known the waters of the West Indies and the

29

Great Lakes under a half-dozen different names. In her time she had been sailed by an amorous Italian industrialist and later by a more serious group of American scientists. I liked to think that this was her most extraordinary voyage.

The members of the expedition joined me at the rail as we sailed through the barrier reef which rings Ra'ivavae. Jim Scott began talking about the unique beauty of the island, with its mountainous backbone rising precipitously from the sea like a great turreted fortress dominating the waters for miles around. Jim had seen other islands—Guadalcanal, Guam, Iwo—for he had been a Marine. But now he was the artist of the expedition. He carried his materials in a simple paper bag and even as we moved up the lagoon he began to sketch the dramatic contours of the island before us.

Zenie was silent. She was the only woman on the expedition and I had written to her months before to ask her help on the trip. Part Tahitian, widely traveled, fluent in the native tongues as well as in French, her presence was necessary if my researches were to be successful. Life among adults in Polynesia is characterized by strong segregation between the sexes. Once a man takes a wife he gives up almost all social contact with other women. In fact, he rarely makes an appearance with his own wife in public. Thus Polynesian men know little of the intimate details of female life. Of necessity, I had to deal with the mature men of the community, for I was in my thirties, married, and interested in such subjects as religion, sex, leadership, and economics. Yet I needed to know what went on among the women. Polynesian matriarchs are a powerful force in the life of both family and village. This was to be Zenie's job; and, as we shall see later, she did it with uncanny skill.

For Alan Seabrook, the approach to Ra'ivavae let loose a flood of old memories, for it was here that he and Stimson had worked together twenty years before. Alan is one of that breed who prefer living in Polynesia to anywhere else in the world.

He is a thinker, a writer, an intellectual, who now works a beautiful plantation in one of the far valleys of Tahiti, where he lives with his wife. I had persuaded him to join me and give me the benefit of his experience and his contacts on High Island. And just as he had gone with Stimson in the old days, so he came with me.

Besides Jim, Zenie, and Alan, I had two full-blooded Polynesians with me on the trip; Tautu and Tioti. One was to return with Captain Temari'i on the *Mareva* when she sailed back to Tahiti. But Tioti stayed and he was to prove of enormous value.

Soon birds began to swoop around the ship and we started to pick out details of the reef islets, the hills behind Ra'irua, and the slopes and cliffs of Anatonu. The morning sunlight glinted from the wave-tossed surface of the water as we ranged the markers of the channel through Tetobe Pass and entered the lagoon. As our craft moved rapidly to the long pier which marks the main village and administrative center of Ra'irua, the waters became completely still.

The "Ra'ivavae welcome" is notorious throughout Central Polynesia. On other islands the population crowds down to the landing place to cry greetings, sniff the new arrivals in the Polynesian *hongi*, and to ask for the latest news from the outside world. But the people of High Island are curiously restrained. Even when a relative arrives it is commonplace for kinsmen to sit nearby on the shore for a long period before going over to shake hands. No exception was made for us. There was scarcely a sign of life in the village. Not an adult was to be seen; no one was at the dock to help us tie up. Just as we made fast, a few children trotted down to watch us solemnly with their great dark eyes. There was a curious emptiness about the scene, a tantalizing lack of life which contrasted strangely with the high spirits of other Polynesian places.

Our stop at Ra'irua was brief, merely long enough to pay

our respects, deliver the mail to the gendarme, and to meet
Taupoa, the medical aid man who had been a friend of Zenie
during the war. I had previously decided that the best location
to set up headquarters would be at Anatonu, the village where
Alan and Frank had worked a generation ago. It was the largest
and most active of the population centers—with the biggest
church on the island. Moreover, Piahuru, the man who might
turn out to be our chief informant, the only French-speaking
inhabitant of the island, lived there. Besides, I knew that
Anatonu was bright and clean, a good place to live and work.
By noon we had completed our administrative formalities and
headed round rocky Vaianaara Peninsula, the northernmost
point of land jutting from the heart of Ra'ivavae. Ahead of us
and to our left were the *motu*, reef islets of many sizes. To our
right ranged the mountainous backbone of the island, crowned
by Mount Hiro, the tallest peak—height 1,434 feet—a silent
witness to the long history of High Island.

No one knows who discovered Ra'ivavae originally, but
there is a rich lore surrounding the island. Long ago, the myth
goes, one of the Polynesian Sea Kings, the *Maninikā*, com-
manding a boatload of the Children of the Sea, fished up this
lovely island out of the Great Ocean of Kiva. Behind him in the
west—a direction still termed *muri*, "rearwards,"—lay his ancestral Havaiki, famous in song and tale. Nothing is known of
this era, but it is possible to infer that Ra'ivavae was the heart-
land from which later voyagers spread out to the rest of Central
Polynesia. The first name of the island was Ragiha, "sacred
Heaven," and later Tahiti Nui. Nearly five hundred years ago,
when the young priests and royalty—the first-born sons—departed to extend their sway over the other nearby islands, they
remembered it with sad nostalgia as Rangivavae—"Sundered
Heavens."

Over the centuries the inhabitants of Ra'ivavae multiplied.

32

The descendants of the original settlers intermingled with those who came later; some, explorers like themselves, others, voyagers and fishermen who had been blown off course into the haven of Ra'ivavae. As the population increased, the valleys were gradually terraced and irrigated so that the staple food of Polynesia, the taro root, could be cultivated. Lines of allegiance and kinship hardened, and some groups took authority over others. Soon more massive divisions arose. Tribes were segmented and subtribes multiplied. Land grew scarce and time hung heavy. Warfare became a constant activity, with certain tribes extending their sway over others, and then being completely wiped out by massacre or migration. By the seventeenth century Ra'ivavae was the home of adventurers who sailed their ships to other lands—to the nearby Austral Islands of Tubua'i and Rurutu, to faraway Tahiti and Ra'iatea in the Society Islands, and even to mist-hung New Zealand. Raiders moved back and forth between the Tuamotus, contemptuously bringing their womenfolk, and even now specific details of the Anaa warriors, "the killer sharks who overrun the seas," are still recounted by the old folk. The history of Ra'ivavae is filled with tales of conquest and defeat, valor and treachery, invasion and defense. The names of the heroes still echo in the tales of the islanders—Narai, Mauri, Tangihia, Te Ehu. From their loins stemmed the generations of today. But between the heroic days of the far past and the lackluster life of the present which we were to witness, there is a terrible abyss.

On February 5, 1775, the frigate *Aguila* and the bark *Jupiter* came to this island, rich in color and adventure, already filled with the memories of history. In command was Lieutenant Commander Don Thomas Gayangos, en route from the abortive Spanish attempt to colonize Tahiti. In the parochial view of Western history, he is officially credited with the "discovery" of Ra'ivavae. The brief offshore visit of the frigate's yawl was substantially aided by two Tahitians who were being carried to

South America. They could make out a few words of the local tongue and persuaded the inhabitants that the Spaniards had not come to war upon them. Indeed, the exploring boat had deemed it wise not to land, but rather to lay offshore. When the hundreds of "Indians," as the Europeans called them, heard that the white men had not come to fight, they swarmed out to the boat and tried to steal anything they could lay their hands on.

"Our people saw themselves obliged to repel them with feints and blows," wrote Don Gayangos in his journal. "But finding this treatment failed to instill any fear in them, and that they did not desist in their efforts, they hove up the grapnel and lay off under oars some distance farther out to make it more difficult for the Indians to reach them. They are so daring, and such thieves, that they collared the coxswain of the boat and likewise the Master's apprentice cheek by jowl and snatched the caps off their heads, diving hurriedly into the sea and making off with their booty to shore, where they skipped about with delight at their exploit. Others grabbed the oars and tried to carry them off: in short, they had no other aim but to rob and make off with any of the many objects, so strange and unwonted in their sight, that met their eyes."

This audacious thievery was the main reason why the Spanish commander was reluctant to remain for a longer period near Ra'ivavae. A charitable and sensible officer, he believed that the behavior of the natives stemmed from curiosity and a natural desire to possess strange things rather than from any evil intent and he wanted to do them no harm. However, the two native Tahitians had difficulty in carrying out extended discourse, even with the chiefs, and succeeded only in learning that the name of the island was Oraibaba (the Spaniards called it Santa Rosa), and that their "ruler" was Tarabaroai. The Spaniards concluded that the natives had never before seen a European vessel.

34

A few observations were made by the captain of the bark, Raimundo Bonacorsi. He reported that his men had received a mother-of-pearl necklace, a paddle, and a spear "which looks as if turned on a lathe" in return for some nails and small knives which seemed completely unfamiliar to the Ra'iva-vaeans. He noted that the hilly but nonrugged slopes were well timbered, with fertile red soil. Breadfruit, plantain, ironwood, chestnut, candlenuts, and hibiscus extended halfway up the hill; groves of coconut palms stretched along the beach. He commented on the fair skin of the inhabitants, some of whom "look like Europeans in hue," and saw no tattooing upon their bodies, which were tall and well made. The hair was worn tied into a tufted topknot on the upper part of the head. Long beards and large perforations in the ears were common while clothing was similar to Tahitian wraps, of dark gray, red, and yellow. The men of the island carried well-made wooden "pikes," and certain short "cudgels," but gave no intention of harming anyone or of making war. Although no villages or houses were seen it was thought that the island was thickly populated. The five or six canoes sighted were twin-hulled, with bows and sterns which sheered upward. Not only were they better constructed, but they were of finer wood than those of Tahiti.

In all of the literature about Polynesia there is no indication that another European arrived on Ra'ivavae for almost fifty years following the Spaniards. This is one of those strange omissions of written history. For we know that by 1819—the date of the next recorded visit—the place was known as High Island and had a reputation among whalers and other seafaring men for the fine craftsmanship of the ceremonial paddles, bowls, food scoops, spears, drums, and other souvenirs. These articles had been traded for over a quarter of a century. Sailors brought home to their families these beautiful mementos which now fill museum shelves and cases throughout the world. Like other islands of the Austral, Society, and Marquesas archipelagoes, Ra'ivavae had become a regular port of call for the men sailing the Pacific—crews hungry for a touch of land, famished for women and recreation. Surely if one could search the unpublished logs and journals of New England whalers, ample testimony to such visits could be found.

Don Thomas Gayangos may have discovered High Island, but the next visitor who has a place in history was to change Ra'ivavae and its way of life completely. He was Pomare II, who had already made himself King of Tahiti and various other Society and Tuamotuan islands with British missionary support. In 1819 Pomare decided to extend his domain (and that of the Lord God Jehovah) to the Austral Islands. Supported by Captain Samuel P. Henry, an American trader-shipowner who sought sandalwood, the King, his Queen, several of his chiefs, and followers of both sexes embarked for Ra'ivavae on the three-masted ship *Arab*. He arrived at High Island to find the inhabitants at war. One tribe had already fled to the hills.

Pomare's reputation had gone before him, and through the force of his personality and an elaborate tracing of genealogical connections, he was able to bring the defeated tribe from the hills, enforce a state of peace, and obtain an oath of loyalty to his rule. He then converted the entire island from paganism to a rude form of Christianity. It is recorded that his stay on the island was a continuous celebration, though in retrospect it is hard to understand why. Despite the professed Christianity of Pomare and his followers, they were enchanted with the place and took enthusiastically to the customs of Ra'ivavae. The officers of the *Arab*, on the other hand, were reported to have been revolted and scandalized by the natives' behavior, for they "gave themselves up without scruple to all the pleasures of sensuality." The American captain was particularly unhappy, for he failed to obtain sufficient sandalwood to satisfy his needs.

Pomare left one of his Tahitian chiefs, named Para, on Ra'ivavae when he sailed. Variously described as a "political agent" or "native missionary," he seems to have done his work well. Eighteen months later when Captain Henry had occasion to call in at High Island, he found the natives piously assembled at their newly built church. Under the direction of Para they had not only defaced their ancient gods, but had even converted many of the divine images into stools for the church. The good captain was much impressed. In a letter to Boston, he reported: "There were 88 assembled at the church for Christian worship to the universal God. The very quiet and orderly manner in which they conducted themselves, not only in church, but during the sabbath, awakened my highest admiration. The whole of their gods are mutilated; removed from their maraes [or places of worship] and even converted into stools at the entrance of the church, which is very neatly built; the ground is covered with grass, and provided with a sufficient number of forms; its length is 117 feet; and breadth 27. There are only twenty-five on the island who have not adopted the religion of the Saviour, but who have nevertheless removed idolatry. They say, 'We have no books, or proper missionary to instruct us, and we will wait till one comes before we become Christians.' "

They did not have to wait long. Shortly thereafter three Polynesian missionaries from the island of Moorea were sent to replace Para, who had failed to satisfy the English missionary leaders with his knowledge or practice of the doctrines of "the first principles of Christianity." Inspectors Daniel Tyerman and George Bennet, who landed on Ra'ivavae on Christmas Day in 1823, were strong in praise of the three good men. "The gospel as preached by them, not only with their lips, but by their lives, has evinced much of its power directly and indirectly, in the moral and social improvement of the people, who gladly received it." They had supervised the building of a new chapel, this one of wickerwork and lime, one hundred and eighty feet long and forty feet wide. The eighteen-foot-high walls contained "forty three windows for light and ventilation and three doors." Fifteen pillars, some with wreaths of human figures carved out of the solid wood, supported the ridge pole; other pillars were ornamented with varicolored matting and other devices. In other districts the chapels were equally beautifully ornamented, and the inspectors commented upon the beauty, ingenuity, skill, and good taste involved. They also noted the images of the deposed gods which were exhibited nearby, remarking that despite their large size they were by no means despicable examples of sculpture.

Tyerman and Bennet probably stayed longer than any of the other early Europeans. They remained until after the first of the new year, giving services in the various churches, baptizing new members, and exploring the island. Their favorable report caused later writers to regard the Ra'ivavaeans as "less cruel, and, in some respects more ingenious" than the other South Sea Islanders whom they resembled, particularly as "infanticide is said to have been unknown to them." The two inspectors were particularly pleased to see that the greater proportion of ground toward the northern and southern shores was planted with taro, and the valleys—which were of several hundred acres in extent—were in good order and well cleared. They explained this by the large population of "over two thousand people." Their visit was culminated in good Polynesian fashion. On January 21, 1824, a new chapel was opened in the presence of sixteen hundred persons, twelve hundred of whom were seated within. The district king and his wife, dressed in crimson cloaks, received tribute. Among this were a number of the famed carved ceremonial paddles, thirteen full bales of the best doubled black tapa cloth (in sections twenty yards long) and mounds of coconuts, bananas, taro, and fish—a "larger quantity than had ever been given as a present in Tahiti and the Society Islands." It was all presented as a farewell gift to the inspecting missionaries; together with a parting promise to provide house and garden room to future missionaries who might settle there.

The next year Rev. John Davies arrived to find the three native "teachers," as he termed them, hard at work, together with their wives. He was pleased to find that the natives now read their service in "good Tahitian, but with the accent of Ra'ivavae." In general, however, he took a sterner view of things than the preceding inspectors. His journal is rather an astringent affair with entries such as this: "In the afternoon a meeting was appointed with the baptized, as I wished to see them all, and converse with them. About 122 adults, including the seventeen selected as candidates for communion, had been baptized here by Mr. Henry and others. Most of them attended, and after singing, reading and prayer, I called over their names, and asked them various questions, but cannot say that I was satisfied with all their answers. I then addressed them on the design of baptism, and afterwards admonished them to attend diligently to their learning, to the instruction of their children, and other relatives as well as personal duties, and encouraged the teachers to go on with their work, looking to the Lord for a blessing, giving them such directions as to the mode of carrying on their work as appeared to me proper."

Mr. Davies must have forgotten something, for within a short time after his departure in 1826, Ra'ivavae was crushed by disaster. A contagious epidemic brought in from Tubua'i ravaged the island. Ten to fifteen deaths occurred daily and often whole families died at the same time and were buried in a common grave. Of the sixteen communicants of Mr. Davies' Christian society, twelve were dead by 1829. Two English visitors reported: "Never have we witnessed a more melancholy spectacle; houses are left without inhabitants; land without owners; that which was formerly cultivated, has now become desolate." Even now memories of this terrible period still haunt the island. Descendants still tell of the horrors of a time when survivors were too weak to bury the dead who lay exposed alongside the island paths, food for pigs and dogs. By 1830 there were but one hundred and twenty survivors of the more than three thousand inhabitants who had sworn allegiance to Pomare in 1819, and in 1834 the explorer J. A. Moerenhout counted less than one hundred. The glories of Ra'ivavae were gone. Its rich pagan past snuffed out. Only tantalizing memories of a culture saturated with erotic ritual and religion remained and even these had begun to wear thin. The survivors had to adopt a new kind of life.

This most aesthetically satisfying of all of the Central Polynesian ways of life had been built entirely on oral knowledge. There was no writing, no means of passing on the rich, complex culture. Knowledge could only be transferred by the lengthy and tedious technique of memorization; and when the teachers died suddenly, there could be no more schooling. All of known history, from the time of the birth of the gods, was irretrievably lost when the repositories of this lore died. The crafts of wood carving, stone cutting, feather mounting, and artistic plaiting had rested in the nimble but aged fingers of the Tahunga who had absorbed the knowledge through decades of practice. With the death of the old men came the loss of economic techniques: when and when not to fish; when and how to plant the taro patches, and when to let them lie fallow. Lost, also, were the marvelous pagan art forms. Even more stunning was the death of social control and the basis of customary law. Discipline disappeared; and the sudden drop in population wiped away the need for social sanction. Political control and religious inspiration now had to come from a new source. The significance of these facts only came upon me gradually, as the days wore on and I tried to analyze what had happened.

In 1842 France assumed the protectorate over Tahiti, and Ra'ivavae (as part of the kingdom claimed by the royal descendants of Pomare) became a French Protectorate; in 1880 it became a part of France proper. Oddly enough, the wave of death which swept the island did not undermine the power of the London Missionary Society. Louisa Barnes Pratt, the first Mormon woman missionary, wrote rather tartly about the efforts of one of her fellow missionaries to establish a toehold on Ra'ivavae: "There is great contention on Ra'ivavae about the Gospel; through the influence of English missionaries, doors of public worship were closed against him. He is anxious to leave there, and go where he can do more good. Those who have embraced the truth are greatly disturbed." Ra'ivavae remains staunchly Protestant until this day.

Politically, the French went about the business of organizing the government of the island with typical Gallic neatness. For administrative purposes the several districts of the island were amalgamated into two, Ra'irua and Anatonu, and these were provided with a full French colonial paraphernalia: chief, assistant chief, three councilors, and five assistant councilors, police agent, and schoolteachers. All of these served under a gendarme who was not only chief of station, postmaster, civil-affairs officer, and head schoolteacher, but was charged with the unwelcome task of supervising the collecting of taxes and acting as chief of police. He in turn was supervised by the lieutenant in charge of the government schooner which periodically visited the island. Geographers of the period reported that some two or three tiny trading vessels visited the island each year in order to pick up arrowroot starch, sweet potatoes, rosewood or sandalwood perfumes, or the newly planted coffee, oranges, tobacco, or cotton—or to buy livestock and produce for their own use. There were some years when no trading

41

vessels arrived. The blustering local wind and the poverty of
the population discouraged them. Although the islanders were
considered more hospitable and harder working than Tahitians, visitors discontentedly noted the women *"moins correct"*
than Tahitian girls, their hair less well cared for, and their
untidy dresses dirty. For the rest, the dry official reports which
are our main documents about life on Ra'ivavae until well into
this century tell little. They do not describe how the people
lived, nor what sort of island they were living on—except in
the broadest terms. More important, they give no sense of that
intimate relationship between man, his land, and his climate
which is the basis of understanding a society. True, I was in
search of the past—a life now vanished—but to reach this goal
I had to understand the present, and this is where I began.

Chapter Two

HIGH ISLAND

A S THE *Mareva* moved around the northern peninsula of Ra'ivavae and coasted under the peak of Mount Hiro, I caught my first glimpse of the village of Anatonu, in the shape of a large white church. This introduction was an appropriate one, for the church was the reason for the village's existence. During the pre-European period people lived in small thatched houses within the borders of the family planting lands. Today, they still maintain the pandanus plantation house, as a place to rest during the heat of the day, or even to sleep in for several days on end if their taro patch is some distance from the village. But the main life and hopes of the family center in the town, for everyone wants to be near the church and take part in its continual round of services. With the money from a good coffee crop, the families take pride in improving their iron-roofed limestone or frame houses, purchasing the windows, doors, mirrors, beds, and heavy, closet-like *armoires* from Tahiti.

Anatonu means "cave of the giant fish." It is the name of both the village and the district around it, but no one could tell us exactly why such a name had been given. Of the four villages of the island Anatonu was the most vigorous and densely populated, although it was part of the least fertile section of Ra'ivavae, lacking the rich valleys, extensive taro fields, and more plentiful waters of the others. As we neared the shore we could see ahead of us the scattered reef islets to the east. On our right, to the south, the mountainous backbone of

Ra'ivavae stretched out in a long line of vertical cliffs and steep talus slopes; the houses, the fertile taro fields, the streams and fields, all lay on a narrow strip of coastal land which was hidden behind the young ironwood, or *toa*, trees which fringed the shore.

Within a few hours after our arrival on Anatonu we found a headquarters for our work. A solemn, taciturn old man named Toāri'i, whom I was to know well in time, offered to rent us his wooden frame house. I accepted the offer on the spot, since I could see it was located right beside the church and was thus ideal for my purposes. The rent was modest, and the house—though old—was completely satisfactory for our particular purposes. Like its twin to the right, it had been built during a "coffee boom" shortly after the turn of the century. Set upon posts, it was by now somewhat rickety and swayed with every wind and each footstep. But it was tightly constructed and the European-style windows not only kept out the wind and rain but let in a good amount of light. There were both front and back porches, a large central area which we used as a combination living, dining, and study-work room, and three bedrooms. We converted a fourth room into our kitchen. (The Polynesian habitually cooks and eats in an area apart from his sleeping house, but this practice, which is fine for keeping rats and ants out of the bedroom, takes too much time for hard-pressed European field workers.) When we arrived at our new house it was filled with the many beds which Toāri'i had provided for members of his numerous family. But within two hours our landlord had cleared out all the extra ones and left a well-swept and tidy building in which we could immediately set up our apparatus and go to work. We started moving our supplies and equipment in from the *Mareva*, anchored offshore in the channel, landing them directly on the beach with our little dinghy. By the end of the day we were settled in our new home. Only then did we dis-

cover that we had set up shop in the same house used by
Frank Stimson just twenty years before.

One of the first lessons an anthropologist learns is that things
are often different from what they seem to be. I had this lesson
driven home when I climbed down the notched log from the
back porch of our new home and entered the *fare iti*, the small
outhouse in which some wag had cut a crescent moon. Carefully closing the door to keep my privacy from the children
who now were starting to cluster around, I suddenly discovered
that there was nothing there but the exterior frame. It was as
much a sham as a movie set—a good beginning and nothing
more. The villagers preferred the seashore in the early morning.
Toāri'i and his sons, however, soon realized our plight, and
within a few hours had constructed a handsome large combined outhouse and washhouse from some galvanized iron they
had stored away. They covered the sandy floor with dried coconut leaves, and finished it off with towel rack, washstand, water
jug, and a companionable two-hole *chic saler*—foreign to Polynesian ideas but well suited to American tastes. Ours was the
only outhouse in all of Anatonu.

Before the *Mareva* was to sail away, Tautu had the idea of
leaving Tioti behind with us to handle the cooking. At first,
I did not realize how important a step this would be, but
within twenty-four hours he had proved himself to be so in-
valuable that I don't see how we ever could have gotten along
without him. Another most fortunate move was to hire
Toāri'i's daughter Pogi to act as a sort of girl Friday. She,
too, soon proved her value. Working closely with Tioti, she
was on the job before we rose in the morning and carried on
until bedtime at night. She helped in the kitchen, served all
the meals, made the beds and swept out the rooms, kept the
yard picked up, did all of the laundry—and together with her
twin sister was one of Zenie's most useful sources of informa-

tion. She was quiet and withdrawn but had an attractive though exceptionally fleeting smile. (Zenie also noted her cleanliness and remarked that she alone of all the local girls lacked the characteristic smell of fish and cooking smoke.)

Once all our supplies and equipment were ashore, I made my final inspection of the *Mareva*. Toāri'i had sold us a pig in order to give our men fresh meat during the trip back to Tahiti, and Tioti roasted it for them before they left. We paid off the crew, cursing the overtime and double-time system of pay which has now reached the islands and caused the payroll to total more than twice what we had expected. I hauled down "Peabody," a nickname Zenie had given to the museum's flag, and sent the good boat back to Tahiti. Finally we were on our own!

Fortunately all of our supplies came through in good shape. It was only when we began cooking and housekeeping that we discovered the trivial necessities that had been overlooked. A small funnel may be nothing at all, but try to pour kerosene from a five gallon tin into lamps and stoves without it. At moments like this Tioti proved his worth, for he knew how to cope with tasks which would have taken us ages. His first chore was to fashion a small stove from an old gasoline drum. On this he could boil water, cook taro, and perform other heavy jobs. The gasoline camp stove I had brought along turned out to be inadequate.

A day after we arrived, Jim became very sick. We put him to bed at once and started him on a course of the powerful drugs which I had brought with me. He needed quiet and rest, but this turned out to be a difficult thing to secure. Right in the middle of one of Jim's low moments a young chap walked into the room, trying to sell us a cowrie shell. Although I angrily sent him packing, I soon realized that we had become the center of attraction for a crowd of curiosity-stricken children and adults. There is almost no such thing as personal privacy among the sociable Polynesians. Used to living out their lives in the midst of a large family packed into a single small room, they do not conceive of our need to be alone. In self-defense I had to draw a "privacy line" around the exterior of our house. We made it clear to our new friends that our needs were different from theirs, and that privacy was one of them. This achieved some results, but every so often, I could catch a glimpse of staring eyes peering at us through the slits between curtains, or through open doors.

The household soon settled into a regular routine. We asked Tioti to set up our little portable dining table early each morning with a buffet breakfast of coffee, biscuits, cheese, or whatever other cold food was available. Thus those who wished to get off to an early start on their individual projects could begin the day with something in their stomachs. Once he had recovered his health, Jim was usually off to paint while the day was still cool. Zenie either went with Pogi to the river to gossip with the girls or called upon some of the many friends she soon made among the women of the village. Alan spent most of the morning talking with Piahuru, who was a fount of information. He did his writing during the evening, or in the early hours of the morning before the rest of us were about. I generally brought my notes up to date the first thing after breakfast, and then went off on my village rounds or had Piahuru or Tauira'i come to my room for our discussions.

Periodically several of us would make a trip around the island, working over the ancient temple or fortress remains, studying the local system of raising taro, or otherwise searching for information. What we found is in this book. But what I remember most fondly about those days were the late afternoons, when work was over until after supper and Tioti had a tin of hot water for me, heated upon his homemade stove. As the first cool breezes of the early evening came whistling through the crevices of our iron outhouse I would take a luxurious sponge bath, for hot water was a luxury which could not be enjoyed even in the posh hotels of Tahiti.

I hold many memories of our life together: Alan working at our writing table, hat pulled low over his eyes to shade them from the Aladdin lamp; Jim returning from a painting tour with another work to be hung on the walls and discussed; Tioti and Pogi contentedly at work on the back porch; Zenie telling us with enthusiasm of her adventures. We lived and worked with professional intimacy and friendship, and we soon discovered that the villagers were fond of us too. Although Ra'ivavaeans generally were not fond of Europeans who had come here, they found us "simple and friendly to everyone." They pitied us for not speaking the language fluently or fully understanding the church services, but within a few days after our arrival they spoke possessively and boastfully of their visitors when they talked to people of the other districts.

Before I settled down to the hard business of immersing myself in the ways of High Island, I wanted to have a panoramic look at my new home. True, I had studied the few available maps of the island. There was one which Alan Seabrook had drawn with meticulous care when he worked there with Stimson. It was a beautifully precise affair on which the rivers, valleys, peaks, and temple sites had been carefully situated after a personal visit to each place. Then there was another which Henry Pambrun of the Bureau of Lands in Papeete had kindly furnished me. It was a detailed map of the landholdings for Ra'ivavae, a necessary aid, for every foot of land on the island, however sterile, is the property of some person or family. In fact, every piece of land is named. Yet these were not enough. They were good maps, but they told me nothing of the environment of earth and sky, of wind and water. They gave me no knowledge of the life-zones of the island. To learn about this I had to spend weeks strolling, trudging, and exploring. But first I wanted to see the island in one panoramic sweep and for this I had to climb to the topmost peak of Mount Hiro, the highest point on High Island. It is not much of a mountain by the standards of those who live on great continents, but a young Ra'ivavaean, overwhelmed by joy at seeing his homeland again, once chanted:

> Oh my mountain!
> —soaring to the domed skies above.
> From thy cloud-capped peaks the dotted lands,
> Rising above the ocean's rim, become visible;
> There beside thee falls thy mighty shadow
> Upon meadows blooming with high-climbing flowers
> of the gods.

That was in another age. Nowadays, few native Ra'ivavaeans bother to make the arduous climb, and I had to turn to the friendly gendarme, Georges Arnaud, to lead us up the mountain. Besides understanding just what kind of weather would insure a dry enough terrain to make the climb possible, he knew of a path.

On the day of the climb, our party gathered for a predawn breakfast. Outside our headquarters little groups of men passed by on their way to the fields, and somewhat later the church bell rang, summoning the oldsters to the thrice-weekly dawn service. Georges was carrying a small, ancient .22-caliber rifle, a weapon which aroused great excitement among the young men whom he had invited to make the ascent of Mount Hiro with us. They, it seemed, were less interested in the opportunity to see the mountaintop for the first time than in the possibility that the trip might mean wild goat to eat that night.

The path turned out to be a combination of a goat trail and an imaginary direct line to the ridge top. We made the preliminary ascent in less than thirty minutes from the flat shorelands to the knife-edged ridge which led to the peak. By the end of this I really knew what the Polynesians mean when

4

they liken the journey of life to a mountain climb. One moves up to a peak of physical and sexual ability and then inevitably begins sliding down the other side. I was truly in the midst of my "slide down," and I wheezed and puffed and my heart thudded as I hauled myself up, tugging at the tufts of grass or small bushes which grew from crevices in the soft vertical rock. Many of the carefree young chaps, who climbed like the goats which could be seen on the rocks around us, made a good deal of fun of my predicament, but one of the quieter youths gave me a helping hand.

The comparative ease of the first vertical climb was more than balanced once we began the delicate feat of moving up the razor-back ridge to the peak above. The sun had now risen and below there was a sweep of magnificent color: the deep-blue ocean, the white wash of the wave-smashed reef, the turquoise hues of the lagoon, the red earth of the eroded foothills, and the rich colors of the mountain flowers. The arid vertical northern face which we had just climbed differed markedly from the much gentler slope to the south. This had received most of the rain which fell from the predominantly southern winds and was covered to the rim with rich vegetation, huge tree ferns, guava bushes, and orange and candlenut trees.

During one breathing spell, as we neared the peak, I had a moment of horror. One of the boys disappeared from view, and I thought he had tumbled over the precipice. Instead he had spotted a tropic bird nesting on a tuft of vegetation which grew a hundred feet down the vertical face of the cliff. As we watched from the brim with fascination, he moved like a spider over what seemed to be bare rock. Nearing the nest he suddenly reached out and took the white bird before she had a chance to move away. He calmly pocketed the egg on which she was sitting, and then floated back up. His first move, upon reaching the top, was to pull the two long red filamentous tail feathers out and stick them in his hat. Then he showed us the quivering bird. Her feathers glistened like white satin, and fear caused her tail to curve out in a lovely fan. As we discussed the tropic bird and its habits in a rather detached academic fashion, the young chap suddenly beat the bird's head on a rock, tore a hole in its throat, ripped the skin and members from the still-squawking body, and stuffed the carcass in his hip pocket. When we protested, too late, he only grinned and threw away the unwanted skin and limbs. This was not the last time that we were to see a sudden eruption of brutality toward animals.

Perhaps we should not have been so horror stricken. This chap and his fellows must do the same thing to the fish they catch almost daily. Periodically they also must wring the neck of chickens, or cut up still quivering carcasses of pigs and goats for their family larder. And was not our gendarme's gun (and the possibility of fresh meat) the inspiration for their climb today? But later we again had to helplessly stand by as they gleefully stoned to death a young kid which had fallen to an inaccessible stone outcropping below. Despite my groping for justification I could not help but feel these brutal acts were a residue of that bygone era when their ancestors had raided enemy tribes in the night, thrust spears into still-sleeping women and children, and then boasted of these acts in the vaunting songs of a victory celebration.

As we moved upward, many small flat goat stands and winding goat paths became noticeable, and we now could use the animals' trails to make our own way. In places we moved along a ridge with precipitous drops only inches from each side of the slim trail. After a final breathtaking and difficult stretch we reached the pinnacle of Mount Hiro.

Below stretched Ra'ivavae—a small island only four and three-quarters miles long and no wider than a mile and three quarters at most—a world in itself. To the east of our route the mountain peak sloped down to a great saddle-shaped plateau

—a mountain meadow upon which escaped horses and bands of goats ranged. Running down in a direct line between Mount Hiro and the village of Anatonu, which lay far below us to the northeast, was a rush-filled ravine which ended in a small pond at the very brink of a precipice.

The contrast between the grass-covered meadows of the eastern half and the precipitous western ridges and cliffs is as great as that between the northern and southern sides of the dividing range. To the north the only vegetation other than grass and ferns seemed to be the miniature gnarled Metrosideros trees, with lovely red flowers whose spiked petals are tipped with gold. On the southern hills great blackened areas could be seen. These indicated that the islanders knew nothing of the disastrous effects of burning over the soil. To be sure, the French have made a law against this practice, but no one pays much attention to it.

But I was not interested in scenery alone. In one sweep I could grasp something of the complex pattern of life which marks this island and relate it to the areas where each activity is carried on.

Encompassing all are the dark-blue waters of the Pacific. The ancestral knowledge of these ocean deeps, however, is known no longer to the present-day descendants of the Children of the Sea. This is the greatest and most poignant change that has come over Ra'ivavae. Where once the ocean was understood and loved, *Te Moana Nui o Kiva* is now feared. Christian though they are, the Ra'ivavaeans still feel that the sea harbors *tupapa'u*—demons waiting to drag them down to the spirit lands which lie below—and they dare not brave this danger. They still tell stories of a witch-woman of the sea, ensnared by fishermen of a preceding generation, who was mated with a High Islander and left her human descendants to multiply here when she returned to her former home. But now, only the ships of foreigners sail where once vessels of discovery, war fleets, and venturesome fishermen regularly embarked upon Kiva's Ocean. Even during the turtle season few canoes venture beyond the reef to hunt the beasts which were once so hungrily sought. The island is passive, receiving what the Pacific washes up on its shores: an occasional iron buoy torn from foreign harbors, dozens of green glass Japanese fishing floats, and great trees from other lands. Moreover, the intimate knowledge of the fish-bearing ocean currents and the grounds and holes where different kinds of fish could be caught has vanished together with the ironwood spear and club.

It is the barrier reef which provides the boundary which sets off the familiar from the strange. The work of myriad minute animals, this massive defense encircles the island a mile or so from the shore. The exterior slopes form a subterranean coral plateau which blunts the waves rolling in from far distant seas and protects the shallow waters and fertile shorelands within. Most of the wide reef is shallowly awash with the sea, but at irregular intervals some forty sand banks rise sufficiently high above the ocean to form atollons or islets. These are called *motu*. Most are covered with vegetation and for centuries have been a major economic asset. All are owned and the lots are neatly marked off with boundary stones. The primordial cover, which once provided great groves of *toa* for the war spears and pandanus for both house construction and food, is now being burned off and replanted with coconut trees in order to provide another source of cash revenue. Immense gnarled *toa* trees, split and warped by centuries of exposure to the wind, are being given up to fire. One can still walk through knee-high depths of pandanus leaves and ponder the fertility of the seemingly arid bare coral.

Once these reef islets were the site of pagan temples and houses. Now their only permanent inhabitants are the rats which live there in large numbers. But the islanders still visit them to collect pandanus leaves or coconuts, to search for mar-

ketable sea shells, or to grill a few fish when en route home
from their excursions into the lagoon. The Ra'ivavaean woman
who otherwise seldom sets foot in a canoe occasionally sails
out to gather shellfish or a special variety of the sea slug. There,
the men seize great numbers of ocean crayfish for which
Ra'ivavae is famous throughout the central islands. When the
tide and sea are right one can easily walk from islet to islet
along the reef, listening to the roar of the surf, the crashing
breakers which cause a fine mist to hang in the air. Though
the coral base is sharp and rugged, banks of pure-white sand
extend far out into the lagoon. Two breaks in the reef, probably
a result of fresh-water runoffs from the steep northern and
western slopes, provide navigable passes at Tetobe and Totoro
Ahau through which strong currents surge. These passes could
be valuable assets to the island's commerce.

During our weeks on Ra'ivavae we were to make many visits
to the lovely islets, looking for temples and habitation sites,
trying to understand the economic cycle and varied life scenes
of the people. We found that the clean white sand was actually
composed of countless fragments of broken sea shells, most of
them bleached white by the sun. Surprisingly, this sand provides a rich soil for growing fine coconut trees, better than the
poor ones which are to be found ashore. In all, the barrier
reef was the equivalent of a full-scale atoll of the kind that
make up such Polynesian island groups as the Tuamotus, the
Northern Cooks, or the Tokelaus. This means that the few inhabitants of Ra'ivavae have economic assets which are usually
found separately in other places. They can enjoy the advantages
of a high, volcanic central land mass comparable to such islands as Tahiti. And they can reap the fruit of the barrier reef
—the southernmost of Eastern Polynesia—the full equivalent
to such atolls as Hao or Anaa.

The barrier reef also forms a deep lagoon between the *motu*
and the fringing shore reef. The channel of the lagoon, though

studded with huge coral heads, provides a passage through which a schooner can reach most of the island. Varying in depth, the lagoon offers a great variety of fish to the present-day High Islander without driving him to the danger of the deep seas.

Toward the shore is another reef, the very shallow fringing variety. The seaward face of it is higher than the shoreward surface. This keeps out the waves which form in the lagoon and provides a calm belt of water around the island. This is Ra'ivavae's chief avenue for getting from one place to another. Every part of the island is rapidly available by canoe transport. Heavy and bulky loads are easily carried in canoes, which are propelled by poling rather than by the more arduous labor of paddling. The shallow and sandy waters also provide needy widowed women, the aged, and the infirm with an endless supply of easily accessible shellfish and sea slugs.

At the heart of this series of concentric rings set in the broad Pacific is Ra'ivavae, less than eight square miles of bristling land. An easy morning's walk will bring one entirely around it, save for the precipitous western extremity, which lacks a path and must be visited by canoe. A range of mountain peaks splits the island in two from east to west, and, in turn, this jagged backbone is divided in the western part by mountains rising to the north and south. These heights form several relatively segregated lowland areas which slope to the sea and which were the natural bases for the boundaries between the independent districts into which the island was divided. The many rivers and the runoff from the mountains are the source of five great taro-growing areas. These are subdivided, in turn, into many smaller valleys by steep ridges which finger out from the major hills almost to the lagoon shores. Just offshore from the eastern tip of the island is the twin-peaked high islet Hotu Atua, whose bizarre shape is the subject of many numerous folk tales. Now it is a place where the islanders stop and rest after their trips into the lagoon.

Over the years, the narrow shore plain was formed by runoff from the steep hill slopes above coupled with a slight over-all emergence of the island from the sea. Nowadays this slender belt of land is the site of all habitation and of most economic activity. Once, great taro fields were scattered throughout the island, rising in man-made terraces well up into the hills. Now they are modest affairs handy to the needs of a more apathetic, greatly reduced population. Permanent homes are scattered along the inland side of the narrow path which parallels the shore of much of the island, but most tend to cluster near the churches and singing-houses which are centrally located in each of the four subdistricts of Ra'ivavae. The muddy, poorly kept trail with its shaky pole bridges spanning the small streams is mainly used for foot traffic or an occasional horseman. There is not a motor vehicle or even a wheeled cart on Ra'ivavae.

Splendid as it is, seen at certain times, there is a depressing look to High Island. On both sides of the tawdry path there is a string of lime pits dug at intervals of a few hundred yards. Lime is made by burning coral chunks from the lagoon together with huge quantities of wood. This produces a fire which is sufficiently hot to reduce the coral to pure lime. Over the years, these pits have consumed much of the rich vegetation which once covered Ra'ivavae.

Landward are great masses of hibiscus trees, used by the islanders for a variety of purposes, from fashioning bandages from its bark to interlacing its leaves to make blankets. But even these trees cannot redeem the air of neglect which seems to have overtaken that part of Ra'ivavae where people live and work. With the change from the old ways of growing taro in water to the modern "dry-land" cultivation, the finer points of island agriculture seem to have been forgotten. The streams, which now pour from the hills and form foul backwaters and malodorous pools, are used for both baths and laundry. How different from that fervent past when people chanted:

Clasp—ever clasp us in thy lover's embrace,
  O Pool-reflecting-the-white-clouds!
Thou whose cold waters are gazed upon each day
  by the young women.
Thou art caressed by the chill fingers of the
  highland breeze,
Wafted from the brow of the bold mountain
  named of old Ridged-crest-of-the-awakened-one,—
A breeze heavy with the fragrance of kavaro *flowers,*
  Drifting,
    Drifting
  Drifting down
    into the pool reflecting the white clouds of the sky!

The loss of a sense of beauty, together with the degeneration of pride in order and cleanliness, have lead to the replacement of order by disorder and of loveliness by ugliness. Even nature herself was affected by contact with the West. For with the whalers and missionaries came weeds and new flowering plants. And the ornamental plants, lovely in the domestic gardens of Europe, escaped from the cultivations of man to become monstrous weeds which turned picturesque parkland valleys into tangled morasses.

In the foothills that rise up from the inhabited coastal strip there stand occasional banana plants, and here and there breadfruit, candlenut, chestnut, and banyan trees. But the ancient upland taro fields and the temple and assembly grounds of old are overgrown with the coffee tree, now the main economic mainstay of the island.

Beloved by Ra'ivavacans for their beauty, the mountains have little economic value. Their steep ridges have been thrust up through fractured layers of both igneous and sedimentary rock, and the resulting caves serve as refuges when hurricane winds and high seas smack down the coconut trees, flood the taro beds, and flatten the frail houses. Once, splintery outcrops of the volcanic uplift provided ready-made phallic uprights for the temples and slabs for the altar walls. White layers of sedimentary coral-sand rock, easily split into squares, were used in the decoration of the marae and now make excellent building blocks for home or church. The talus slopes of mountain debris support a few guava bushes, and though coconut trees sprout from the crevices in the face of the cliff, their fruit is contemptibly small and lies rotting and unused at the bole of the trees.

Bands of wild goats ranged on the grassy plateaus and saddle-like tops of the mountain ridges which spread out below us. Before their ancestors were forced to these heights there was more forest land and a higher water table than at present. But years of grazing wiped away the cover, and where once the verdure-clad mountaintops held the excess rainwater, now it runs off in torrents during a storm—lost to nature and man.

And just as the ancient vegetation had gone, so had the land birds. Not even the pesky European mynah bird, now a normal part of the wildlife in other Polynesian islands, disrupts the stillness of Ra'ivavae. Occasionally one of us would startle a blue heron into stately flight, and frequently, as we worked over the hills and ridges, a red and white tropic bird would soar around us. On the mountains there were exactly three wild ducks. Georges had taken pains to prevent their extinction, hoping that they might propagate.

The cold wind from the south whistled around us as Jim sketched, Georges watched for game, and I pondered. I was trying to visualize the difference between the ways of life of those Polynesians who lived on the high islands such as we were now exploring and those who lived on the sandy atolls similar to the barrier reef and *motu* which surrounded Ra'ivavae. I realized that despite the dramatic beauty of these mountains, despite the economic value of the stone for making adzes and altar walls, they had little if any greater cultural significance than did the central lagoon of the low islands. For the mountains were barren and impeded communication, while the lagoon provided fish, shellfish, pearls, and pearl shell, and was a convenient ocean waterway. Although the valleys of high islands could support taro and breadfruit and provide a more constant source of water, dwellers in the low islands raised their essential Polynesian foods on the *motu* and dug wells for their water.

This brought me to the conclusion that the term "Children of the Sea" was more than a boastful self-appellation of the Polynesians. They are essentially a sea people, not a land people. Whether dwelling on the narrow strip of humus soil which encircles the mountainous cones of Ra'ivavae and Tahiti or living on the atolls of Anaa or Hikueru, the Polynesian is never more than a few yards from the sea. He either spends hours a day fishing in it, or imbibes it in the salt-water sauces which accompany his daily meals. He once sprinkled it on temple pavings to render them sacred; he still uses it to heal the newly superincised penis of the adolescent boy and to cleanse and soothe the woman who has just given birth.

The sea is the most permeating element in Polynesian life. So important is it, I learned, that one does not seek the embrace of women before venturing upon its surface, or defile it by allowing a woman in new menses to pass over it. He who plans to fish over the reef is careful to abstain from relations with his wife the night before—and if a wife betrays the fisherman at sea, he will not be allowed any catch.

From these revelations I realized that in Ra'ivavae, despite the great beauty, despite the geographic complexity, we were dealing with a typically Polynesian culture. Certainly the local geographic condition had affected to some degree the way of life derived from the original Polynesian ancestors, but I knew that in making my analyses I could rely upon my knowledge of Polynesia and upon comparative material from other islands to aid me in comprehending the local way of life.

Chapter Three

FRIENDS, NEIGHBORS, AND SAGES

IN THE village of Anatonu there were only two hundred people, not many as towns go, but enough to offer a cross-
section of High Island society. They turned out to be as varied
and unusual as any that one might find in any other part of the
world. Within the tight confines of this village one could find
every kind of human being.

On one side of us lived our landlord and friend, Toāri'i, the
head of the most substantial family on Ra'ivavae. Anni Mervin lived on the other side of us, and she was almost as prominent, but since the death of her husband and the illness of her
son, her family had crumbled in status. She was related to
Toāri'i, but the difference in their fortunes caused certain jealousy between the two households. Anni was the daughter of
one of the great families of Tahiti, had married into Toāri'i's
family when she was young, and had been mistress of her
household since the First World War. Of course she was somewhat chagrined that we had chosen to live with Toāri'i rather
than with her, but she turned out to be a good neighbor nevertheless, sending us such delicacies as *popoi*, *po'e*, watermelon,
and *'ape* when the spirit moved her. I was always disturbed
by these gifts since I knew that the family was occasionally
reduced to eating wild taro and sea slugs. Anni, however, never
paraded her troubles.

Another of Anni's great charms was her granddaughter, who
spent a great deal of time with us during our stay on High
Island. She had two names, Rita and Louise, which were used

interchangeably, but to us she was Giggles, for the nervous laugh which kept bursting out. I gave her the name when we arrived and it stuck until the day we left. Throughout our stay she remained a good friend to all of us. Zenie, who was somewhat put off by her habit of eating lice taken from the heads of smaller brothers and sisters, recognized her many fine qualities immediately. Giggles was goodhearted and competent. She was the best singer in the village and could weave fine hats, cook well, and keep house. She had even made a journey to Papeete.

Toāri'i was obviously a person of substance. He was a deacon of the church and wielded great influence. In speech he was calm and deliberate, almost to the point of monotony. His dignity was heightened by glasses which gave him great trouble. At first I thought that this was because he had left the price tags on each lens in customary Ra'ivavae fashion. But it turned out that they were simply no good for his eyes. He found Alan's spectacles more suitable and he borrowed them when he wanted to read something of importance.

Toāri'i had eight handsome daughters, including our Pogi, and two sons. Only two of the daughters were married, but these happily to hard-working and devoted husbands. The others were much sought after, but Toāri'i had so far refused to let them get married on the grounds that the suitors were not well enough off. The girls agreed with him; they not only received a share of the family coffee money, but they had much more freedom than the other girls of the village. Toāri'i was always happy when his daughters had a chance to enjoy themselves.

Our landlord was descended from a royal ancestor, Teri'i O Tahiti, but he had achieved his present eminence by his own hard work. Even in his twilight years he was the active head of the family, working in the fields, tending his animals, repairing and painting his large fishing canoes. He had pigs and cattle to sell and the family coffee lands produced one and a half to two tons a year, giving him one of the highest cash incomes on High Island. He was a generous yet stubborn man; when he let us have his main house, he moved to the smaller limestone house in back of the church.

Toāri'i was on the best of terms with us, although he never presumed to intrude upon our privacy. He and Tioti became fast friends, despite their difference in religious beliefs (Tioti was a Reformed Mormon pastor) and soon our general facto- tum was to be seen at Toāri'i's house giving the daughters the benefit of his familiarity with the Bible. Whatever favors we did for our landlord were always scrupulously returned in kind. I can think of no greater praise for him than to say that he was a true Christian, whose happy and healthy family reflected his good and sensible ways. Yet to my great surprise, many High Islanders regarded Toāri'i as a "bad man." This may have been due to the normal Polynesian jealousy of anyone who is suc- cessful. "No head or shoulders should be above any other," goes the proverb. But more probably because Toāri'i led a disci- plined life which was more Christian than Polynesian in character.

Among the many friends we made in Anatonu, my favorite was Mama Iē, whom we visited almost daily. She was the vil- lage live wire, combining a salacious sense of humor with deep religious feelings and steady church attendance. This was an unusual combination, but it made her one of the most impor- tant women in the village.

When I met her, Mama Iē was poor. Her husband had died years before and she had never had any children. Although there was a young cousin who was supposed to bring her food, he often forgot her. Young people tend to forget the old in Poly- nesia. The result was that Mama and the twelve-year-old "feed- ing daughter" who lived with her often had to forage for themselves. She fished, ate taro tops, and even gathered puny sea slugs from the lagoon.

Now that she had come on poorer days, Mama had moved from her former big house at the eastern end of the village to a rotting frame house more centrally located. It was a remnant of the first coffee boom, and the galvanized iron roof was rusting through, the millwork coming apart, and the cookshed virtually roofless. A good new limestone house for Mama had been started by her adopted son, but he had died in Tahiti the year before. It was now another hulk. Despite these misfortunes Mama remained hospitable. She always welcomed us with a loud *Haege mai, haege mai!*—"Come hither, come hither!" We usually found her working on the floor in a curious sitting-kneeling posture, one withered breast hanging limply outside her ragged clothing. If she remembered she casually tucked it under her *pareu*. I was fascinated by her white whiskers and firm Polynesian jaw and the way she used her eyes and chin to express meanings. Despite an asthmatic condition which made her look older than her fifty-nine years, she still had great presence.

I remember one poignant visit with Mama. Her lovely, dark-eyed adopted daughter was in smiling attendance. A flock of neighborhood children lingered outside the door watching us with wide eyes.

I had brought with me pictures of Mama and her relatives that John Stokes had taken two generations before. Mama held her photo and said, "Not good—I was beautiful when I was young, and this picture is not beautiful." Her voice rose as she talked, looking long at each photograph of a departed relative, and soon she was weeping. I noted how thin and worn her clothing was, how little the younger girl had to wear, how—despite the cold evenings on High Island—Mama had nothing warm to throw over her shoulders and no medicine to help her asthma.

Her simple one-room house was furnished with two ancient iron beds, and at the rear of the room, between two locked sea chests, was a table with a few cracked dishes upon it. In the center, a strange and striking contrast to the dark household, was a bowl full of huge roses.

We talked through the morning. I was interested in learning the location of artifacts, but Mama said that other visitors had taken great loads away. True, the villagers were continually finding spears, staves, tapa beaters, poi tables, and stone objects in the swamps, but these generally fell into the hands of children who broke or burned them or lost them in the sea. Mama knew a good deal about the past. Her family had specialized in making tapa cloth, particularly for pregnant women, and she was well versed in the craft. Her house, moreover, was on the site of an ancient archery court and she herself had seen the stone images standing on the nearby marae when she was a child. She had a wealth of vague information and a wonderful sense of comedy. Invariably when I left her house she gave me presents—sea shells for Zenie, a fragment of a pre-European stone tool, and neatly shelled coconuts.

At the other end of the village of Anatonu lived the "Widow-in-brown," as we called her, because she wore the same brown dress at every church service. She was a pillar of the church, one of the small group of older people who supported the religious activities of the town with all their energy. As one might expect, she had a firm belief in the efficacy of prayer. However, she practiced what she preached, a trait I found particularly admirable. Although she had many children of her own, including a son who had lost an arm, the widow adopted a young orphan baby whom no one else wanted. The mother of the child was from another island and had stopped off at Ra'ivavae en route to Makatea. After a disagreement with the baby's father, she had decided that she did not want to be bothered with the little boy anymore and offered it to various people on the island. Polynesians usually pay little attention to anyone not related to them, and the young mother found no one who would take the baby. When the ship sailed she simply left the child behind her on the dock.

Now the child was two years old, a sober infant who would sit solemnly without moving for hours at a time, waiting for his foster mother to return from the taro fields. Since the widow was poor, she had no clothes for the child except on Sunday; then he wore a little suit made up from one of her old dresses. We later learned that the father of the child showed up and tried to claim him, but the widow had grown so attached to the unfortunate babe that she refused to give him up.

At the same end of the village lived Tamaiti Pa'apa'a, whom I renamed "Uncle Bert" after a favorite uncle he closely resembled. Tamaiti was a councilman and churchgoer. He, too, had been photographed by Stokes, and he was an amiable companion and a constant source of amusement. Like Mama Iē he fulfilled an important social function by keeping the population constantly amused with his salacious quips and stories. We periodically bought a chicken from him at an exorbitant price. Invariably the fowl was skinny and meatless, but when I complained that it would take six of his chickens to properly feed us he merely said, "You shouldn't eat like pigs," and asked for another cigarette. I liked him.

Down the path from us lived Tino, a small vigorous chap with Portuguese blood in his veins. He attended us constantly, in a rather obsequious way, and was our principal source of supply for adzes and antiquities. Whenever there was something to be done he seemed to be there, ready to lend a hand. He obviously did the same thing in his own household, for though he was already a grandfather by the first of his eleven children, he told me that he was just now beginning to take life easy. But despite some assistance from his children he never could be seen loafing. He was always at church, and his

66

house and lands were the neatest and cleanest in Anatonu. His tiny wife spoke little, smiled much, and was constantly busy plaiting hats or mats.

Not all of our friends were Polynesian. There was the gendarme, of whom I shall have more to say later, and another European couple whom we saw periodically. His name was Gounin, a Frenchman who suddenly decided, when he reached middle age, that civilization was going to hell. With this he pulled up stakes and took off for the South Seas. Tahiti turned out to be too civilized and too populated for him, and he had gone on to Tubua'i. But there were five other Frenchmen there, and he grew tired of their constant bickering. He then moved on to Ra'ivavae. For a while he managed quite well as a small trader, farmer, and functionary in the French government. When I saw him he had become fed up with the gendarme who had taken over his duties and was about to sail off to the remote island of Rapa, where there were no Europeans at all.

His wife, Madeleine was a Frenchwoman he had met in the islands. During the Second World War she had fallen in love with and married a Tahitian soldier. She returned to the island with him but soon tired of the Tahitian demonstration of affection, which involves weekly wife-beating as a proof of continuing love. Leaving her man, she tried school-teaching, but this did not work out. When Gounin met her, he offered her a partnership in his little trading business and she accepted. They even adopted a young boy from Tubua'i. She soon brightened up his household and her feminine touches combined well with Gounin's beehives, vegetable gardens, and ingenious farming methods. Although they lived very simply in the local stone house which they had converted into a combined store and home, she turned out excellent bread, cheese, pastries, and other delicacies which we enjoyed. They introduced us to the virtues of crushed sea-salt crystals, and did their best to be hospitable. Madeleine used to obtain chickens from the natives in trade for tins of sardines ("they tell us that it is easier to open a tin than to cut up and cook a chicken"). We often benefited from this exchange.

Their home faced the beach at Mahanatoa, where there were few other houses. It had a superb view. The small building was divided in two. On one side was the stock for the store while the other was reserved for the extensive shelves of paperback books which were Gounin's chief joy. In contrast with the Chinese stores, which are full of lounging locals at any time of the day or night, Gounin sold his merchandise through an opening in a small cage which enclosed the customers' entrance. This discouraged loafing.

The terrible storm which had hit Ra'ivavae the year before our arrival had hurt his honey crop (from which he occasionally made beer) and his business as well. In former years he kept as much as 400,000 francs worth of merchandise in the store and was accustomed to sell 60,000 francs worth in one day. But this year his shelves were almost bare. Since Gounin did not give credit and money on the island was scarce, he saw no point in restocking the store. He was not overly depressed

68

by the situation and told us of his plans for installing a wind generator, a kerosene refrigerator, and an electric stove.

Gounin's competitors, if they can be called that, were four Chinese merchants, all established in the village of Ra'irua, which has a dock and good anchorage facilities. Two of them were successful; the other two were not. The latter eked out a very precarious existence selling soap, tea, flour, tinned beef, and other staples where the profit margin was small. Whatever success these two marginal merchants had depended upon their ability to gauge the character of their clientele. They had to know to whom to give credit in between the coffee-picking seasons, since most families live on the expectation of the next year's crop. Gounin solved the problem by giving no credit at all and handling a smaller clientele, but the Chinese, facing greater competition from their countrymen, could not afford the rigors of a cash trade. Moreover, when they gave credit they had the sole right to sell the debtors' coffee beans—another way of making a small profit. Generally the stock of all these stores was so limited that one often had to make a tour of all four to make a purchase.

The prosperity of the two more successful Chinese merchants rested upon their bakery business, which they carried on in addition to normal trade. Following the coffee crop, when there was money on the island, this could be lucrative. When there was little money about or when flour ran out between boats—the daily baking was dropped. Despite their problems, the Chinese (most of whom have taken local wives) occupied a useful and necessary place in the modern life of High Island. Polynesians are not accustomed to work as traders because they had no previous system of either cash purchase or of direct trading. Indeed, there were few pre-European foods or artifacts which were suitable to store or trade. Moreover, the close-knit family system of the islands, which permits any member of a family to ask another for something he doesn't have, means that few Polynesians can successfully operate a store.

One of our most useful friends in Anatonu—and Zenie's most particular friend, was the village gay lady aptly named Ta'oto—"to lay down." We made her acquaintance during the first evening of our stay on the island. Jim and I had gone to the government faucet to get water shortly after dusk. While we were playing with the children there, I noticed three women going by, returning from a fishing trip. Forgetting my Polynesian manners, I asked the woman with the fishing pole if she had gotten any fish. To my dismay, my request obligated her to give me a string of her catch. It was obvious that she needed it more than we did. The next night as she walked by the house, I called to her and gave her a packet of cigarettes—hoping to make amends for my thoughtlessness. She and Zenie began talking, and Zenie took a fancy to her. In fact, she tried to give her a hand by arranging to have her do some of our laundry since there was too much for Pogi to handle. From that point on the friendship ripened. Ta'oto was a frequent visitor to our headquarters, giving Tioti and Pogi a hand in return for a highly welcome dish of food. She ate this as if she were half-starved. Soon Zenie was spending a lot of time gossiping with our new-found friend at her tiny shack.

At first I did not approve of Zenie's constant association with the village loose woman. I felt that it might prejudice her relationship with the more respectable local women. I was wrong. Ta'oto was a mine of useful information and moreover she seemed to be on friendly terms with the "Widow-in-brown" and other highly respected people.

Ta'oto had never been away from the island of Ra'ivavae. As a young girl she had fallen in love with a sailor from the government vessel that periodically visited the island. He jumped ship, and she kept him hidden in the bush for six months, bringing him food and necessities. He was eventually dragged off to Tahiti. After this she had further love affairs with visiting Tahitians and local men. Although she had never been married, she had a couple of children whom she was trying to raise. She also had a young niece who lived with her and obviously was following closely in Ta'oto's footsteps, such as they were. These days the young men in the village who lack the courage or the opportunity to engage in the courtship custom of *motoro* are always after Ta'oto. They sometimes wait in line outside her house. Ta'oto also sleeps with married men on occasion, either in the bush or on the *motu*. But despite her private relations with them, she is the public butt of jokes and ridicule by many of the men in the village.

If the immediate reason for Ta'oto's downfall was the Tahitian sailor, the villain of the piece was a former chief of the island, who is still alive and is quite popular "because he always helps anyone who needs him." Ta'oto's parents died when she was young, and when the family lands were distributed this chief got her to sell her land for almost nothing. (He must have been very good at such real-estate deals because now he is the biggest coffee producer on Ra'ivavae.) By the time her surviving relatives had heard of the unfair deal it was too late to do anything about it. These days the Bureau of Lands in Papeete tries to see that this sort of thing does not happen.

As a landless woman with little family, Ta'oto had a hard row to hoe. No man was likely to be tempted to take her in marriage, or even to bring her home to live with him. Thus she had to find her livelihood with her own hands. Moreover, without land there was no way to raise food for herself, and without a canoe, no way to look for good-sized fish. Ta'oto had to be content with the few tiny fish she could snare from shore, with wild foods from the mountains, and with the taro and *maniota* which she and her niece were forced to steal from the lands of others. The gendarme was well aware of their plight.

As he remarked: "They are brought before me by other people who charge them with theft every one to three weeks."

Even I had personal experience with this one Sunday. Tioti was reading his Bible on the back porch and we were busily writing in the house when Ta'oto and her niece arrived. Ostensibly they were there to pick up laundry, but Ta'oto's niece was clearly in trouble. With a sheepish look she told how she had taken a few roots of *maniota* from a nearby field. The owner of the property had noted the theft, gone directly to Ta'oto's house, and found the roots. She then rubbed the inside of the girl's mouth with the highly acrid skin of the *maniota*. Not content with this she brought the young girl before the village policeman and demanded one hundred francs compensation for the food—a price far beyond its real value. The policeman had approved this unofficial fine, which the girl had absolutely no means of paying. We felt sorry for her and gave her the money, saying that she could work it off by helping around the house.

All of our friends and neighbors were sources of information about life on Ra'ivavae, and most of them helped as best they could to provide us with the material we were after. But like most ordinary souls anywhere in the world they had not looked very deeply into the life around them nor observed it sharply. Moreover, their memory of the past was slim, indeed. Since our aim was to dip back into the history of High Island as much as we could, this presented a problem.

By a great stroke of luck, however, all of the persons who had been Frank Stimson's and Alan Seabrook's main informants when they worked on Ra'ivavae a generation ago were still living and available to us. They were the ones who had provided Stimson with the vast amount of material which he analyzed in his epic manuscript. They were the "authorities," the "sages," the "leading people" whom he had tapped for his strange masterpiece.

*Ra'ivavae
at dawn*

The Mareva, *the expedition's yacht, lies at
anchor*

At the end of each
I returned to my c
to write out my f
ings

Virginie Richmond, the Tahitian member of our group whom we called
"Zenie," queries a church gathering about women's activities

(ABOVE) *Jim Scott, our expedition artist, sketches temple ruins watched by two curious Ra'ivavaens*
(RIGHT) *F. Alan Seabrook, senior expedition member, fully understood the meaning of life in the South Seas*

Sharp cliffs and rugged slopes mark the terrain of Ra'ivavae

On his voyage to Ra'ivavae Frank had taken care to have these men themselves write down their stories and replies to his questions in their own hand. Then he went over their work, recording additional information and inserting necessary diacritical marks and amplifying details in a different colored ink. He had once been accused of falsifying and misrecording information, and believed that this method would enable him to be above any suspicion. My visit to Ra'ivavae would allow me to check this material in my own way as well as get any other information I needed from these people.

Frank had first worked with a French-speaking, local ex-schoolteacher named Piahuru, who not only furnished him with data but helped enormously in putting him in touch with the learned people of the island. It was to Piahuru that I first turned in my own research. I suppose I would have gone to him in any case for, as the only French-speaking native on the island, he was entrusted by the administrators with the care of the civil records—those of birth and death, legal marriage and political election—and I was particularly interested in these aspects of Ra'ivavaean life. Moreover, he was now quite aged, although still mentally very alert and physically active, and his knowledge of life on High Island extended over almost three generations.

Even before leaving Tahiti I had heard much of Piahuru. Frank was particularly fond of him because he was a descendant of a famous pre-European Ra'ivavaean who had won the hand of a local "princess" in a rather striking way. The young charmer, who was sought after by many men, had announced that she could only accede to the ardor of a man who could copulate with her while she danced. Piahuru's ancestor waited until a major public affair; then, while everyone looked on, while the drums and gongs thundered, he approached the princess as she danced, whipped his kilt about the two of them, and in time to the music of the dance he succeeded in fulfilling the arduous condition.

Stimson was also impressed when Piahuru gave a farewell dinner to a group of visitors. The centerpiece on the banquet table was a bowlful of poppies from Mount Hiro set in an unusual but familiar-looking receptacle. "What is that?" one of the guests asked. Piahuru casually replied, "Oh, that is the helmet I wore in France—a place called Flanders Field, I believe." I was thus prepared to meet a rather unusual character.

Soon after we arrived at Anatonu, Piahuru came to call upon us and renew his friendship with Alan Seabrook. His yellow-white hair showed that he was in his seventies, but his rounded face beamed with health, intelligence, and good will. He was obviously pleased at our arrival. I soon found out that although he had wanted to go off to war, he had not been able to because of his age, his children, and his family responsibilities. We talked for a long time, for I wanted to size him up as rapidly as possible. He had walked miles to see us despite a wounded leg which was swollen and hot from an infected cut. Moreover, he was hungry since he had not eaten since early that morning and his children neglected to provide anything for his excursion.

We began talking about the ancient names of Ra'ivavae and soon moved to the subject of the sage Tauira'i and his famous book. Obviously there was some rancor between these two old gentlemen. Piahuru said that Tauira'i believed that the ancient name for the island was 'Oromona-i-haua. Our visitor insisted that it was Vavitu. Though Piahuru and Tauira'i had frequently worked as a pair in giving information about the past (Tauira'i reciting old tales in Ra'ivavaean and Piahuru translating into French), our new friend was quite contemptuous and antagonistic in referring to his erstwhile colleague. He flatly stated that Tauira'i *must* have a book for reference, obtained from his feeding father, for "He is younger than I am. How else would he know? The book is there!"

Piahuru told me that he had not bothered much about passing on his knowledge of the old days, since "No one wants it." We were an exception and he seemed delighted at the opportunity to work with us. Soon we settled on a stipend adequate to satisfy both his pride and his meager needs, yet which was within our limited means to pay. I was very pleased with what I saw of Piahuru, though I had reservations as to the extent of his knowledge of ancient lore.

When I first went to work with him, Piahuru and his family were living in their plantation house a mile or so down the path from the village. The wattled, coconut-leaf-thatch sleeping house was elevated above ground to the height of a coconut log, and was divided into two rooms. The freshly laid sweet grass on the floor of the sleeping room proper was covered with pandanus mats. In the front section he had set up a large table covered with a freshly laundered cloth, surrounded by several solid chairs. Pen, paper, and ink were laid out in readiness for work to begin. Both the sleeping house and the cookhouse, together with the grounds about them, had a fresh clean look, although there were the usual bothersome mosquitoes and flies.

I spent the morning there, first chatting about matters of general interest, and then passing on to specific details from a list of questions I had prepared. To my surprise I found that Piahuru was Tahitian on his father's side and Ra'ivavaean on his mother's. This explained why he had had the advantages of attending the Viennot school in Papeete. It was there that he gained his command of French. Piahuru returned to High Island and was made schoolteacher. Unfortunately he not only got involved in a family quarrel with the then ruling governor— a descendant of the Pofatu royal family—but had exposed himself to criticism by taking a new woman after having legally

married his previous partner. This gave his opponents a
chance to revile him to the far distant administration, who
promptly removed him from his position. Piahuru had never
gotten over the effects of this blow to his prestige—as I was to
find out in the weeks to come.

Piahuru had a long record of working with ethnologists. Two
generations before he had been one of the several local men
who accompanied John F. G. Stokes in his field expeditions
here. The work was mainly concerned with excavations. People had not given Stokes information about the pre-European
period, he said, because they thought that like other previous
visitors and administration officials he had only been interested in the more material remains of temples and images and
other curiosities. Piahuru noted that Stokes impressed people
as a very fine dignified man (in contrast to many other less
respectable European visitors), but he thought that the eth-

nologist's poor command of French and Tahitian had hindered his work. During the period of Stokes' visit the famed sage, Tauira'i was only a *taure'are'a*—an irresponsible youth, and the problem informant Hapai, senior to Piahuru by several years, had not been seen with the field group. It was not until Alan and Frank arrived, with their dual command of both the colloquial and classical Tahitian and other Polynesian dialects, that anything about the old days had been recounted to foreigners.

Archaeologists left by Thor Heyerdahl had used both Piahuru and Tauira'i to tell stories of the old days. Piahuru said that the Chilean leader of this group asked questions in Spanish which a Norwegian companion translated into French for Piahuru's benefit. The latter then asked Tauira'i the question in Tahitian—and the answer traveled back over the same devious route. (Tauira'i later told us that he was sure they had gotten the information straight, for they then took the precaution to re-recite his answers back to him via the same circuitous fashion—an admirable example of tenacious field work!) Piahuru again spoke rather contemptuously of both Tauira'i and Hapai, and noted that at the recent "christening" of the football field the former came and recited a story of the "old days" which our aged informant thought he might have gotten in Tahiti.

From personalities we passed on to the work at hand. Specifically I wanted to test Piahuru's knowledge of ancient days and his reliability as an informant. I was particularly interested in tattooing, for in contrast to the reports of the early Spanish and French explorers who stated that this was one of the few islands where tattooing was not practiced, Stimson's informants had written of elaborate tattooing customs here. Piahuru was sure that there had been tattooing, for his mother's father had been "tattooed all over his body." But he claimed that he had "never heard of a woman being tattooed on Ra'ivavae." He went on to discuss musical instruments, telling of drums, gongs, jew's-harps, resonant stones, and nose flutes. He had never heard of clappers, however. He talked about the various weapons of war—the many types of barbed and unbarbed spears, the slings, and the skull-smashing clubs. Bows and arrows and shields were not used, for fighting was body to body. As I asked for more details I found that Piahuru was very vague. He knew nothing of skeletal internment in caves, nor the preservation of skulls, nor did he know of any cranial or skeletal remains in the vicinity. Later I was to find human remains which stuck out of the altar foundation of a temple site on Piahuru's own land.

Although Piahuru deprecated Stimson's Ra'ivavaean dictionary (a dictionary of which he had himself been one of the principal sources), saying that it was "full of new Tahitian words," he did not know most of the ancient words with which I tested him. Neither could he pronounce the characteristic Polynesian velar nasal "ŋ," which occurs in Ra'ivavaean but not in modern Tahitian, nor did he know anything of the special or "secret" languages of the ancient days.

During this first morning, I gradually reached the conclusion that Piahuru had no real knowledge of the pre-European period. True, he knew fragments of folk tales and the more obvious bits of history, but there was no coherence or consistency to his data. Yet it seemed to me that he had one unique value which set him apart from most native informants: when he had no knowledge or was not sure, he was frank to say so. He did not try to bluff us or to dream up answers. And at the same time the combination of his knowledge of French, his custodianship of the official records, and his familiarity with patterns of behavior over three generations made him useful in our quest for the picture of present-day life. Even in these fields, however, I was to find vast discrepancies between the accounts of this seemingly honest and simple old man and the facts which we observed ourselves or learned from other informants who had absorbed fewer European manners.

But what of Stimson's great informant Tauira'i, the man who was spoken of throughout High Island as "the one who knows"? Everyone we met on Ra'ivavae—including old Mama Iē—said that "no one else on the island knows anything about the old days except Tauira'i, even the oldest people." It was he who was called on to tell of the old days at certain births, christenings, marriages, and deaths. They were certain that "his knowledge comes from a book" which they believed he had gotten from his feeding parent. But no one had even seen it and Tauira'i denied owning it.

Book or no book, Tauira'i always had a literary touch. Even when Stimson just had met him—a young walking encyclopedia who could answer any question about High Island's history or culture—Tauira'i preferred to write down his information rather than discuss it in person. He liked to be given a handful of blank notebooks, so that he could "go home, think over, and write about," the questions which Stimson' posed. For this he was paid a few francs for each piece of work.

I met Tauira'i within a few minutes after we arrived at the administrative center of Ra'irua. He was quick to doff his hat, give me a huge smile and a flabby hand, and tell me that he had heard that I was coming. He seemed to know all about my plans. I said that we would meet again soon and probably work together. It seemed a wise course to go very slowly in my relationship with him. Moreover, his obsequious manner to me, coupled with his imperiousness to his fellow High Islanders of lesser stature, offended me. He seemed to be saying "I am the only one here who can give you—the inquiring rich foreigner—what you wish to know." Nor did I like the brusque way in which he greeted Alan, who was obviously not the leader of our expedition. I gather that he had been as obsequious to

Stimson twenty years before and as offhand with Alan even then.

A few days later I traveled to Ra'irua to meet the boat which had come in from Tahiti. There was Tauira'i, acting the great local man in the midst of a parcel of politicians who were touring the islands seeking election. We could easily believe the local gossip that he—along with our other informant Piahuru —aspired to be the *Tavana* or chief of High Island one day. But again he was quick to doff his hat to me and smile pleasantly with his lips, if not with his eyes. Tauira'i was one of the island councilors, and again and again I was to see him playing the role of popular politico, when he was not putting on airs as a learned sage or a sanctimonious church deacon. But I never saw him tilling his lands, nor did he exert himself to work with us in the field. I had to agree with Zenie—whose subjective reaction I learned to trust—when she called him *"prétentieux."*

When we finally arranged to work together, Tauira'i wanted to turn out more notebooks, but I insisted that he have some formal discussion with Alan and me. (I needed Alan's command of the language, and relied heavily on his judgment.) At the first one, Tauira'i brought me an example of a genealogical record, a mnemonic device of knotted hibiscus-bark cords which he claimed to be the ancient means of recording and tracing ancestral descent. He had written about this for Stimson years before. Despite the fact that Piahuru claimed to have seen one of these in an ancestor's trunk many years before, I was not at all sure that this was a pre-European concept. It seemed too simple. On the other hand there were similar concepts employed in the wooden genealogical devices of the New Zealand Maori and in certain knotted cords of the Marquesans (which our informant could have seen in the Papeete Museum). Tauira'i also claimed that the ancient sages had not lived on the marae, but taught there in special houses. They devoted their time to instructing their students in genealogy and history, using the knotted cords as memory aids.

In trying to check on Tauira'i's competence I found that he could translate few of the ancient words about which I asked him, nor could he remember the native terms for many of the concepts he discussed. Like Piahuru he also seemed to have a complete block about sexual information. Not only did he deny any pre-European connection between the temples and sex (in contradiction to the material evidence which we have in the museums) but he also denied having any knowledge about present-day sexual practices—some of which, according to both Zenie and Tioti, would be too far-fetched for a Polynesian not to know.

Indeed, Tauira'i accused Europeans of having exaggerated the sexual aspects of the ancient images—a detailed accusation which I checked and found wanting. He talked of god names and temples, but much of what he said seemed to be the result of not-too-well-educated guesses. I asked him to write down a prayer couched in the ancient language, one of the so-called "unalterable chants." This he did, but it might have been written by any good Christian as a prayer to Jehovah.

Throughout all this, I did not feel that Tauira'i was deliberately falsifying information. But it seemed to me that he might be doing what Hapai, Stimson's other chief informant, had been accused of—turning out information to order. Later I was to revise this view when I went back and compared the material he had given Stimson with what he was doing for me. Tauira'i's early work had mainly consisted of retelling old legends, tales, and sayings, besides such general information that might well have been passed down from grandparent to grandchild (the Polynesian chain of transmission) or written down in the genealogical account books kept by every sensible family in the last century. These earlier accounts rang true to my ears, for they were in accordance with what I knew from a detailed survey of the general Polynesian cultural patterns. Moreover, they seemed gospel truth to Alan, who independently confirmed much of the material with his own compilation of Rurutuan data. But when Tauira'i tried to answer specific questions which diverged from what he knew by rote, or when he attempted to generalize from the meager details of the folk tales, his lack of imagination and disciplined reasoning led him to the accounts which I doubted.

As a final note to these first impressions of Tauira'i, I must admit that the problem of his celebrated book had me buffaloed. The volume (or volumes) was talked about by native and European alike through all of Central Polynesia. Yet to me as to all others, Tauira'i denied its existence. He admitted that he had a book, but it was one in which he was presently writing down his own knowledge for the eventual benefit of his son. The local populace believed that he could not admit to ownership of the book, for it reputedly had belonged to his feeding parents rather than to his Ra'ivavaean mother and Rimataran father of blood. This would make it the property of his foster siblings, and if he admitted its existence he would lose this source of periodic revenue. I must confess that I went along with the others in believing that Tauira'i had some kind of a book. One day, in fact, he had let slip to Alan that the information he had just given him was something he "had heard, it was not out of the book." Alan believed that if we offered him a sufficiently large cash sum he would produce the volume. I did not have the cash available, for one thing. For another, I really didn't believe the mysterious volume could be that important now.

In any case, the closest anyone seems to have come to obtaining the book was a French pharmacist named L'Herbier, a hero of the First World War. I heard his story from his own lips in Tahiti shortly before his death. Just before the Second World War he decided to retire on Ra'ivavae and built a home on one of the reef islets. Tauira'i wanted to sell "the book" to him at that time for three thousand francs (Mme L'Herbier and Tauira'i's wife were friends). The druggist agreed. Tauira'i was on the way to L'Herbier's house with "the book" in his handbag when he was stopped by Pastor Timaru, who at that time virtually ruled the island by threatening to bring down the wrath of God on any opposition. The pastor, who later admitted to L'Herbier that Tauira'i had such a book, categorically forbade the informant to sell it to the European.

I had many other friends and neighbors on Ra'ivavae, some of whom we will meet later on. But Piahuru and Tauira'i occupied most of my time for understandable reasons. As we will see they are two of the central characters in this book. Another one I was not to meet until the end of my expedition and the fourth, Hapai, was dead when I came to the island.

Chapter Four

CAVE OF THE GIANT FISH

IF THERE is one thing that I have learned above all else in ten years of field work it is this: an anthropologist in the field must use his feet. The time when the inquiring ethnologist could have the "beastly heathen" brought to his front porch, to be formally interrogated through the medium of an interpreter, has passed. Just as the reporter in search of a story must get out and walk—and talk—so the field anthropologist must search out and mingle with the people he is studying. And just as the neighborhood cop regularly walks his beat, alert for any sign of change in local activity as a clue to possible danger to the community, so the field anthropologist must set up a beat to search for clues which will lead him to hitherto unsuspected facets of local behavior.

On Ra'ivavae my beat was Anatonu, Cave of the Giant Fish. My work was simplified by the village layout. Owing to the very narrow strip of land between the inland talus slopes and the sand beaches, where the houses were strung out along the path which encircled the island, much of what went on in Anatonu could be seen in the half hour that it took to stroll from one end of the village to the other—a distance of less than a mile.

Although there were periods when I spent hours systematically pumping Piahuru or Tauira'i for answers to my prepared questions or caring for my expedition "family," I made every effort to walk my beat at least once daily, usually with Zenie. Part of the time she sought answers to questions which I had given her from women and girls at the washing pool. But more frequently she walked her own beat through the village searching for the sort of information readily obtainable by a woman. From these patrols there gradually emerged a picture of modern life on the island, for in this manner we obtained at random not only the significant details, but also the all-important social and geographic context of the total environment in relation to the picture we had of life in the past. Also we obtained occasional striking insights into life on Ra'ivavae, triggered by witnessing unplanned incidents.

The layout of Anatonu was relatively simple. Our headquarters was located beside the church, the physical and social center of village life. This building marked the boundary between the two religious work groups, or *pupu*, each of which represented, in theory, one half of the village. These were the only organized non-kin groups in Anatonu. Walking east, toward the twin-breasted islet of Hotu Atua at the end of the island, I would pass first by the old wooden house of our neighbor Anni Mervin. Somewhat farther on, beyond Piahuru's small limestone town house, I would come upon the home of the chief of the island. This brightly painted small frame building was set on a little knoll, well back from the path that rose directly below one of the peaks of the steep precipice that stretched like a stone curtain behind the village. Beside the house there was a tall flagpole, but I never saw the tricolor flying there. Opposite the chief's house on the sea side of the path was the village water supply, a faucet which was fed from the headwaters of a stream dammed by the Public Works Department of Tahiti. Its location near the chief's home was a convenient coincidence of centralization and prerogative of rank.

A small stream, bridged by a few rotted poles, ran between the chief's house and the neighboring plot of land. Similar to others that cut through Anatonu, it had its origin in the slopes and cliffs behind the village, and provided the water to dampen the taro fields to the rear of the house compounds. Though muddy, the streams were the general source of drinking and working water for the village, and in the scattered pools the people bathed and washed their clothes. Few people used the government faucet, despite its greater cleanliness, for using it meant a longer walk and a chance that the faucet had run dry.

Farther along the path, by the households of people with whom we did not become intimate, loomed the compounds of our friend Tino and of the old woman who was to be involved in an incident of witchcraft, the pastor's unpretentious home, and, at the very easternmost end of the village, the small and ancient homes of Mama Iē and her aged cousin, our most beloved informants.

Fond as I was of our several friends who lived in the eastern half of the village, I preferred to walk in the western direction, beyond the church meeting house and its new village sports ground. For there I was met by a colorful peasant brightness, neatness, and gaiety which seemed psychologically to set off both the western sub-village and its inhabitants from the more somber eastern part. Indeed, for no other reason than its gay effect, we nicknamed this "the fishing village." Here, more than elsewhere in Ra'ivavae, I frequently saw men at work painting and retouching the outside of their houses, using a paint-wiping rag with professional dexterity. Here the houses were more amply furnished, with bigger beds, and larger mirrors than elsewhere in the village. And here, amid the close-cropped grass of the village green lay more marae remains than in any other village on the island, including a still erect altar wall. If I continued walking west, I encountered the homes of the unfortunate Ta'oto, gamy old Uncle Bert, and the Widow-in-brown, and following the path beyond the point of the peninsula which marked the boundary of Anatonu, I could in fifteen minutes reach the plantation house of Piahuru, and in another hour or so arrive at the town of Ra'irua.

The most striking sights of modern Ra'ivavae are the many hulks of *ma'atea* and limestone scattered through the villages, houses in all stages of construction and disintegration. Some were incomplete owing to a lack of practical knowledge of how to finish an overambitious structure. Others were simply "in process." Red curbstone taken from fallen temples could be seen in the steps and the unfinished walls. The basic materials for continuing work on these hulks lay in the dozens of lime pits located throughout the village and along the path.

In the yards, usually close to the houses, were tombs for the family dead. The older ones were of heavy stone and lime; the newer, set off with flower plantings and freshly strewn sand, were less massive. Despite official French urgings, there was no community burial ground on Ra'ivavae, which reinforced my impression that there was still no concept of the community as a social force; the family was still the focus of all loyalty.

Most High Island houses are built of heavy coral and lime,

with a galvanized iron roof and milled windows and doors. Some are clean, brightly painted, and differ from those around them in appearance and in landscaping. A few of the homes are well built in European frame style, but most of these are very old by island standards, and the paint has faded to lovely pastel tints. But walls of limestone replacements are rising beside them, and timber and iron are gradually being accumulated for future homes. Other than the cooking and eating shacks, set apart and hidden from the road by the larger sleeping houses, there are no thatched or wattled buildings, for these are restricted to the plantations. Some of the house clusters are separated from the rest of the village by fences of peeled poles, but more frequently hedges and flowering bushes are used. In some areas no divisions may be seen at all.

During the day, while the people are at work on their plantations or gathering materials from the reef islets, the houses are closed and shuttered. And except for the early morning and late afternoon, when children play in large noisy groups, the village is usually quiet.

When Zenie and I walked the path on our morning rounds, we would see clothing and blankets set out on bushes to air and dry in the sunlight. Occasionally we would meet a chap coming home from an early-morning stint at the plantation with a bundle of firewood and a basket of taro, or a young man, clad only in blue-jeans and hat, or perhaps with only a *pareu* around his loins, cantering his horse in the special "Ra'ivavae dog trot" along the path. During the late afternoon circuit we could expect more life and spirit, for vigorous football scrimmage took place on the playground in front of the meeting house, and much of the population was in attendance. Those who did not attend could be seen dragging a mat out in front of their home, where they and their neighbors sat and strummed idly at guitars, chatted, or dozed. These people, when in their own setting, seemed more truly Polynesian than those on any other island with which I was familiar. We soon made friends with the children and the old folks, although it was some weeks before we could overcome the painful shyness of the teenagers and the young people.

We soon learned that there was more to the household setting of the average Ra'ivavaean than the building in which he slept, and upon which he pridefully lavished his spare energies. Particularly significant was how the cluster of family dwellings seemed to be related to the layout of the family taro fields and the streams. Tino's place, neater and more openly situated than any of the others, provided the nicest example. His whitewashed limestone house stood clear of the surrounding flower bushes, a convenient distance behind the fenced-off path. To the rear of this was the neatly thatched work shed and eating shack, and off to one side were the hulking remains of his father's more pretentious attempt to build a house.

To the rear lay the varied green patches of the taro fields, separated by tall stands of sugar cane, and in the distant foothills open patches of sweet-potato and arrowroot plants stood surrounded by coconut trees in orderly array. The whole complex, together with the lagoon upon which it faced, was the setting from which the High Islander obtained his means of food and shelter.

We soon discovered that the house compounds similar to Tino's reflected the largest social and economic groups to be found in Anatonu, for the village itself was merely a collection of houses clustered about the church. There was no village social structure, no mayor or selectmen, no council. Although the members of the church were divided into two competitive work groups, these were concerned only with the operation of the church. The only meaningful social ties in Anatonu were those of kinship.

The web of kinship is all-encompassing in High Island life, as it is elsewhere in Polynesia. Generally speaking, all kinsmen, *heti'i*, are regarded as "good," all non-kinsmen are considered strangers and "bad." The distinction made between kinfolk and other persons is strikingly clear in the grammatical pattern of the Polynesian language itself. Persons and things which are intimately a part of one are referred to with the form of a possessive word "my" which contains a vowel *o*, as *tō'u māmā*, "my mother," *tō'u mana'o*, "my thought, idea." In contrast to this are possessives which are not intimate, and which—although belonging to one—are in a sense foreign to one's person. These contain the vowel *a*, as *tā'u peni*, "my pen," *tā'u puta*, "my book." Yet although blood kinsmen and children are always *tō'u* and intimately possessed, one's own wife is *tā'u vahine*, "my woman"—a foreign, nonintimately possessed person.

The great extended families who once lived together in a single open house are now gone. Yet most of an individual's home life still takes place in a single sleeping room and a single cooking shack in which grandparents, odd uncles and aunts, and hordes of children sleep and eat and talk together. There is little "privacy." And despite the tremendous Polynesian emphasis upon the rights of the individual, one cannot escape being labeled as being of "that so-and-so family." Although in Anatonu it is universally stated that "all families are good," I only had to listen in on a few conversations to know that true feelings run otherwise. I often heard, "that family are idiots" . . . "so-and-so's family are drunkards." Mama Iē told me, when pronouncing upon some hats and mats we had just purchased from the in-laws within the household of her cousin, "That family always makes things badly." Piahuru stated that, "all families are good"—but two minutes later said that "the best families in the village are always Toāri'i and Anni Mervin." He went on to say that the only "bad family" was the small household of the village fancy lady, Ta'oto—but later stated that "a good family must own a good house and have good land, work the land well, and live together without fighting, beating up one's womenfolk, or getting drunk within the house"—assuredly not all families in Anatonu village are blessed with this complex of qualities!

The wealth of a family helps to make it a "good" family, although—as in the notable case of Toāri'i himself—the person responsible for achieving the wealth may be held to be a "bad" man. But to attain status and prestige involves working hard, owning cows, canoes, good houses, and land, and staying out of disputes. Bad feelings exist between many families, but explode openly only when women bicker or animals are stolen or cause damage to a neighbor's food crops. Each feud I traced back to its source was usually a long-standing disagreement between families over land! Much of the argument is "talk," but whenever possible the members of one family will take the opportunity to injure the other family. Our literate informant insisted directly that there was no such thing as jealousy or envy here, yet at another session gave the term *pohehae* as "the feeling one has at regarding another who has a prettier wife or greater possessions than one's own"—and Piahuru had originally stated that it was the jealousy of others which had brought about his own removal from position. Yet despite these strong biases introduced by family ties, there is recognition of each individual's knowledge, ability, and general worth to the community. Life is a freely open book on High Island, and there is ample opportunity for each person to evaluate and comment upon how another plants, keeps his animals, and discusses the Bible in church meetings.

There is little indication of conflict between in-laws; a respectfully formal relationship is maintained. High Island literature contains no Polynesian equivalent of our stock "mother-in-law" stories. The young couple generally lives with one or the other of the parental families, and which side is chosen for residence depends upon the relative rank and merits of the two families. The decision rests with the young people.

One exception to the tendency of keeping within the family and regarding all others as strangers lies in the custom of making bond friends, *hoa*. When two people (generally of the same sex) enjoy each other's company, the parents may formally recognize the bond. A feast is given and the *hoa* is announced. As such a bond is generally made between people who reside on different islands, this provides a practical means of obtaining food and lodging when traveling.

The biggest social group today is one's loosely defined "family"—the *'ōpū ta'ata*, "people of the belly." It is the *'ōpū* which brings man into the world and eventually buries man's remains. This set of relations includes all of the people to whom an individual is related by blood, although today, with the effects of French law, more emphasis is placed upon paternal relationships. Within the *'ōpū*, marriage and the placement of orphaned or adopted children is discussed. These kinsmen also meet to aid a dying relation return to his place of birth. The women gather to prepare feasts and the men work as a group to build a house or a canoe. One does not take a wife or mistress from within the *'ōpū*, yet visiting and hospitality must remain within the family. Except for the family there is neither clique nor club for the Ra'ivavaean.

Within the 'ōpū there are no uncles and aunts, only "mothers" and "fathers." All brothers are termed "father," and all sisters are termed "mother." It may be necessary to speak of the "mother of birth" to specify the biological parent, or of the "feeding father" to distinguish the foster parent. The first-born child, who in ancient times was most likely to inherit title and leadership prerogatives, is still given the special term *matahiapo*. Brothers and sisters have different terms for one another: a younger sibling of the same sex is the *teina*, the older is the *tua'ana*; regardless of age differences a sister speaks of her brother as *tu'ane* and he refers to her as *tuahine*. In other words, within the Ra'ivavaean family the important distinctions are between the sexes, and one's age relationships within one's own sex. Grandparents and all other ancestors are spoken of as the *tupuna*, but older persons use a series of distinctive terms for each different generation level, as far down as great-great-grandchildren, reflecting the Polynesian concern with youth rather than age.

Perhaps the most important family phenomena is reflected in patterns of adoption. In striking contrast to European custom a large proportion of all High Island children are reared by other than their biological parents. Generally the parent "gives" the child shortly after birth to a grandparent, a sister, or a brother of the mother or the father, or even to a more distant kinsman—but always within the family group of either the mother or father. Commonly it falls to the grandparents to raise the children.

The extensive shifting about of children (and the same parents who give their child to a relative to raise may shortly thereafter accept from another relative a child to rear) helps maintain the immense feeling of family solidarity. It also gives freedom to the young parents to carry out more arduous labors and gives company to the old folk in their more sedentary life. It also allows the passing of grandparental knowledge of Ra'ivavaean customs to the young.

Now that war and overseas voyaging have disappeared, now that all forms of artistic expression and craftsmanship are gone, and history and legends are forgotten, and even the local dialects have been supplemented by Tahitian, the major link with the past is to be found in a shallow hole in the ground by the cookhouse. Should a Ra'ivavaean of the prehistoric period visit Ra'ivavae now, it is only in the *umu*—the earth oven dug near every kitchen shack on the island—that he would recognize a segment of his own way of life. For with the loss of almost all of the nonutilitarian patterns of life, the struggle for existence on Ra'ivavae has focused the greatest attention upon the filling of the stomach, as we shall see in a later chapter. And as the family is the center of social life, so the cooking-eating house and its earth oven are the focus of most family life. The culmination of each day's work, the net end of each individual's contribution to the group, is eventually interred in this hole in the ground. So it is today, and so it was in yesteryear, as reflected in the ancient wail of a father to his son, the inefficient oven-maker:

Alas! alas! for your earth oven!

It is extinguished.
It is slow to burn from too much moisture;
The food is underdone—it is unevenly cooked;
There are hard lumps in your baked breadfruit paste!
Why ever did you build an underheated earth oven?
    O my son!

Alas for you, whom I brought up to be my oven maker,
To line my fire pit with leaves so that the packaged food
    be well-baked!

99

Now indeed you have become a careless fellow,
  looked upon with scorn by all the people of our homeland!
Be sure they will spread your ill repute abroad.
Such incapacity as yours has become a deep humiliation for me,
  your father.
    O my son!

You have become a public shame in the sight of all eyes,
For you are contemptuous of the customs of your own homeland!
When you build your earth oven
Be sure that the heap of stones
Glows with the intense heat of the fire which you have built;
Make yourself over into an assiduous and capable workman,—
    O my son!
      O, thou my own child!

An example of this everyday activity in the household was
offered to me shortly after our arrival on Ra'ivavae. I had
stopped in at Toāri'i's while on my daily patrol, and found
him getting ready to make his earth oven. One of his sons was
busily scraping the ashes and remains of the previous day's fire
out of the shallow pit, laying bare a round depression about
two feet across and eight inches deep. In this, Toāri'i carefully
arranged sticks to heat a series of round stones laid over them.
(The oven stones are of an especially tough variety of rock
which will stand the effects of being heated and cooled over
and over again in a moisture-laden atmosphere without flying
to pieces, as do other stones.) The fire was ignited by matches
on the occasion when I watched. But in times of shortage
Toāri'i and any other man on the island can still draw fire in
a few seconds by rapidly rubbing a hardwood stick against a
piece of dried hibiscus wood. The erotic rhymes which once accompanied these suggestive movements of the fire plough, however, are no longer chanted.

After the fire had died to a bed of coals and the stones were red-hot, the remaining butt ends of the sticks were snaked out of the way and Toāri'i's son spread the stones evenly over the coals with a long pole. Then Toāri'i, seeing the arrangement not to his liking, grasped the hot stones with his bare fingers and set them exactly where he wanted. Tin dishes of leaf-wrapped arrowroot-starch pudding, po'e, were put in the center, and fish wrapped in ti leaves were set around the edges. Over the whole an interlapped set of hibiscus-leaf mats was laid. Toāri'i used several burlap bags to cover this, although his forefathers would have had a set of special pandanus-leaf mats on hand for this purpose. The whole pile was then covered over with a thin layer of dirt and left for three hours.

Making the earth oven is now, as it was in pre-European days, the job of the males in the family. The women may boil water in the iron pots hanging over the open fireplaces, but more regularly they concern themselves with the preparation of food, peeling the taro corm and pounding out popoi.

As the days wore on, our notebooks and sketchbooks became filled with details which rounded out the ethnographic description of modern Ra'ivavae. And from these details, and by comparing our knowledge of life in the past with what little we knew of the events in local history, we could form our first impressions. It was obvious that the first really clear-cut picture of the effect of the clash between the old and new came in the sphere of economics: the relationship between man's changing wants and needs, his resources, and his means of exchange and distribution.

When Europeans first arrived on Ra'ivavae there were many kinds of buildings: double-apsed, rectangular, and round houses; varied structures of the nobility, the aristocracy, the middle class, the commoners, and the slaves; special buildings for the priesthood, for warriors, for adolescent boys and pubescent girls; houses for military training and religious instruction; canoe sheds and work sheds. Each of these was of a distinctive design and size. But all houses had one common characteristic: they were constructed with the easily available leaves, branches, and trunks of local bushes and trees. But when the missionaries arrived High Islanders began to reconstruct, using the old techniques with one significant difference: the newcomers taught the Ra'ivavaeans to make lime to plaster the wickerlike walls of their new structures. And the only structures built were the family's sleeping house, cookshed, and plantation house and the new village's church and meetinghouse. This pattern continued for three quarters of a century.

Toward the end of the nineteenth century the few trading vessels which touched at Ra'ivavae began to buy the coffee beans, gathered from the plants introduced by the Europeans, allowing the Ra'ivavaeans to construct frame houses and use millwork, glass windows, doors, and galvanized iron for roofs.

Iron roofs eliminated the need for the pandanus-leaf or coconut-frond shingles, and the glass doors and windows let light
in while keeping cold Ra'ivavaean winds out. More signifi-
cantly, both because of social stigma and as the desire to match
or exceed one's neighbors was achieved, more and more land
was planted in coffee bushes, and more and more time was
spent in working the coffee plantations to obtain money to buy
more materials and to build new houses.

After this first coffee boom, when most families converted
to the frame houses, it became apparent that the new homes
had some disadvantages. Wood rapidly decays in the tropics,
and is subject to the attacks of many kinds of insects. Frame
houses soon became rickety. But about this time, early in the
twentieth century, someone brought from other islands the idea
of a stone house, which would not rot or fall down. These
houses were relatively simple to make, requiring only two or
three flat boards, some notched sticks, boulders or coral heads,
earth, and lime. Soon each family on Ra'ivavae was beginning
a new house. Then each village decided to build a new church
and meeting house.

Ra'ivavaeans had been taught to make lime in the most elementary fashion. A pit was dug, huge quantities of firewood
arranged in it, and certain types of coral from the lagoon
placed on top. When the fire was lit (and it might burn for
a full week) the ensuing intense heat converted the coral to
lime. As time passed more and more lime was needed and more
and more timber was cut to fill the demand.

During the centuries of Polynesian occupation there had
grown up around the shores of Ra'ivavae a belt of ironwood
trees, *toa*. Over the hundreds of years of growth they had
reached immense proportions, and served as effective wind-
breaks for the exposed coastal lowland strip of the island where
both taro and coffee are grown. As the demand for lime increased, these trees were felled, for they were conveniently

located where coral heads were brought in from the bay. Being practical people who thought in terms of present ease rather than future needs, the Ra'ivavaeans made their pits right by the *toa*, the largest and most available source of wood on the island. In some cases the trees were so big that they had to be girdled and coral brought to them to be burned *in situ*. The trees which once formed the windbreak were burned in the communal lime pits to provide building materials for the new churches.

By the time of my first exploratory visit to the island in 1955 the belt of trees was almost entirely wiped out, and each side of the belt path was pock-marked with old and new lime pits. A world-wide demand for coffee had sent prices soaring, and most of the available lowland interior of Ra'ivavae was covered with coffee plantations. The cash income of Ra'ivavae shot up to unheard-of heights.

In 1956, the year before our expedition's arrival, this tiny island exported one hundred and ten tons of coffee beans. Several stores were immediately opened by Chinese merchants from Tahiti to serve the High Islanders' new needs. The Ra'ivavaean had cash, but he did not know what to do with it. Storekeepers sold cloth by virtue of high price rather than quality or value, together with guitars, phonographs (for which there were few records), toy mechanical helicopters for children, and gold-plated watches and plastic household wares for the women. Ominously, less and less taro was planted as the newly rich Ra'ivavaean grew to rely on the bread he bought daily from the Chinese baker.

The trade winds, so steady in other parts of Polynesia, are somewhat unstable in the Austral Islands. Storms from the south, especially when the seasons change in February, are reinforced by the steep mountains of Ra'ivavae. With the loss of the ironwood windscreen the effect of these winds had become dangerous, and with the increased dependence upon cash crops the susceptibility of the island had increased. The first warning was the death of most of the breadfruit trees on the island, once an important source of food. Quickly panox hedges were planted, in the hope that they would help break the force of the wind. But too late!

On the 23d of September 1956 a storm broke up the stone pier at Ra'irua and wiped out the entire orange crop. And then on a March afternoon during the following spring a high wind blew a salt spray over the now unprotected lowlands and wiped out virtually the entire coffee crop. By the time our expedition arrived on High Island, despite drastic efforts to replant, living had been reduced to a hand-to-mouth existence. Storekeepers' shelves were bare, for without coffee to sell, the Ra'ivavaeans could not afford to buy goods. Half-finished houses were abandoned. There was no money with which to buy materials, and time which might otherwise have been devoted to work on the home had to be used for fishing and planting. In many families the people were reduced to a desperate quest for wild foods and to eating the contemptible sea slug in order to survive.

And so our expedition worked on Anatonu with a once great, once proud people now reduced to economic oblivion by their own improvident ambitions.

Chapter Five

A MOUNTAIN FORTRESS

ONE of the particular things about Ra'ivavae that interested me was the report that it once had "sanctuaries,"
places to which those who had offended society or been defeated in war might retreat and be under the "inviolate protection of the gods." Hapai had told Stimson about this, but I
was not satisfied with the account. It seemed to me that his
story of temple-like refuge areas where victorious or vengeful
opponents dared not enter smacked of Biblical influence. On
the other hand, I had heard of mountain sanctuary sites in
Tahiti and in other places in the Society Islands. Alan had
encountered the concept in Rimatara and on other of the
Austral Islands. He believed that these temples of refuge were
a natural development in an area which lived under constant
fear of raids and massacres, and where extended warfare was
chronic. Lacking defensible deep valleys, there was literally no
place for defeated parties to retreat or defend. He understood
that the refugees lived in grass huts on the sanctuaries, where
their women were allowed to take them water and shellfish
during the period of war.

During my first visit to Ra'ivavae I had traversed the lovely
hills through the center of the island. In the distance I could
clearly see that one of the knife-edged ridges which jutted out
into the rich taro beds on the southern side of the island had
been altered by pre-European man. There, where no one now
lived or worked, the entire face of the hillside had been artificially terraced. The cuts were not suitable for agriculture, and

when I checked the hillside location against Alan's map of the archaeological sites of the island it proved to be Mount Hatuturi, one of Hapai's so-called "sanctuaries." Alan had partially investigated the site a generation ago, and Stimson's notes contained sketches of the cuts. There were references to it in folk tales and traditional history. It was manifestly impossible to study the role of the fallen temples themselves as sanctuaries, but we might learn something from the more specialized mountain retreats. I determined that Hatuturi would be a primary site of investigation. We were particularly fortunate in that the site had partially been cleared by some previous visitors, who spoke of it as a mountain village.

Piahuru had little information to give about the Hatuturi sanctuary, although he stated that it had been discovered by John F. G. Stokes. When Piahuru was a young man people on the island didn't know that the remains existed, but Stokes' archaeological techniques brought them to view. When in Honolulu I had talked with Stokes about the site, and he noted that although he had sketched the observable cuts, he had not been able to make the ascent to carry out actual excavations. On both of the occasions when he had made the attempt, heavy rains had made the steep climb impossible.

We had hoped to have Tauira'i with us to discuss the remains when on the actual location, but he felt that he was "too old and soft" to go along. However, he did say that Hatuturi was only one of several mountain fortresses. Tauira'i believed that these so-called "sanctuaries" were actually homes for defeated clans; for "there was no safety from enemy warriors other than by hiding or getting up into the mountains." He indicated that water was available to these defeated groups further on up in the hills.

Jim, Alan, and I started off without guides. En route to Hatuturi, which lay halfway around the island, we stopped here and there to renew our knowledge of marae already visited, and to uncover and record new ones. On this trip, as on many others, we were soon followed by a troop of inquisitive boys and young men. Three of these young fellows were more persistent than the others and stuck with us even after we had left the temple areas below and commenced the ascent. It was our good fortune to find that one of this group had been the straw boss for the group that had cleared the site.

Even the outlying foothills proved exhausting to climb, for the crumbling rock outcrops and the decaying boulders and pebbles which covered the surface provided insecure footing at best. There was nothing to hold on to, for the grass and brush was so shallowly rooted in the stone that it would bear no weight. Brightly glittering among the brown stones were the remains of thousands of little tridacna clam and turbo shells. This was interesting, since this seafood called *pahua* and *ma'oa*, is the classic staple of impoverished Polynesians. Obviously the shellfish had been carried by those who were hard-pressed for time, for the Polynesian customarily smashes the shell on the reef in order to carry home more easily the meat which lies within.

When we arrived at the first low flattish outcroppings above the brush-covered valleys and the lower foothills, we stopped to rest. We shared our simple lunch of cheese, tinned meat, and wine with our three new-found friends and chatted about the scenery around us. Despite the exhausting climb we were still not far above the temple area; and below us, at the very base where the foothills emerged from the dampish area of the coffee groves and coconut and hibiscus trees, was a row of stone uprights—obviously planted by man. Looking above us at the terraces, smaller than I had visualized them, I could see that they were not the site of house platforms or a village. One could not live for long under such conditions, except under the passing stress of battle.

We moved on slowly up the hillside, ascending what seemed

to be a steep path on the very forward edge of the knifelike ridge. Periodically I moved out to the flanks to check the terraces. Invariably they were the same—stone-paved areas, cut back two or three feet into the hillside, several feet in length. They were hard to approach. Interspersed here and there were what we could only interpret as small shrines or temples, complete with paving and upright *tara*. As we mounted farther a growing suspicion took root within me. My mind went back to Fort Leavenworth, Kansas, where only a few months before I had been a student at the Army's Command and General Staff College. Day after day we had pored over maps, moving divisions of men over terrain which we had to gauge with intimate accuracy. As we disposed of companies, regiments, and divisions in our theoretical maneuvers we were never far from one basic precept: take and hold the high ground, cover the area with cross fire. The stone-paved platforms, set in an ideal pattern of covering defense, could be nothing else than fighting platforms. Men who held this ridge could indefinitely hold off an attacking force of any size, even if they had no weapons but the rocks at hand. With the delicately balanced and lengthy spears which they were accustomed to wield, with slings which could hurl stones with terrific and well-aimed force, a besieged tribal remnant could be secure. It seemed that Tauira'i was right!

But as we reached the flattened top of the ridge we again had to revise our opinion. Here, on a horizontal ridge which had been completely leveled off, was a series of miniature marae. Stretching out longitudinally, one could see the altar, the upright columns—even the red stone curbings. High winds whistled around us as we carefully photographed and sketched the remains in detail. From the background of this temple we could clearly see all of the slopes below us, and again check the brilliantly laid-out covering situation of the fighting platforms. Clearly the Ra'ivavaeans used a double-edged concept of defense, much as they wielded double-pointed spears. Obeying the ancient injunction that "The Lord helps those who help themselves," they were careful to propitiate the gods while manning an almost impregnable defensive position.

It was Jim who finally clinched our picture. Above us was an almost vertical slope, with towering crags forming either side of it. I couldn't conceive of an attack from that direction. But Jim decided to climb it. As he moved up the slope like a mountain goat, I thought of the famous chant of a Ra'ivavaean father to his son:

> Go forth and reconnoiter!
> Now swiftly scale your mountain lookout!
> May your lungs be long-winded—
>   filled with your exhaustless breath!
> May your body be tense—
>   straining with the violence of your exertions,
> And the veins of your legs
>   distended with your racing blood!

I called him to return, but the ex-Marine did not hear. With a groan I went up after him, for I couldn't let the Army down, even in such a situation. When we arrived at the top the entire picture came into clear focus. This was the final rise, and the ridge here dominated the entire terrain for 360 degrees.

Pulling up the grass which covered the suspiciously flat surface we found the entire top of the ridge had been leveled and then paved with flat stones. To the rear there was a final rise, a sort of "crow's nest." From here the entire southern half of Ra'ivavae could be seen in detailed panorama. Crawling downward, Jim found that a deep man-dug foss completely cut off the entire fortress from the mountains behind. The ridge was so set that an attacker from the rear must ascend the mountain backbone of the island, move down open slopes subject to sling shots from the besieged, and then again move uphill

—only to find a steep ditch with a defending spearman above. The entire jutting ridge was an impregnable mountain fortress. Except for a few youthful goat hunters who stopped here now and then to build a fire and cook a young bird, we were the first men to rest on this citadel since pagan days!

The three of us sat long in the "crow's nest"—Jim sketched and Alan and I were busy with our own thoughts. As far as this particular location was concerned, I was satisfied that we now had the answer: this was not so much a "sanctuary" in the classical sense as a mountain fortress. It fitted in with other well-known Polynesian mountaintop fortresses such as the one on nearby Rapa, the palisaded heights of the New Zealand Maori *Pa*, and the fortified areas of Tonga. The European battle commander might worry about water and provisions; the Polynesian—knowing that his opponents lacked the cultural and psychological determination to wait and starve out an opponent, simply manned his positions and stole out at night (or else awaited his *tapu*-protected womenfolk) to bring in food and drink. Eventually the enemy tribe would tire of battle, or someone in authority would sound the drum of peace.

Sitting here it was easy to visualize Frank's accounts of the training of warriors, and to bring to mind his superb translations of Ra'ivavaean war chants. His interpretations, when reviewed from my present site, snapped into vivid focus. For the ridge upon which we sat and the area over which we looked represented much of the destiny of the Ra'ivavaean male. Here upon these fortifications, as attacker or defender, he fulfilled the destiny set for him from childhood when first his mother rubbed his vital organ with the potent unguent—

Never let yourself become as hibiscus leaves,
Blown by capricious winds into another's land,
For you have been anointed with the valor-bestowing lotion
  of the sweet-scented mountain fern.

May you display your warlike prowess in some
foreign land,
As proof of the strength of your mother,
Until the time of your death.

From boyhood the warrior was trained in the use of the javelin
and the thrusting spear, the sling and the club. Upon the com-
bat-training marae he was bred for war, taught to scream his
lineage in the face of his enemies and to shout his prowess:

> *I am a warrior hero—*
> *A towering breaker*
> > *Dashing upon the land,*
> > *Bursting in tossing spray upon the skies—*
> > *Thundering onward!*
> *A mighty surge towering on high!*
> *A flying crest!*

Combat and courage were the order of the day, redeemed by
the softer virtue of companionship, for upon the narrow dikes
of the taro fields, and probably upon the fighting platforms of
the fortresses, men fought as close-knit teams of two—one to
offensively wield his spear and the other to use his own weapon
to parry enemy thrusts.

Although there were continuous individual trials of strength
and skill between warriors, the organized raids and the formal
battles were an affair of state. From our seat in the highest
position in the fortress I could see below me the basic cause
of battle: the rich taro fields. When the population was at its
pre-European peak, each square foot of the black, water-covered
mud was zealously guarded—and as zealously coveted. For
more dangerous even than the assassination of a member of
another tribe was the shifting of boundary stones or desecration of the temples. It was the desecration of these which
caused the war drums and gongs to sound, and the trumpets

to blast the call to take up those arms stored in sanctified buildings. And old men shrieked with passion—

> A *war of just vengeance—*
> *Let the enemy be routed—*
> *May their high priest be devoured!*
> *Let him be dragged before the altar of our God,*
> *Let him be disembowelled—*
> *Let him be flung away upon the Waters of Death.*

The lore of Ra'ivavaean combat and death, raids and battles, filled hundreds of pages of Frank's field notes. In them are recounted tales of individual valor and of the courage of women, of acts of treachery by noble men and acts of heroism by base men; of the killing of women and children and the repulsing of warriors from foreign islands.

But as I sat in our eyrie, gazing at the deep ocean, the reefs, the rich lagoons, and the still-fertile taro fields, I pondered the question of leadership and of how men are ruled. I had come to Ra'ivavae hoping that among other things I could gather comparative material with which to give depth to my forthcoming detailed study of the power-laden island of Mangaia. I wished to compare the role of the *Tavana* of High Island with the king and six *Kavana* who controlled the Village of God on Mangaia.

But on Ra'ivavae I could find few traces of leadership. I saw the island *Tavana*, the chief, disregarded and mocked; heard him spoken of with contempt. When he gave his thoughts in the *fare himene* even little children ignored his words. Piahuru spoke of his *Tavana* as a mere tool of Tahitian political parties, a man who left any decisions up to the resident gendarme and who "just sat and pocketed the money" which accrued to a man of title. Where the chief once judged the disputes over land which constantly arose, these were now impartially decided by jurors from another land. Indeed, after

the most careful of investigations the only reasons I could dis-
cern for the *Tavana's* election were that he was one of the very
few "real Ra'ivavae men" who were available—and that he was
weak.

For on this and most Polynesian islands with which I am
presently acquainted, there seems today to be an actual fear
of real leadership. The men who display true ability are often
forced to move elsewhere to find outlets for their energies. The
Polynesian of today, when given a choice, displays his aggressive democracy by electing a person he considers inferior to
himself rather than superior. He pushes to its limit the ancient
Polynesian dictum, "No man's shoulders should be higher
than those of any other man." But there are deeper reasons.
With the development of dry taro cultivation and the conse-
quent lack of rigid social control of water, with the breakup
of the large pagan home into smaller Christian-approved
groups, with the passing of all warfare, sea-voyaging, adventure
—there seemed no need for leaders any more. Only the church
needs them and even here the strong pastors are trained elsewhere.

Things have changed. Our friends on Ra'ivavae are now
citizens of France—although few are really aware of this fact.
Certainly none of them fully realized the responsibilities and
rights which are implied by the idea of citizenship. On the
island a native calls himself an "Anatonu man," or "Vaiuru
man." Away from Ra'ivavae he would talk to other islanders
of being a "Ra'ivavae man," and in addition would feel some
sense of kinship to Polynesians of Tahiti or the other Austral
or Tuamotuan islands. However, even the relatively nearby
Marquesas and their inhabitants are considered something
apart. A few semiliterate persons such as Piahuru consider
France as "the mother country," but most regard France as
being as unrelated as America or Britain.

France gives far more than she receives to these distant citizens. All medical services, including the costs of passage to Tahiti and sojourn in the hospital there, are free of charge. Costs of radio service, road, wharf, and other public-works construction, schooling costs (which loom large)—all are borne by the administration. Even houses, dogs, and guns—formerly subject to a small charge—are now untaxed. Only storekeepers and commercial interests pay any charges to the government. The basis of all law is French law, although the resident gendarme does no judging. There is no jail on Ra'ivavae. The gendarme does attempt to settle disputes and difficulties which arise, but anything really serious is passed on to the Austral Islands Administrator or to the other superiors in each field—the Gendarmerie, the Treasury, or the Post Office in Tahiti.

Ra'ivavaeans had once been a proud and independent people. But now the depopulation, the long years of colonization, the nearly complete severance from the past, and the lack of responsibility to one another, has transformed them into aimless dependants of France. Temari'i, captain of the *Mareva* and one of the shrewdest Polynesians I have known, talked with me about this. His evaluation of his fellow Tahitians was much the same as my own summary of the leadership situation on Ra'ivavae: the Polynesians, unprepared now by either experience or schooling to assume their own responsibilities, were losing all sense of independence. Mothered and protected by France, who gave without demanding a return, they "ran to the government when they wanted anything. And if the request was beyond the government's means to give, they tended to blame the government for their plight, rather than working to obtain things for themselves."

We grew fond of the local gendarme, Georges Arnaud. He and his little family were both pleasant and attractive, and we saw them often. Georges was an Algerian who had formerly been stationed in Indochina and elsewhere in the French colonies. Life here was difficult for his young wife, whose first child had been born in Tahiti just before she arrived. She had absolutely no one to talk to save her husband and the youngster; consequently the latter was smothered with affection. One of Toāri'i's daughters gave her reliable household assistance, and Georges kept an excellent garden in addition to raising chickens and rabbits. (Even he was affected by the great windstorm, for it wiped out most of the island's banana plants. Since these are the normal food for the island's rats, they started attacking his livestock—eating fifteen chickens and six rabbits within four nights.)

Although Georges' duties were not arduous, they were bewilderingly diverse. He had to serve as gendarme, postman (in a "post office" which has stamps but no weighing device), radioman, even an aid man when none is posted here, in addition to supervising the general health and school services of the entire community. The Gendarmerie had given him no special training for his tour here, but the choice could not have been more fortunate. Although he does not speak the language, Georges has a genuine liking for Ra'ivavaeans and a talent for getting on. In our various trips and talks together I noted how he seemed to know both individuals and families and the idiosyncrasies and reputations of both. He handled the native language far better than he would admit. His two local policemen each serve a day on and a day off with him, and together they periodically make a tour of the island on horseback, checking the condition of the path and bridges, killing sick animals, and keeping a watch over the entire situation. We frequently ate together, sometimes sharing in the preparation of meals, sometimes as one another's guest. We benefited from his wife's excellent Parisian cooking and his own version of the native Algerian dish of *kuskus*. We were, in fact, somewhat honored by their attentions. Georges, in the tradition of independent French citizens, was very particular as to whom he invited to his home. He had been known to refuse to entertain the Governor of French Oceania or the Administrator of the Austral Islands, for, he said, he "did not like *grand persons*." One entertained them, but they never entertained one in return—why bother? Fortunately we were able to help him out by loaning our generator when that of the government radio transmitter broke down, and Jim did a fine water color for them of the little boy.

The gendarme is in fact, if not by law, the "strong man" of the island. As the representative of France he could (unofficially) overrule the native chief if the situation ever arose. It is he who gives orders to the police, not the island councilors, and it is he who hires local men to work on the roads when necessary. During the latter half of the last century, there was almost always a gendarme on High Island, supposedly stationed in Anatonu, though Georges believes that it was in Mahanatoa. During the economy era following the First World War the post was combined with that of Rapa and Tubua'i and the gendarme was stationed on the latter island. However, in these days of increasing colonial restlessness the Gendarmerie in Tahiti has been increased, and for the last two years a French representative has once again been in residence with his family upon High Island.

Ordinary disputes, whether they involve land or not, are taken before the local policeman. If he cannot settle them the matter may be brought before the *Tavana* and his island council. If the person concedes his guilt he may be fined, and—if he has no money—may work the fine out. If no solution can be reached, the gendarme arranges for a trial by a judge from Tahiti but does not officially try cases. (Unofficially he keeps matters well in hand, and seldom bothers his superiors in Tahiti.)

However, with such a highly reduced population (there were still only a bare seven hundred men, women, and children on the whole island at the time of our work there), seldom does a major quarrel arise. This current situation is far different from the complex period before the Europeans arrived, when there were continuous arguments and fights, bloodshed and warfare, between districts and tribes, even within families between father and son. These ancient quarrels were sometimes settled by bare-handed combat, often resulting in death, or by more formal wrestling bouts or spear play. Sometimes arguments were adjudicated in frightful bone-breaking contests in which the combatants stood on either side of a sharp-edged slab of stone, clasped hands, and then attempted to smash one another's arms or backbone over the rock.

Arguments over land were even more serious, and led to formal judgments by old men learned in genealogies and boundaries. At times mere knowledge would settle the issue, and at other times magic, witchcraft, and the use of oracles was brought into play. All of these represented an outlet for social contact within the tribe. When the arguments took place between individuals of differing tribes, and when woman-stealing was involved, the result might be a night raid, a skirmish, or a full-scale war, which could result in the complete extermination of one of the opponents. The loser and his supporters often fled to another island to escape the vengeance of the victors. But if the winner had obtained his victory by uncondoned means, or had let his temper allow him to seriously injure a brother or near relative, he, too, would be expected to sail for far lands.

The tribal authorities had means of enforcing the by-laws of their society. Disobedience led to corporal punishment, as did "free riding" on the great fish sweeps, or lack of adherence to ancient custom in canoe construction or communal house-building. Penalties ranging from deprivation of food or light beatings to death by the disemboweling spear were meted out for tampering with boundary stones, breaking the *tapu*, or desecrating the temples.

Today's authority is the gendarme, who is aided by a paid native secretary of civil affairs (our elderly informant Piahuru) who records births, deaths, marriages, and the like, as well as by a Tahitian director of schools and two other imported native instructors, and an aid man—also an imported trained native from Tahiti. The latter, whom I have already mentioned, was our steady friend and the husband of a relative of Zenie. This jovial Tahitian, Taupoa, had come to know Americans through his wartime service on a French gunboat which operated through the Guadalcanal-Solomons area all through the war and had American liaison personnel on board. Hence he was well accustomed to our ways and was of great value in helping us learn about local aspects of fishing, medicine, and witchcraft, as well as sexual behavior.

Taupoa not only did an excellent job of cutting our hair and frequently entertaining us at dinner, but he also ministered to our ills. One always had to watch his sense of humor, however. A local Chinese merchant came to him one day, asking Taupoa to write an affectionate letter to his Tahitian wife who had gone up to Papeete. He wanted her to return quickly to him. Instead Taupoa wrote that as the Chinese storekeeper had found a new and more attractive woman, she need not come back to the island. She has not been back since!

The educational system on Ra'ivavae has had a varied history. Before the arrival of European administrators a century ago, the children of High Island learned by doing, generally under the tutelage of their grandparents. Special craft techniques or specialized knowledge such as carving, medicine, or unique fishing skills were held strictly within the family. Since knowledge was passed along orally from grandparent to grandchild it meant that it did not pass through as many generations as if it had gone from parent to child. Hence it was more likely to be preserved intact, a fact of some importance for us.

Following the conversion of the island to Christianity, it was the native pastors who taught the entire community—men, women, and children—to read and write. Later they taught the children, although all the instruction had a religious purpose. When France became responsible for the island she saw to it that there were school instructors. At times these were Tahitians or other Polynesians; at times the gendarme's wife held the position. During the economy years of the first part of this century, however, school lapsed and a whole generation grew up without learning how to read, write, or figure in either Tahitian (which a century ago began to replace Ra'ivavaean) or French. Some effort was made by local pastors to teach the Bible on Saturdays, but the traditions and equipment of the old church schools had long since gone. The schoolhouse decayed. In 1939 the Governor of French Oceania paid a visit to the island and promised a schoolteacher. The schoolhouse was immediately reroofed, but the war intervened, and it was only in the late 1940's that formal education recommenced.

Even before I came to Ra'ivavae I had heard about the school from other visitors. It was a white-limed, red-roofed building situated in a beautifully secluded location, fronted by a curving white-sand beach and shallow lagoon. High-spirited children filed into the school building through two doors, shepherded by a male and a female teacher, each wielding a ruler to maintain order. The schoolhouse and its location formed a lovely picture, but there was only one school to serve the entire island. This meant that each day the children of Vaiuru had to cross the great mountain range which splits High Island, braving the blasts of the strong and chilly winds which perpetually sweep the hills. The teachers, I gathered, were pleasant and intelligent—especially the woman of the pair—and everyone who met her was charmed by their daughter Jasmine.

When I arrived on High Island things had obviously

123

changed. Poor little Jasmine was still there, but when I first saw her she was sitting on her mother's grave, kicking her heels idly and staring moodily off into space. Now there was a flashy new Tahitian instructress to take her mother's place, sexily dressed in the fashion of a European demimonde, who spoke very little but played a handsome guitar of *tou* wood which set off her handsome body. The natural setting of the schoolhouse had been destroyed by enclosing the play area with a "fence" of upright dried coconut leaves in order to create a "football field." A roofed-in spectators area contrasted drably with the white building. On the other side of the island a new school had been built near the village of Vaiuru, its modern architecture nicely calculated to fit in with the huge bowl of the taro-growing valley. It was complete with a radio and loudspeaker system for letting the entire village listen in to the Radio Tahiti weekly broadcasts. An efficient motherly instructress rules over it, aided by her Tahitian husband. Already they have planted a row of *toa* trees by the path as a future windbreak. Frequently we met their students on the way to school, carrying luncheon packets of *popoi* or drinking-nuts, and were greeted with "*bonjour*," the most obvious benefit of their education. Occasionally one would see the teachers and their pupils, divided up as to boys and girls, out in the woods with their slates and pencils taking a "nature walk."

Just as the educational system has drastically changed from that of pre-European times, so has the system of rank and social structure. Although the royal families retained power long after the conversion of the island to Christianity, French concepts of democracy and a lack of any precise function for the nobility undermined the inherited rights of the district kings. Indeed, after the drastic depopulation of the island, intermarriage between everyone became a commonplace and most High Islanders can now trace their kinship into the royal family if they care to. But today nobody worries about royal rank. The

Our beloved friend, neighbor, and informant, Mama Iē

*Uncle Bert,
the jovial Deacon*

*Tioti, the Tuamotuan
cook, doctor, pastor,
and major-domo of
the expedition*

The Orphan. There is no greater misfortune than for a Polynesian to be without parents

A son-in-law of Toārīʾi with his daughter

*Our maid Pogi, daughter of Toāri'i, whom Ra'ivavaens called the "Virgin."
She was most unique among the older women of Anatonu, for she had
yet to know the love of a man*

old hierarchy which separated the island into the several ranks of king and priest, judge and master craftsman, warrior and middle-class landholder, commoners or slaves, has vanished. There are only citizens of France, of equal rank and status.

The *Tavana* or "government chief" of Ra'ivavae lived in the village of Anatonu. I frequently saw him and chatted with him, and watched him in action at church meetings and as presiding deacon at certain services. He was relaxed and friendly, handsome and pleasant, but I always wondered how he became the elected head of the island of Ra'ivavae, for he seemed to demonstrate few qualities we ordinarily associate with the office. I tried to find the answer since I was interested in the problem of leadership, and it was not a simple one.

Following the first visit of Pomare and the evangelization of High Island, the three dominant royal families of the major districts still retained power as sort of "father-protectors" who operated within the framework of the London Missionary Society church. They settled land disputes, judged arguments, and untangled inheritance claims. Even when elections became the mode, it was the descendants of royalty who were elected to office.

Under French administrative control the chiefs of Ra'ivavae have been elected for many generations. Indeed, until the economic pressures of the depression made a cutback mandatory (the chief draws pay from the French Administration rather than from local resources), Ra'ivavae was divided into two autonomous districts, each with a full political apparatus, and supervised by the single gendarme who oversaw island affairs. The democratic process is observed throughout the island, with all persons over twenty-one voting for officials, from church deacons to alternate members of the island council. The elections take place in the house of the presiding chief (High Island has yet to construct a "government house"), under the supervision of the Secretary of Civil Affairs. Individuals go into a room which has a table bearing a pile of slips. These have been written out by individual candidates or their political parties and bear the names of the political contestants. The voter chooses a slip and puts it into an envelope. He then returns to the room in which the rest of the voters are assembled and drops his envelope of votes into the ballot box under the eyes of the rest of the group. It is said that only five or ten of those persons eligible to vote do not exercise their privilege. Names of the candidates for office must be submitted a week before the election is held. One does not need to vote for all the officials up for election. The Civil Secretary says that there is plenty of "soft-soaping" during the elections and there is also some interest expressed by the several political parties of French Oceania, headquartered at Papeete.

The political parties solicit card-holding members (and contributors) at election times, but otherwise they are seldom in evidence. Lines and shifts in Ra'ivavae follow those of the main parties at Tahiti. The groups are not only interested in having members elected to local offices, but also to other elected positions such as the delegate for the Austral Islands to the Assembly at Tahiti and the delegate to the French government at Paris. There are no practical voting requirements. As one friend put it: "If the voters can't read, others will read for them whatever is necessary."

In point of fact our present *Tavana*, Te-ua-ari'i, did not win his election. But Ro'o, the man who did, decided that he lived too far from the center of things to carry out the duties of his office and the island council elected Te-ua-ari'i in his place. His main distinction seems to be that he is one of the few present-day island residents who is generally recognized as being "a real Ra'ivavae man" (i.e., descended from Ra'ivavaean parents on both sides). Members of the other political party accuse the council of "high-handedness" in making their decision, but there is little doubt but that the procedure was generally correct. Nevertheless the fact remains that the present *Tavana* is shown little respect when he is talking to the people or when he is being talked about. Political opponents and disinterested Tahitian administrative personnel alike condemn him as being a "cipher who knows and does nothing." Opponents say that "he is an ignorant man who does nothing but draw his pay and put the money in his pocket."

It was difficult for us to disagree with these comments. The *Tavana* neither reads nor speaks French or English. In the weeks of our stay we never saw him bedecked with the red, white, and blue sash of office. We did see and hear plenty of him at meetings, and were unimpressed. His wife and daughter made and sold us baskets for our own use and as museum specimens. But our general consensus was that he was a weak man who could not control a dispute. He was so soft that people no longer listened to him. His kinsmen say that he is a "good" *Tavana* because he "smooths over trouble without the need to send people to jail." Essentially it seemed to me that he reflected the Polynesian tendency I have seen on other islands: never elect a man of ability to office, for then he will use the office to get himself and his family ahead.

In more active areas such as Tahiti the chief has a real function and great influence on local affairs. But this is not the case on High Island. Particularly when the gendarme is in residence, the situation is such that at best the *Tavana* can be but a rubber stamp. The same is true with the *muto'i*, or island policeman. Although he may settle minor arguments within the village, the issue may be taken over his head to the gendarme—particularly if the disputants are from a family which is traditionally at odds with the family of the policeman. Zenie witnessed a typical situation at the village clothes-washing place by the taro stream.

One girl of about twenty accused the daughter of the *Tavana*, who was her age, of stealing her bar of soap. The latter was rather timid and retreated to her father's home. The first girl was not up to invading the chief's home, but she was fully capable of standing in the road daring the other girl to come out and fight. "I'm going to twist your arm off," she screamed. Finally she was so exasperated by the other's unwillingness to stage a public brawl that she reverted to the ancient Polynesian custom of facing away from her opponent, raising her dress, and baring her bottom at the enemy. (This gesture was once practiced by warriors as a sign of contempt, or when neither could defeat the other in combat, as a sign of equality.) "How do you like my bottom?" she raged.

The chief's daughter summoned up enough courage to shout back, "It's a stinking bottom!"

About this time the crowd of neighborhood women who had gathered around noticed Zenie, and one shouted at the belligerents, "Haven't you any shame, baring your bottom in front of a stranger?"

Far from feeling shame the more aggressive girl then came to Zenie, appealing to her to take sides in the argument. When Zenie would only tell her to "forget the whole affair," she flounced off, angrily stating that she was going to get the policeman and have him force the chief's daughter to pay for her soap. Two hours later she appeared before the *muto'i*, who immediately chased her back home. He told us that the women here were continuously getting into such arguments (over bars of soap, a thimble, or a bit of cloth), many of which wound up in hair-pulling contests.

We saw a good deal of this same policeman during our stay in Anatonu. Like the other village *muto'i*, he had been appointed by the administration in Tahiti, following his own application submitted through the supervising gendarme. He had worn his red-banded cap for five years. One day I remarked that there was no jail and asked what sort of trouble he met. "Oh, there is never any trouble here," he replied, candidly adding, "a good thing there isn't, for if there was I wouldn't know how to handle it." We did not doubt the latter, for our friend was more noted for his smile than for his intelligence or initiative.

Ra'ivavae proudly boasts that there has never been a major crime on this island, and I found no indication to the contrary. Murder is unknown, and though once in ten years or so a charge of "rape" is brought, this is generally a case of one family taking advantage of a European code of law to spite the son of another family. Most of these cases seldom if ever come to a real trial or even go before the local council. The main function of the *muto'i* seems to be to listen to quarrels over food-stealing or arguments about and by women.

Chapter Six

THE BASIS OF LIFE

O Almighty spirit of the glistening rainbow!
May our fishing canoe be filled with all kinds
of fish,
May they become nourishment for our children—
from the full grown to the tiniest babe.
May they feed all to repletion,
from the aged masters and middle-aged sages
to the youngest acolytes,—
So shall it be!
O ardent and upright God!

WHAT shall we eat today?" is the gnawing question which preoccupies the Polynesian every day of his life. On High Island in particular, where the population has been so terribly decimated, almost all labor must be devoted to the never-ending business of finding enough food to keep the family alive. All other goals of existence are subordinate to this. Even when the men are not working they gossip about fishing and planting for hours on end, wondering about next week's weather, the way the sea will run, the winds and the rain. For it is the weather which rules life on Ra'ivavae, weather which makes the difference between going fishing or not—and having fish to eat or not. And because weather is variable, all life activities in Polynesia must be subject to immediate change. Man must adapt his activities and his life to the vagaries of nature. There can be no such thing as "scheduled activity."

The sole exception to the natural relationship between man and nature is the one imposed by the Christian church. Although the great purpose of Polynesian worship is to propitiate God so that he may provide good crops and plentiful fish, the High Islander follows the calendar laid down centuries ago by our own Christian forefathers. He lives as nature dictates—or permits—for five days of the newly introduced Western week; the sixth is devoted to preparation for the seventh, and the seventh is (for the most part) devoted to the worship of God.

On Saturday the women of the family do the weekly laundry by the taro beds and then, with heavy charcoal-fire irons, press the clothing for the entire family for hours on end, for these must be fresh, starched, and neatly pressed for the morrow. Besides, the yards must be swept, the house cleaned, and more than double the usual supply of food brought in. This means that the men must visit plantations and spend most of their time there gathering and harvesting, while the most able fishermen in the family spend a good part of the day in the lagoon— if the weather is right. Should the family be old-fashioned enough to hold to the interdiction against cooking on Sunday, all of the cooking for the weekend must be done on Saturday.

In any case, when Sunday arrives there is not a person in Anatonu who will work, despite the most pressing needs of the plantation or the likelihood of luck in fishing. For one day in the week God's schedule overrules the dictates of nature and the earthly needs of man.

Come Monday, life resumes its normal course. Let us take one of the younger and smaller families in our village of Anatonu and follow it through a typical day, for in this way the basic activities of island life become clear.

At dawn the crowing of a rooster may wake the man of the family, who then sits quietly thinking about the day ahead and the work to be done. He then calls to the children. The household comes alive, slowly. The calls of nature are answered, and

the parents—especially the women—are careful to wash their privates. Then while the parents bow under their blankets to pray silently, the half-grown daughters start a fire and hang a water kettle over it, while a younger brother sits around and watches. Someone husks a coconut on a sharp, upright stake, cracks the nut, and grates it. It will be used for cream in the coffee and is ground by any of the family who has a free hand. A bowl and a pot, unwashed the previous evening when darkness fell, are now scrubbed. The boiling water is poured through a cloth strainer to make drip coffee. The only one who does not take part in these morning chores is the father. He goes out to his tethered hog with some leftover food, changes the grazing for his horse, and comes back with a five-gallon kerosene tin of water for the day. By this time one of the children has laid a banana leaf on the floor, and all sit around while the father says grace. With the coffee there may be a morsel from the day before—taro or manioc, *popoi*, an orange or a banana. Occasionally there is bread. But nothing special is made, for the Austral Islanders eat one real meal a day, an hour before sunset.

Like everywhere else in the world, there is apt to be a baby or two to clean up, and a young child to be packed off to school. A girl's hair plaits require the mother's attention, and some food must be folded in a leaf wrapper for the school child —a morsel of *popoi* probably. A drinking-coconut often makes a nice box lunch. After drinking the milk the film of young flesh on the inside can be scraped out for a quick snack.

By this time the man is off to his plantation work. If he only has a garden adjoining his house by the shore he may postpone tending it for an hour while he tries fishing for the meal of the day. But if the plantation is a substantial one inland he is more likely to tackle its chores while his strength is fresh. If the son is old enough he can help his father, but if he is too young he is left to play as he likes. Dressed in denim shorts, torn undershirt, and a hat of pandanus leaves stuck with fishhooks, the father of the family goes off to work carrying a brush knife, a sack, tobacco, and a pandanus-leaf cigarette wrapper. He is apt to light his cigarettes with either a hard chunk of wood glowing from the breakfast fire or from a fire made by rubbing sticks together. His work may be planting (if the moon is right), or clearing and burning brush, hilling-up sweet potatoes, tending his taro patch. During a long, hard rain he plants coffee, for at that time the young seedlings can be pulled up without stripping their rootlets too badly. He works, smokes, picks a papaya or a guava for a quick meal, and watches his sun time-piece for high noon. Then he stops; fish must be found for the evening meal. But before he leaves, the father, the provider, stocks up on staples which may be needed at the house: taro or a few coconuts, a papaya or a banana, even a small load of firewood. "Never come back empty-handed" is a saying of the Islanders who work in the valleys every day; and when the family sees the worker returning from his plantation carrying his load on a shoulder stick, "fore-and-aft," they know that there will be something to eat.

138

By the time he has returned, the wife has put her house in order, airing the bedding on the crinum hedge, washing clothing that cannot wait for the regular Saturday laundering, weeding the miniature flower bed. Now as the man throws down his load outside the cookhouse, the woman begins a new task, helped by an old grandparent or an almost-grown daughter or, even, a reluctant son who will soon quit to go fishing with his father. If it is just twelve o'clock, an earth oven is started and the taro is pared of its rind and wrapped in leaf parcels while the stones slowly grow hot. If it is later in the day, a pot is hung over the fire and everything is boiled in a hurry.

The man and his boy throw their fishing gear in their canoe and put it into the water, then work out along the nearby areas of the lagoon. What they want is a small mess of fish, quickly, a half-size parrot fish, a young grouper, or a rudder fish. If there were no boy in the family, the man would have to find some neighbor to paddle the canoe and a double quantity of fish would have to be caught. Usually the fish can be found near the surface but if this does not happen the fisherman drops his pronged spear, takes the short, single-steel one without a barb, his water glasses, and goes overboard, sinking quietly into the water on the outrigger side of his canoe.

In this half-lit submarine world studded with strange limestone formations he tries to corner fish. If the two men in the boat are equally skilled and familiar with the passages in the particular limestone "cavern" they are exploring, they may try to block the openings on one side and drive the fish out into the open. But father and son of equal power are uncommon and the usual practice is desultory, a stabbing at whatever luck puts in the way. Even there, if luck fails there is a last recourse —tridacna, the rather tough giant clam. Tridacna has always been a second choice, but it is better than nothing and with night falling after an unlucky afternoon something must be found. Formerly, tridacna were abundant in foot-deep shallows, but now the work of prying them loose from the coral with an eighteen-inch iron crowbar must be done four fathoms down if a fair-sized catch is wanted. However, rather than being a food brought in by women when stormy weather prevents men from regular fishing as before, they are now eaten frequently.

Even if he has luck and the fish and taro are in the earth oven early, the man will not return to his plantation in the afternoon. Waiting for dinner he sees to his hog, changes his horse to fresh grazing, and works about the house or rests in the doorway with a baby in his arms, waiting for the school-age child to return and play until dinner is ready.

Just as soon as the food is cooked the whole family sets it out on banana or crinum leaves in an enthusiastic burst of activity. After rinsing their hands all sit cross-legged around the fish helpings, the taro, the bowl of coconut sauce in which all is dipped. After grace by the father, the hands pick up the food, rapidly, neatly; fish bones are separated in the mouth and placed on the leaf table. There are no courses. Fish may be eaten from one hand and bananas from the other. A nursing infant sleeps a few yards away, snugly wrapped, but babies a size larger sprawl on the mother's lap and get morsels of fish or taro, but not the raw tridacna.

When fish is plentiful, a sizeable leftover may be wrapped again and hung up for the next day. Smaller scraps go to the pig or dog. The banana-leaf platter-table may go to the pig as well. The bowl and pot are left to be scrubbed in the morning if it is now dark.

After the meal comes the evening bath in some pool beside a nearby taro stream or at the new main-street faucet. On cold-wind nights a splash from the water remaining in the kerosene can will do. Only the baby gets warm water. Fishing people are not dirty, but Austral Islanders have not the Tahitians' reputation for cleanliness.

There is now an oil lamp for putting the children to sleep, replacing the candlenut light of ten years ago. When the father's prayer is done the house goes dark, and sleep comes quickly. But the grown-up, unmated children retire later. Their guitars sound under trees for a while, they laugh and run as silhouettes against the lagoon. They may play for two hours or more, without protest from the parents. Suddenly, all are gone. Anatonu is still, without a light.

On Ra'ivavae, as everywhere else in the world, however, there are vast differences between families, and these show up most clearly in the way each handles the daily meal which is the focal point of most economic activity. I remember with pleasure the extraordinary neatness of my friend Tino's cookhouse, beautifully constructed and thatched. It was divided into two equal parts by a coconut log, the cooking section covered with neatly raked white sand, the eating section with pandanus mats over a cushioning layer of sweet grass. All of his well-scrubbed utensils were hanging in order in an easily available place. On the floor the "table" consisted of green leaves laid out in a neatly overlapping regular series, and for each person in the family there was a plate and eating utensils —again regularly laid out. Set in the center was a big bowl of taro *po'e*, the fermented paste so favored by Polynesians, and roast taro was laid out at each individual place. Tino himself was frying up strips of wild goat meat to serve to his dependants and he bustled from fire to family serving the young people who waited patiently.

Across the street there was another family, as well-to-do, as prominent, even larger than Tino's. But the cookshed was old and dilapidated, with great gaps in the roof through which the sunlight showed and rain could pour. No separation was made between eating and cooking place. Sloppiness prevailed, and the shack was full of unpleasant odors. Dogs, cats, and chickens skittered about and the family pigs looked on from the side.

Yet despite these variations in personality and behavior, which are good-naturedly accepted in the Polynesian world, each member of a family knows the part he will play from the time he begins to walk. The relationship between sexes and age-groupings still reflects ancient patterns. Young girl-children, themselves hardly out of the toddler stage, guard and carry about with them smaller children. Small boys and girls carry tins and kettles of water from the stream to the home, kick-

ing a homemade pandanus-leaf football about as they wend
their playful way from one place to the other. By the time
the small girl has reached the age of five or six she is able to
thump her own laundry with a tiny club in accomplished fashion and the boy can wash a used roasting pan. Both may keep
a watchful eye on smaller children, lug bunches of dried banana leaves to the taro patches, pick up coffee beans in small
tins. Children learn all of the regular ways of life by doing, by
imitating the parents as soon as they can handle the tools involved.

Between six and eight, the division of labor between the sexes
becomes more obvious. The boy is more likely to be spading in
the taro patches or carrying home bundles of firewood—even
trying his hand at fishing. The sister becomes more dependable
in guarding smaller children, washing clothes, and doing a
modicum of cleaning. At this stage girls may also start to plait
mats and hats, and learn the few types of needlework still
practiced by the women of High Island. Even such subtle matters as how much firewood should be burned to heat the stones

of an earth oven and how long to leave the oven covered are grasped at this age.

By nine a High Island boy is casting spears at beach targets to develop his eye for fish-spearing, and going out with his father or uncle to learn the habits of fish. But even so, he is less dependable than his sister, spending more and more time away from the house playing with his age mates. He may still work from time to time in the taro fields, may fish a little, but he is not asked to assume any steady responsibility. Perhaps it is in anticipation of the heavy burden he will later take up as head of a family that the boy is allowed to pass through a privileged period in which he may play the guitar at any hour of day or night, kick a football, sleep while his parents work, drink, experiment sexually, and generally "sow his wild oats." His father did the same before him, and so he will allow his own sons to behave similarly when they reach this age.

The daughter on the other hand is more and more restricted to the home and the work around the home—washing, cleaning, pounding out *popoi*, doing errands—always in the company of smaller children. One may see the older girl and half a dozen of her brothers and sisters of all ages from two to twenty working together on the squash patch or sweet-potato garden near the house. All squat busily over the work, the youngest searching for sticks and branches to make a little windbreak on the seaward side, older ones hilling up the young plants, all under the direction of the shrill-voiced elder girl. Here they learn the pleasure and importance of family labor (as contrasted to the lack of family social life) which will characterize the rest of their lives.

By their mid-teens both boys and girls know enough about the basic facts of life to assume the responsibilities of mating and raising a family. Yet it may be ten to fifteen years later before they will give up the relative independence of life within the confines of their own family for marriage—and this only after months or years of trial living with one or several partners, as we will see later. Once having made the decision to settle down to the responsibilities and restrictions of raising children, the man and woman work smoothly and efficiently as an economic unit. Truly heavy labor is handled by the man —spading up new taro beds, carrying sacks of coffee gathered by the rest of the family, building the limestone houses and making the lime, constructing canoes. The man also has the sole responsibility for catching those fish which must be taken by spearing or from canoes over deep water; women confine their lagoon activities to gathering shellfish, groping under rocks for smaller varieties of fish, or using a light rod and line along the shore. For their part, women make the clothing, mats, and hats, do most of the laundry, and handle some of the chores connected with raising children. All preparation of food, however, is a joint affair. As in Toāri'i's household, the men do all the heavy labor of making the earth oven, the women prepare the food which is to be cooked in it.

When life on Ra'ivavae was in the full splendor of its ancient civilization, when there was sufficient labor to spare, the pattern of daily living was far different. Then the women of lower rank carried out most of the work in the taro fields and plantations, leaving their men free to fish in the lagoon and deep sea. In the upper ranks the women kept busy fashioning bark cloth for wear and for household use, while the higher-ranking males practiced the more artistic expressions of Ra'ivavaean life: the continued rehearsal with weapons required by the warriors, the craftsmanship of workers in wood and stone, the construction and sailing of vessels of exploration and war, the practice and periodic exposition of dance, oratory, and music.

But with the drastic decline in population on High Island, such specialists could no longer be supported. Persons of all ranks and all ages had to occupy themselves with satisfying the daily search for food, and fit in whenever possible the work on houses and crops.

Although the new cloth, more durable than that made of bark, and washable where tapa was not, freed women from the labor of beating out bark, which once had occupied many of the adult years of their life, it was the Christian missionaries who most drastically changed the patterns of life on Ra'ivavae. The missionaries were horrified to find women laboring in the fields, while men fished or made war. They believed that women should be solely employed in the care of children, in sewing clothes to cover heathen nakedness, and in making "respectable bonnets" to wear. Hence it was left to the man to plant and weed and harvest the fields, do the fishing, build the houses, lead the church services, make the canoes, raise the cash crops—and continue to make the ovens, do much of the cooking, and play the same role in the raising of children as they had done before. And as Polynesian children handle themselves to a great extent, and grandparents and the new school system take care of much of their instruction, the young and middle-aged women at the village are left with plenty of time on their hands while their husbands are away in the fields. To this imbalance in the division of labor may be attributed much of the malicious gossip, slander, quarreling, and jealousy which disrupts the village from time to time.

With the plummeting decline in the population of High Island, however, and the Christian emphasis on the nuclear family of man, wife, and small children, there are many enterprises which a small household cannot undertake. Once several generations lived together and worked as a unit, but now the team of available kinsmen for a large job has dropped below the point of efficiency. In its place the *pupu* has come to be of increasing economic significance. It is a "work gang" of men (or women on occasion) who live in the same vicinity and can join together to spade over a taro patch, relash a canoe, make a lime pit, or lay up the walls of a limestone house. They may or may not be kinsmen and the partners may be of any age from fourteen to forty. Fluctuating in membership from year to year, the group takes turns at the work needs of each individual member. Usually the *pupu* works two hours each at two plantations or house projects each morning, breaking up in the afternoon to allow each member to carry out his fishing for the day. The frank comments which are standard within the group keep the younger members from breaking off work when the spirit moves them.

As the High Islander grows older and less active, he remains closer to home, leaving it to the younger men to take part in the *pupu*, go out for fish, pick up and bag the coffee. The older folks care for and aid in the education of the grandchildren, and concern themselves with the religious activities of the group. But the main function of the older man is to impart his knowledge and experience to the young.

Yet how meager this knowledge and experience seems when compared to the rich wisdom which the High Islanders once possessed. Since the problem of finding food is central to their very existence it might be expected that the inhabitants of Ra'ivavae would have amassed a subtle and elaborate body of fishing and agricultural techniques. We know that they did. Once, expert specialists led vigorous bands of men in the construction of great stone fish weirs while other teams wove elegant fishing nets and various types of traps, or fashioned lengthy leaf sweeps to scare schools of fish into waiting hands. Such community co-operation was bound up with strict codes of behavior and with elaborate religious rituals to sanctify the apparatus and to propitiate the gods for favor. Stone images of fish were used to draw fish to a desirable area. One of the two great religious rites of the year, the *Heheru*, was held in November to ask for an abundance of fish during the coming year. Such practical knowledge and the psychological effect of belief in divine favor brought results. Catches were great and were communally divided. Ra'ivavaeans did not hesitate to troll for bonito or albacore, or to fish in open waters with bone-tipped wooden hooks for the *ruvettus*, the grouper, and the tuna. Groupers and the oil fish, *ruvettus*, were set aside for the king; and the gods were also allotted their share.

Most of the ancient knowledge passed away when the island was decimated by the epidemic of the 1820's. Today the High Islander is fearful of the deep sea and seldom ventures beyond the reef. There are no more vast communal efforts. Most fish are now taken by spear, either thrown from the platform in front of the canoe or thrust while underwater with the aid of swimming goggles, introduced by Europeans. Fish are still the major protein element in the diet, but today shellfish and crustacea and even the contemptible sea slug are eaten without regret. Tins of New Zealand corned beef take up the slack. One of the few traditions which remains from the past is the communal division of the catch. Fishermen who work together satisfy their own needs in equal shares from the catch, and their catch is divided among their kinsmen. Fish are never sold. There is a practical element to the division, however. Among a people with no way of preserving food for more than a day or two, it would be wasteful not to give away the excess. And in Polynesia gifts are like bread cast upon the water—they invariably are returned in full measure at some propitious time.

If fishing has fallen on evil days, the noble sport of hunting the sea turtle has all but disappeared. There is a famous song from Ra'ivavae which goes

> *Overturned on the shore are the captured turtles.*
> *Their virile organs are trophies belonging to*
>   *the clan of the diving champions.*
> *Ho!*
>   *Unrivalled Champions!*
> *Full twenty mighty turtles have fallen to their prowess*
>   *upon this memorable night!*

The proud ecstasy of this chant is understandable, for not only was the task of catching the turtle with bare hands in deep water in the black of night a highly dangerous display of courage, but the rich meat was so highly prized that it was generally reserved for chiefs and priests. Moreover, the turtle had a religious and ceremonial significance and it was usually cut up upon sacred marae with appropriate ritual. Now, this risky sport which was once reserved to young men of the aristocracy is gone.

Not only have the youth lost the taste for such activity, but the old experts who knew the location of turtle lairs and the habits of the animals are long dead. There is still some turtle hunting done, but it is done with an iron spear, capable of penetrating the carapace. When the season is right, and if there are sufficient men willing to take the risk, a few canoes may venture into the lagoon or even into the sea in hopes of spearing a turtle. But even if they are successful, only the few fishermen and their families share in the catch, and no one cares, since it is a rare thing indeed.

The passing of the wisdom of the sea is more dramatic than the gradual loss of agricultural knowledge, but the latter has been no less momentous for the life of Ra'ivavae. Though the High Islanders eat breadfruit, coconut, sweet potato, and many other foods, taro has always been the true staff of life, not only for them, but for all the inhabitants of Eastern Polynesia.

Native to that part of Southeast Asia which was probably once the homeland of the Polynesians themselves, the plant has been cultivated so long that one rarely sees it in flower. There are innumerable varieties in the island, most cultivated for their distinctive differences, but also several varieties which have "escaped" from the cultivated state and again have reverted to the "wild" condition. The basis of cultivation is simple; the work itself is arduous. The plant stores foodstuffs in a corm, the bulbous area just above the mesh of small roots

—comparable to the familiar onion or to the lily bulb itself. When harvesting, one merely cuts or breaks off the corm slightly below the base of the stalk. After deleafing the stalk it then may be thrust back into the mud to regrow; six months to a year later, depending upon the variety, the plant is ready for the next harvest. The cycle is perpetual, although varied and increased in yield by the use of young plants which grow out to the sides of the main corm when it is left for more than an optimum period.

Until the beginning of the twentieth century the taro of Ra'ivavae was grown in a complicated set of terraced, water-covered beds—comparable to the rice paddies of Southeast Asia. Entire valleys were systematically covered with a series of small banked patches, so engineered that water flowing from streams at the head of the valley passed from one patch to another, covering the entire area with sheets of slowly moving water from six inches to a foot in depth. Below the water was a foot and a half to three feet of soft mud, in which grew the taro; the deeper the mud and the growth of the roots the firmer the texture and the finer the flavor of the corm. Fertilization was done in two ways: the waters flowing down from the valley above brought a minute but never-ceasing supply of fresh soil; the planter continually pushed the weeds which grew around his taro down into the mud to re-enrich his soil. Yet despite the fine flavor and continuing abundance of this food source there were disadvantages. Both men and women worked the patches, laboring in knee- to waist-deep mud for days on end, not only gathering and replanting the food but keeping each patch spotlessly free of weeds and arranged with geometric regularity. Many developed rheumatism at an early age.

At the turn of the century, a new way of growing taro was introduced to Ra'ivavae which gradually drove out the old "wet" culture. This was a "dry-land" method which is said to have originated in Samoa. The same variety of plants were used, but instead of being grown under a sheet of water the stalks were set out in holes made in the soil. Around the patch there is usually a ditch of stagnant water to keep it moist. Moreover, the dirt between plants is covered with dried banana leaves or coconut fronds to prevent its drying out. The new method gives a larger corm, but it is mealier and tastes flatter than the old-fashioned taro. No one seems to mind, however. The islanders find it a relief not to work in water for hours on end, and they do not miss the elaborate efforts which were needed to maintain those neat beds and embankments which are the most splendid aesthetic byproduct of "wet" taro culture. To them, the mosquitoes which spawn in the stagnant water of the irrigation ditches seem a small price to pay for the comparative ease of growing taro on dry land.

Throughout the history of Ra'ivavae the land has played a critical part in the life of the islanders. Every section of the island that can be cultivated is divided and subdivided—from the mountainsides and the reef islets to the richer soil near the shore. Each miniscule patch of taro is the property of some family, some individual. The power that decides the ownership and allocation of land controls the island, its life, and its people. Once it belonged to the kings of Ra'ivavae, who held it even when Christianity came, for they worked in co-operation with the missionaries who supervised them. They held this power throughout the terrible years when the plague swept the island and the population dwindled away. Only when the control of land tenure was taken over by the impartial and beneficent law of France did royal dominance disappear.

The blessing, however, was a mixed one. French law is democratic, universal. It gives each individual his just rights. But it is too atomistic for Ra'ivavae, whose tradition vested permanent ownership of land in the family, leaving the control of family administration to the leader of the kin group. Once quarrels between family heads over ownership of land and the location of boundary stones led to bloodshed and war, exile and migration. Today the quarrels are less momentous, but they have a vicious, spiteful quality to them, for they are apt to take place within a family as well as between families. Under the new system, where land is divided equally between children, it does not take many generations for some families to breed to the level where plots owned by the individual are too small to support him or his family. Then there are cases where a family dies out and the land remains unused. In former times such land would be reapportioned by tribal authorities; today there is no mechanism for such division. A landless person must either marry someone whose family owns land or must emigrate to Tahiti and find a job.

Chapter Seven

TO FAR LANDS

Every cord is tied,
All is firmly lashed in place.
Bird-carved prows strain
for the long voyage of the Sea Kings!

Now the breeze holds steadily from the land,
And proudly the great ships ride
eager upon the waves—

Oh, heart-stirring sight!

FEW people have been such great shipbuilders and sailors as the Polynesians. In their huge twin-hulled craft, constructed of planks literally "sewn" together with coconut-fiber cord, they set out, shortly before the beginning of the Christian era, from their homeland *Havaiki* to fish up new lands from the sea. These superb navigators with their women and children sailed thousands of miles over the uncharted Pacific before the European had the courage to venture beyond the sight of Continental shores. To plot their course they watched the minute shifts in the colors of the sea and in the patterns and motion of its waves, looked for differences in the colors and movement of clouds which hung over the horizon, kept track of both the migrating and shore-based birds, and most important, relied on an intimate knowledge of the stars and their movements. The captains inherited their knowledge from their ancestors—the Sea-Drinkers, as the Polynesians at times called themselves, and they were sure of their great skill. One of their oldest chants goes:

> "Haul—haul *the great ship down to the shore—*
> *Thence she shall be safely guided to distant lands*
> *By her renowned star-gazer and navigator, the*
>   *unerring one!"*

With a supreme confidence in the skills of man and in the beneficence of the gods who shape human destiny, with contempt for fear and even for death itself, the Sea Kings discovered the habitable islands of the entire eastern Pacific area. Northeast to Hawaii, southeast to New Zealand, fanning out —but always moving eastward, to the rising sun—the Polynesians rapidly settled the Cooks, the Societies, the Tuamotus, the Australs; went thence to Mangareva and Rapa, to Pitcairn, and then—the longest voyage of all—to remote and mysterious Easter Island. Some botanical evidence suggests that they may even have reached the shores of South America.

It is understandable that the white "discoverers" of the Pacific islands overlooked the seafaring genius of the Polynesians, for by the time they arrived in these places the Polynesians' profound knowledge of ship construction and navigation was already on the wane. There was little need for these skills once all of the eastern islands had been discovered and populated. The energies of this vigorous people turned from exploration to conquest. They became less interested in mastering the sea and more interested in mastering their enemies. When the first European explorers arrived, there were no more voyaging canoes, only vessels of war, though tales of exploration and long voyages to far lands were still sung.

Today, to the best of my knowledge, it is only in the poems and songs which Frank Stimson has translated that we can understand the extraordinary sympathy which the Polynesians had for the sea. In these we feel again the passions which beset the sailor as he left his home, the joys of finding a new land, the sadness and terror which came over him as his ships lay beached upon a foreign shore. And in them we can hear a faint echo of what it was to be a Polynesian, living in harmony with the sea and the winds and the waves.

O North Wind!

You come from the Primeval Source
trembling in the first throes of creation,
While the divine seed of life, there—far below,
Impregnates the womb of the winds!

You come, red-washed in streamers of the sunset,
Trailing cloud banners
torn in the consummation of your desire.
Evoke your rapture till the oceans seethe and toss!

All this is gone, but on High Island there still remains a tenuous link which connects with the past. Here the *tahuṇa*, the canoe experts, still retain knowledge of how to carve out the planks, join together seven or more sections, and shape them all into the graceful pattern of the sewn canoe with its flattened elongated bow which serves as a platform for the spearman. Now the Ra'ivavaean makes use of iron bars and plastic cement where they can be used. But he still finds that the sewn-together hull provides a greater sturdiness and cargo capacity than can be found in the craft of the other islanders. These are either the plank-built canoes made of Oregon pine or the older dugout canoes which need huge trees that are no longer available.

When I first saw these sewn craft—the largest canoes I had seen in the islands—I was deeply moved. With their projecting prow they seemed like ancient history come to life. I knew them only from the renderings of the artists who had accompanied the early explorers. At first I was puzzled as to why the canoes

155

seemed to occur in pairs, one with the outrigger on the port side, the other rigged to starboard. Usually Polynesian canoes only have an outrigger on the left side. Then I found out that the canoes are frequently joined side by side to meet the high seas of the open lagoon as they carry huge loads of pandanus leaves or great fishing nets or leaf sweeps from the islets across the wide lagoon. Yet it is not only tradition which makes the High Islander continue to build his complex craft in the old way. Even now they are ideally suited to ply the wide lagoon as far out as the barrier-reef islets. And at the same time they can navigate the shallow fringing reef, carrying heavy loads of coffee, lime, or coral. I appreciated the versatility of these slim canoes when I saw how easily they carried our heavy generator and other supplies from ship to shore. And I have seen seven men poling along a single canoe loaded with pandanus or other materials for house construction a few minutes after it had been used for a fishing trip far out in the lagoon.

Sails are no longer used in the canoes, even in the rare cases when the men of the island venture out upon the deep ocean. The natives feel that the working of the sail puts too much strain upon the coconut-fiber-cord hull fastenings. This necessitates the laborious chore of relashing more frequently than they care to. Although a sail could easily be used on the present craft, the High Islander prefers to paddle his canoe even to the most distant *motu*, saying that he can reach there in less than an hour's time. Obviously he is fond of this craft. Although there formerly was a foreign-built planked sailboat on the island which was used to gather coral for use in the lime kilns, the continuous labor of caulking it with oakum and painting it was too demanding and it was allowed to go to ruin. A few men are content with one of the other types of small dugout fishing canoes, but most own or borrow one of the larger sewn canoes. Only the Tahitian schoolteachers experiment with outboard motors—usually attached to a newfangled catamaran.

During our stay in Ra'ivavae we did not have the opportunity to witness the construction of a canoe, for even with the comparative prosperity of the new coffee economy (sadly hurt) the business is an expensive one, not lightly entered into. It is usually necessary to accumulate from six to eight hundred *tārā* (about fifty dollars) and then employ a canoe "expert," *tahuŋa*, to supervise the job. Each village has one or two of these specialists, but since fifty dollars is a goodly sum for High Island they are not often employed for the full job.

However, we were lucky enough one morning to find a canoe-relashing *pupu* at work behind Piahuru's house. His family canoe had not been resewn for some five years, and the joints were now worn and leaking. The craft was no longer suitable for long periods of work in the lagoon. Piahuru's household was fortunate in that two of his daughters had married into the family of Ronouri, a faithful churchgoer and deacon, who also happened to be the only canoe expert in our village of Anatonu. Thus Piahuru could call upon the resources of the other family to help with the work at hand.

By the time Alan and I arrived on the scene the craft had been disassembled and the men and women of the work group were intent upon their specialized tasks. The women stripped hibiscus bark from nearby saplings to act as temporary bindings, while some men rolled freshly separated coconut fibers upon their thighs. These would be used to make lashing cords. Others cut pegs from the heart of the ironwood *'aito* tree. The more expert carpenters very carefully planed down the worn edges of the separate planks and sections of the boat to insure a good fit. All of this was carried out under the watchful eye of an old *tahuŋa*, who warmed himself by a tiny fire and smoked innumerable hand-rolled cigarettes of pandanus leaves and locally grown tobacco. All he seemed to do was to utter an occasional grunt or flick his eyes, but the entire *pupu* worked together with the smoothness of a well-oiled machine.

When all the preliminary work had been carried out, the more precise task of assembly was begun. The women and younger children now retired to their homes, leaving the men to work and the older boys to watch, learn, and run errands. New dowels were inserted in each section, and the fit of one piece with another was rechecked. After much shaving and trimming, the *tahuŋa* pronounced the fit correct. With scissors and huge bush knives the men then cut an old burlap bag into strips of the proper width to fit between the sections. Section by section the connecting surface of the bottom piece was covered with a black plastic compound, the burlap strip laid down and in turn covered with compound, and the upper piece gingerly placed into position. (One hundred and fifty years ago the caulking was bark cloth, tapa, and the compound was gum from the breadfruit tree.) As each section was added the temporary lashings of hibiscus bark were inserted in the binding holes, and made taut by wedges of soft wood tamped into place. Vertical joints had a dowel inserted lengthwise between the two butts in order to provide greater security.

I was as interested in the men who did the work as in the actual details of construction. The group was from one *'ōpū* or family kingroup, and even the village policeman was a member. All were sons-in-law of Piahuru or their brothers. They seemed to work rapidly and efficiently, and the working leader of the group—the youngest-looking of the lot—rarely acted bossy or referred to the watching *tahuŋa*. He knew his job, for it was he who had supervised the work on the same canoe five years before.

As the men worked they periodically dipped their hands into a bowlful of white coconut oil and water. This prevented the plastic compound from sticking to their hands. When one man called for the big knife the child who brought it in was careful to pass it to him handle first. Meanwhile another group had completed the rolling and manufacture of the coconut-fiber cord and strung it out in a long loop between two trees in preparation for the next day's work. The next chore was to lift the partially assembled craft and rest it on segments of coconut logs, half buried in the ground. And then came the final job of the day. The prow, most complex of all parts, was prepared with cloth and cement, and patiently lowered into place. A curved limb of *purau* was placed below the whole foresection of the canoe, and another above. The two were then connected with many strips of bark and the lashings were twisted by means of a stick in the center, the whole acting as a huge clamp.

When the work stopped I carefully examined this canoe which had been the center of such attention all day long. I was struck by the way the gunwales and seat rests had been neatly cut from the solid trunk and left in relief in the proper part of the canoe. Turning to the outrigger, I noticed how the heavy forward outrigger boom was lashed to the float with an iron "U" bolt, leaving the rear boom more flexible than the one forward. (Outrigger designs seem related to wave and lagoon conditions, which differ from island to island.) And I observed rather sadly that in contrast to so many other craft on Ra'ivavae, this canoe was not painted, which seemed in keeping with the somewhat sloppy character of Piahuru's family. Unlike Americans, for example, who may have messy homes but keep their automobiles in gleaming condition, the High Islanders are quite consistent in their sloppiness—or neatness.

Next morning I was back to see the completion of work on the canoe. The compound had "set," and very carefully—section by section—the temporary burlap lashings were removed and the coconut-fiber permanent lashings inserted. This difficult business involves a complex series of operations by a partnership of workers. The sennit cord is passed through the hole by using a "needle" made of coconut midrib. The cord is then drawn taut by one of the men pulling on it with a Y-shaped forked stick, upon which he lays all his weight. While he is doing this his partner remains on the other side of the hull and then hammers the cord itself to make it draw tighter with each blow. One can see the line move slowly through the hole. A whittled peg then is hammered into the hole to prevent the cord from slipping.

While the work was going on, the *tahuŋa* sat by a fire of tiny faggots, puffing silently on his cigarette. Like any good foreman he held his peace—until there was trouble. At one point, for example, the coconut fiber turned out to be one turn too short. After discussing the matter between themselves the boys decided to leave it as it was. It took but a brief grunt from the father to reverse the decision. One of the young men immediately sat down and started rolling the necessary length of fiber. Obviously the *tahuŋa* allowed no short cuts which would damage the quality of the canoe.

These heavy sewn canoes are exciting because they are a tenuous link with the great craft in which the Polynesians sailed on their epic journeys. But of the high craftsmanship which produced the superbly carved "ceremonial paddles" which can be seen in the ethnographic and art museums of the world, there is no trace. These beautiful objects, covered in the

most incredible detail with stylized pictures of dancing figures
and versions of a sun motif were brought home in great quantities by New England and European whalers during the first
part of the nineteenth century. Now the only paddles I saw on
Ra'ivavae were crude affairs, whittled out of local soft woods
with sharpened table knives. This is understandable, for skills
die easily. But I was moved to discover that the natives of
Ra'ivavae could not even recognize these classic paddles as
products of their own island when I showed them photographs
of notable specimens, much less describe their ancient functions. Piahuru remembered only that it was said of the ancient
paddles that they made a pleasing sound as they rippled
through the water.

But even this was more than any living Ra'ivavaean could
remember of the craft which plied the seas before the Europeans came, or of how they were navigated. One elderly man
said that the only thing he had heard was that there had been
great double-hulled ships, with high sterns and even higher
prows, which had made voyages as far away as New Zealand—
and that the "gods guided them." When I asked him if they
used the stars he said he did not know, but that "if they did
so they must indeed have been wise men, for we don't know
how to do this today." Another elder told me that the ancient
war canoes "had no sails" and offered, at a price, to build us
a model. We did not accept his offer, knowing that the result
would be pointless. Yet some sense of the achievements of the
Polynesians has come down to us. We not only know of their
canoes and ships, but of rafts made of hibiscus log and rush as
well as great floats for transporting the temple stones.

What a formidable job it must have been to build these
craft. It took days of work to cut through the immense tree
trunk with stone adzes, and more days to trim off the branches.
Then all the men in the community had to be assembled to
truss and move the hulk to the place where the major job of

construction was to be carried out. Since the principle of the roller was unknown in the islands, cruder methods to ease the enormous enterprise had to be used. One of them was to use the trunks of viscous trees on which to slide the massive trunk. Smaller sections were moved upon a sort of sled or skid. Construction tools were equally primitive. They included fragments of stone, pieces of coral, fish skin, and conical shells. But the greatest skill and energy went into using these implements. Planks were roughly split out by pounding one stone against another, sharper one, used as a wedge. Days of effort with the stone adzes, whose blades had to be constantly honed upon other stones, produced the necessary planks. But despite the use of sea shells and stone drills rather than the modern bit and brace, sharkskin and coral chunks rather than rasp or file, and pumice stone rather than sandpaper, these impressive ocean-going ships received a far smoother and more decorative finish than one sees on the rough lagoon craft of today. The individual sections were highly polished, and many of them were carved in great detail with shark's-tooth or eel-tooth chisels.

Yet all this was only one part of the enormous labor. There was also the work of preparing all of the paraphernalia necessary for a great ship: the high shed to shelter her from sun and weather between voyages, a special cradle in which to place her, skids and shaulks, rigging, masts, paddles and steering sweep, woven pandanus mat or sewn coconut-stipule sails. Especially important and complex was the carving of the high ornamental prow, *uru*, which still survives in a rudimentary form in the simple canoes of today.

From the very beginning, the construction of one of these old, seagoing canoes was surrounded by a web of ceremony, ritual, and religious law. The selection of a tree for the hull had to be made under the most favorable auspices and various rites were necessary to placate the gods. All during the building of the ship there were special chants and prayers as well as secular songs to speed the work along. And when it was finished there was a special naming song, composed just for the occasion.

These proud craft which sailed the seas, festooned with bright pennants and strings of feathers, must have been sizeable affairs to accommodate the specialized crews which were aboard. From the songs and stories which have come down to us we know that the most important person aboard the ship was the *Maninikā* or "Sea King," commander of the vessel. Under him was the captain of the crew (*unutai*), the navigator (*haiŋa,*) and a complement of warriors, paddlers, and others. The *haiŋa* knew the heavens intimately, both the fixed stars and the guiding stars. He could find the ship's position in a rough sort of way by lining up a series of guiding stars which he knew would rise above the sought-for destination. This skill may have been of little help in the legendary voyages to the Underworld or to those lands inhabited by supernatural beings about which the myths of Ra'ivavae tell. But it was indispensable in trips to the Tuamotuan Islands, and in the great expeditions south to New Zealand and to Hawaii in the north.

There were many reasons behind these epic journeys. Some were made out of the sheer passion for adventure, the desire to find new lands. Others were expeditions of conquest to known islands such as Ra'iatea or Tubua'i. Some men sailed out of the wish to be reunited with relatives in earlier homelands, and others out of shame and humiliation for some unworthy deed or after they had been banished for losing a battle.

In the pages of Ra'ivavae lore which Stimson had gathered there are stories of a father and son who voyaged to all of the Austral and Society Islands and thence to New Zealand and Hawaii; of Taŋaroa-i-Mahara, who visited the Austral and Cook Islands and then returned to rule two districts of Ra'ivavae; of the banished Nahati, who sailed to the Tuamotus and was married to the royal scion of Anaa—and whose warriors then invaded Ra'ivavae; of Narai who raped the wife of his son and then in shame emigrated to Tubua'i; of warriors who lost wrestling matches and sailed away in humiliation. The Polynesians were men of the sea and, as we look back, it seems as if they used any excuse to set sail upon the broad Pacific.

Now, however, there is not a ship on Ra'ivavae capable of even making an inter-island trip. Sixty or seventy years ago, it is said, the people of Ra'irua village owned a European-type schooner with an unusual history. Two Tuamotuan men had pirated a vessel belonging to Pomare, King of Tahiti. They somehow sailed her to Manila, and there took up with a local whore. During a drunken spree they boasted of the piracy to her; later, during a fit of jealousy, she told the police about their theft. Both the men and the schooner were sent back to Tahiti, and from there the craft was acquired by the Ra'iva-vaeans. What happened to the ship no one remembers—and no one cares. The government now subsidizes frequent schooner service to the Australs, so that local craft are no longer needed. Indeed, on two occasions the government has sent the Tahitian flying boat to evacuate desperately ill persons.

These trading schooners, unbelievably filthy to European eyes, erratic in schedule, graceless and uncomfortable, still carry the necessities required by the islanders: flour, sugar, kerosene, cloth, paint, mattresses, dressers, mirrors, sewing machines, onions, and beds. In return they remove the coffee, pearl shell, copra, pigs, and other local products which are given in exchange. They also carry the natives from one island to another in that continuous shift in population which takes place throughout the Central Pacific; and they transport the long-bearded French priests and pastors who together with young American Mormon boys minister to the spiritual needs of the islanders. Most of these schooners eventually wind up on the reef of one or another of the outer islands, but they are rarely missed, for there always seem to be other craft, just as dirty, to take their place.

This, then, is what has happened to that race of great seamen who once flourished on Ra'ivavae. It is a sad story and it has a sad little epilogue which was played out some thirty years ago. By some twist of fate a trio of adventurers landed on Ra'ivavae, a Russian, a promising French artist, and a young American. They decided to build a Polynesian double canoe and sail it to Tahiti. One day the writer James Norman Hall passed by the place where they had been working on the canoe. He was impressed by their effort, but soon discovered that the men knew nothing about seamanship. Hall talked the young American into returning to Tahiti with him on the schooner. The other two set sail, the twin hulls of their vessel laden with antiquities from High Island and with the artist's own collection of paintings.

Nothing was heard of them again.

Chapter Eight

GHOST DANCERS

*The great drums rolled; the rat-tat-tat of the little drums
fell excitingly upon the ear, and Hiro, head and shoulders covered by his cloak, sprang lightly into the very center of the
cleared space and began to dance. At once the Princess joined
him. Stirring indeed was the continuous roll of the drums—
and Hiro bent and swayed in the vigorous postures of his
dance. The young girl paused and stood rooted to the spot
as she kept her eyes fixed upon Hiro, for she was entranced
with the marvelous dancing.*
　　　　　　　—The Adventures of Hiro, the Trickster

THE people of Ra'ivavae are starved for entertainment.
This was one of the most amazing discoveries I made on
High Island.

I became aware of this on the very first night we settled down
in Anatonu. Nobody had shown much interest in our arrival
until we unloaded the generator which we had brought from
Tahiti. Then the husky young men who had been standing idly
around, not helping us at all, suddenly surged forward, crying,
"*Tienama, tienama!*" (movies, movies!). "'*Aita tienama*" (No
movies), I replied sharply, annoyed that no one had lent a
hand. But despite my denial the rumor flashed around the island. By the time we made our last return from the *Mareva*
in total darkness, a large part of the population surrounded us.
The aged and the infirm, the young—even infants—had walked
or been carried to Anatonu to gather around our headquarters.

167

Some had come from the other side of the island. Most were wrapped in large towels or blankets against the cold of the night. Some strummed guitars. Our yard was full of robed figures, and they followed me up onto the porch as I tried to enter the house. I turned and asked what they wanted—"We are waiting for the cinema to begin." As gently as possible I again told them that there was no cinema. There was an audible sigh of disappointment, but from somewhere in the background came a good natured "O.K." The inhabitants of Ra'ivavae are obviously used to disappointments such as this. Once a Tahitian politician promised to bring the cinema to High Island, but nothing happened. He was like most politicians.

Yet in looking back upon our stay I think that we did more to amuse Ra'ivavae than most visitors. Every night crowds of gray-hooded figures gathered outside our house. Sometimes they simply listened to Radio Tahiti. But on other occasions we treated them to a show of color slides which I had made during a brief visit to the island several years before. Even though the showing was never publicly announced, people seemed to get wind of it and came from all over the island to throng our yard and wait patiently until we tacked up a sheet against the house and set up a projector. They were remarkably well behaved as I ran through the slides, although their enthusiasm was so great that they often obscured the screen. To a running commentary by Toāri'i, our landlord, who had taken the trouble to identify the pictures, the islanders shouted their approval. Young girls cried "Nehenehe, lovely, lovely!" and there were bursts of laughter when photographs of familiar persons appeared on the screen. The greatest laughter bubbled up when a photograph of the oldest man on the island was shown. I was at a loss to understand this until Alan explained that it probably seemed inconceivable to Ra'ivavaeans that I should "waste film" on such an aged and worthless person. We could have given the same show every night and still had an audience, but fortunately I finally loaned the generator to the gendarme. For the rest of my stay on the island I had to explain wherever I went that "'*Aita tienama*," there would be no more movies.

This is how it is today on Ra'ivavae and I never got over my first shock at the paucity of entertainment and art on the island. There is no doubt that Ra'ivavae once enjoyed great festivals and dances. There is no doubt that of all the Polynesian islands, this one had been pre-eminent in creating songs and stories as well as wonderful examples of carving, design, and sculpture.

But now the people of High Island no longer compose odes to the beauties of their land; in fact, they do not even remember the ancient songs. No longer do they decorate their recreation fields; there is virtually no recreation. The rhythmic pounding of the drums is unknown, for there are no drums nor gongs nor dancing girls to dance to their beat. No longer does the population sing of the pleasures of a community pleasure house, for there is little pleasure to be had.

Moreover, virtually all the old folk tales have been long forgotten, while the '*ute*, an impromptu chant composed to fit almost any occasion, is no longer sung, though it was heard by Alan as little as twenty years ago. Even the singing of hymns in church was devoid of both melody and spirit. Our next-door neighbor Giggles was the leader of the church singing because of her "beautiful voice," but I failed to find any touch of beauty there. For an island which once sounded to the varied and beautiful tones of drums, flutes, trumpets, slit gongs, clappers —even the bamboo jew's-harp—things had come to a sorry end. When the young people were not loudly singing their improbable versions of songs heard over Radio Tahiti, they were strumming a guitar awkwardly or listening to the few in the village. I don't know which was the most annoying, but even now I can hear the interminable strumming of the guitar—

some of which were made locally out of sardine cans and strung wire.

Of their former mastery of stone-carving, which produced magnificently stylized sculpture in red tufa, as well as the most beautifully finished stone tools and bowls, nothing remains. Only the rough but useful stone food pounder is now made, but it is crudely hacked out with steel ax and rasp. Wood carving has fared no better. Save for the relatively well-shaped, but crudely finished, lashed sections of canoes, no wood-cutting other than simple European-type carpentry is carried out—and most of this by imported Tahitian carpenters. High Island, which furnished the museums of the world with some of their great Polynesian masterpieces, is now an artistic cipher. The drums, bowls, paddles, and other objects, which surpassed anything of their kind seen in the Pacific, now are not even recognized by the descendants of the men who fashioned them. Ivory is no longer carved, bark cloth has not been made for generations, and even the needlework and handwork of a few years ago is rapidly disappearing in favor of store-bought goods. The only thing that is left—and it is rare to find it—are drawings in the sand made by the young. They are geometric and highly stylized but they have some aesthetic power. Unfortunately no one seems to develop this skill after a certain age and it may soon wither away.

This aesthetic vacuum—so shocking for Polynesia—has engulfed even the most prosaic aspects of life. There is only the most perfunctory attention to the niceties of personal grooming and even the boys of Ra'ivavae complain that the girls "smell of dried fish and smoke from the fire." Compared to the women of Tahiti, those on Ra'ivavae take no care with their clothes at all. Nor are the young men much better. This same indifference extends to the houses of the islanders.

Other than the flowers and flowering bushes which are found around every Polynesian dwelling, there is little effort made to decorate the homes. In a few, yellowed newspaper clippings or handbills with the pompous features of politicians look down from the walls, but even this is not common. At the occasional dinner given in honor of visitors, flowers rarely are scattered around the table. All one can say about Ra'ivavae is that some houses are neat and some sloppy.

If the aesthetic sense has dwindled away, the pleasures which come from community entertainment are also scarce. Other than for an occasional drunken brawl, held by the Tahitian schoolteacher to honor the passengers and crew of a visiting schooner, or a rare wedding feast, people almost never gather socially. Even the rites of passage—birth, death—are scarcely celebrated, whereas once they were the occasion for a feast, if not a festival. There are no parties of any kind, and few dances. The last time the Governor of French Oceania called on Ra'ivavae the total contribution for a dinner in his honor was one scrawny chicken and five small crayfish. "We have fed the great man once; why should we do so again?" Nor does a visit from the European head of the church organization which dominates Ra'ivavae elicit any greater enthusiasm. "Neither the people nor the local pastor seem very interested," said one elderly islander.

The French gendarme has made a brave attempt to inject some life into things. In honor of the 14th of July, Bastille Day, he has initiated a small celebration. The school children sing the "Marseillaise" as the tricolor of France is run up, and the four districts send small groups to compete in singing for government-offered prize money. Chinese storekeepers run a few wheels of chance, and a few odd foot races, canoe races, and, more recently, a football match are held. A luncheon is given to the chief and his council and at night the Tahitian schoolteachers and the gendarme and his wife hold a "bal." All in all, it is a pathetic affair, but it is all the gendarme can manage. When Alan arrived on Ra'ivavae a generation ago, people still retained the ability to make up impromptu songs and to accompany these by rhythmic clapping. But by the time we arrived the only music of any nature was the untutored strumming of newly purchased guitars (from the profits of last year's coffee crop) and vague essays at rendering Tahitian songs.

For the young *taure'are'a*—and only the males—contact with Europe has given one substitute for the former excitements of war and voyaging, dancing and singing. The local youths manufacture a virulent kind of "bush beer." The main ingredients are water, three or four kilos of sugar, and a supply of yeast, mixed in a five-gallon tin. Oranges or wild honey are used for flavor. The concoction ferments within a week and must be immediately consumed or it will go bad. Although one drink is potent enough to cause dizziness, the young men swill great quantities once the drinking has commenced. They are likely to sing and fight and then those still able to move when the tin is finished stagger into town to look for women. There is little doubt that on Ra'ivavae, as on the other Polynesian islands which I have studied, bush beer releases three pent-up emotions: the desire to sing and dance, to fight, and to copulate.

However, there is much less drinking now than formerly. When our aged informant Piahuru was young, he and his age mates occasionally planted or fished, but more frequently they "played the accordion, slept, and spent three to four days a week drinking." As he told me, "the real reason we drank was so that we could hunt women." In the last few years drinking has been largely restricted to Saturday and Sunday. Some say the newly introduced football competitions have something to do with this. In any case we found no indication of any alcoholics on High Island. Drinking seems to be a traditional outlet for the *taure'are'a* to get rid of their itches and to prepare for adult responsibilities.

What passes for sport on Ra'ivavae these days is a poor thing indeed compared to the noble pastimes which once occupied the islanders. Then there was surfboarding and tobogganing, archery competitions, javelin-hurling, dart-throwing, foot-racing, weight-lifting. Now the only sport we saw was a local version of kick football, brought to the island two years ago by the new interdenominational religious young peoples' group in Tahiti. Yet the enthusiasm with which the islanders took to it suggests how much they crave something to amuse themselves. The young men have taken to the game with deadly seriousness, practicing every evening; even, on occasion, in a pouring rain. Their womenfolk have made uniform jackets of multicolored patches for them, embroidered with the name of individual teams. Men, women, and children—the sexes separated as usual—watch the play with intensity, particularly when there is an intervillage match. And the children copy the older boys, substituting a *popo* woven of pandanus leaves for the regulation leather ball. So avidly has Ra'ivavae taken to football that a major game seems to be the only occasion when the whole village turns out for a feast. The matches themselves are hard-fought in an informal sort of way and studded with fights and outbursts of bad feeling. The children behave in a much more amiable way.

Besides football there are no real competitive sports on Ra'ivavae, although games for both children and adults are common. During the months I was there I saw the children go from kickball to rope-skipping to stilt-fighting with equal enthusiasm, although they were most skillful at stilt-fighting. Marbles, played with candlenuts, are another favorite, as are variants of hopscotch, mumblety-peg, and knuckle bones. The youngest children amuse themselves with a pig's bladder inflated like a balloon or a meat tin nailed to the end of a stick. Adult games are no more ambitious. From time to time the men of High Island play a Polynesian version of the old shell game. Two of them would sit for hours on end on the sandy beach with four holes dug in front of each player. As it is the world over, the idea of the game was to have the other player guess in what hole a real shell was dropped. But even this sedentary recreation is not too common. As one of Zenie's young informants told her, summing up the usual way of spending an evening: "We meet, tell stories, play cards, and afterward either sleep or go out and chase women."

It is clear from the many folk tales that dancing was one of the great pleasures of ancient Ra'ivavae. There was not only ceremonial dancing of both a religious and secular nature, but there were any number of occasions when purely recreational dancing was the order of the day. The people took any occasion they could to dance: birth, betrothal, and marriage festivals, receptions for honored guests, contests between intertribal or local champions, the completion of any important communal enterprise, the seasonal food festivals, even notable catches of fish or turtle. And just as there were many occasions to dance, so there were many forms of the dance—from the war dances of men to the imitative graceful flower-plucking dances of women, from the seated 'aparima, in which only the hands were used, to the suggestive belly dances of women. The dancer might be a soloist but there were also times when great groups of men and women would join in highly rhythmic performances. Victory in battle was celebrated by the dance, while courage before battle was sought by highly stylized dances. There were several forms of prancing, insulting, and mocking dances to defame one's enemies.

Dancing, in fact, was such an important part of life on Ra'ivavae, that the chief motif of the island's ancient art was a row of stylized dancing figures. It can be found carved in stone and in wood, full size in the old temples, delicately small on the decorative details on wooden bowls, paddles, spears, drums. The dancing female figure with her great collar and pointed

174

triangular breasts, knees spread and arms raised, represented the spirit of pagan Ra'ivavae.

What has happened to the dance on Ra'ivavae gave me a poignant lesson in how completely the past can die—and in what strange ways it struggles to be reborn. Though bizarre, the episode of the ghost dancers was a major contribution to our study, for it illustrated how human needs find expression despite existing taboos.

From the very first evening we landed on High Island we became familiar with the strange spectacle of guitar-playing figures, hooded with blankets or towels, wandering across the landscape. They were to be seen along the village path by day or night—even on Sundays as our little company went off to church. Vague stories about these hooded figures came to our ears. Some that they were seen dancing in the moonlight out on the reef islets. But our housegirl, Pogi, and her friends— all of them in their twenties—swore that no one knew how to dance. In fact, they said, there were no parties or dances on Ra'ivavae—"nothing but work."

Shortly after our arrival, however, the grounds around our little headquarters became a sort of village "no man's land," in which the youth appeared to feel free from adult meddling. Some of them took delight in resting under the house and plucking incoherently at a guitar. There were only a few at first, but soon the size of the group increased, and one night we counted ten boys and five guitars. That evening our housegirl, her sister, and Giggles were sitting on the porch. I urged them to dance, but only one of the girls dared even make an attempt. She was joined by one of the boys but it was clear that neither had ever danced before. When I talked to the boys they claimed that the girls knew how to dance, and that they danced out on the reefs. The girls denied this.

There is nothing like a series of conflicting reports to pique the curiosity. The gendarme himself told me that the girls danced, "but only on the *motu*, and then in complete darkness, with everything but the legs covered up." Old men such as Piahuru categorically denied that there were dances of any kind held on High Island. Old Mama Iē had heard rumors of the dancing on the *motu*, but knew of no details. And, as my curiosity grew, the guitar players continued to come, playing in front of the house, and even under the house when it was raining.

Then, one night, I had the answer to my question about dancing. Supper was over and Alan and I were working on notes. The guitars started up and Zenie drifted out to see if she could pick up any gossip. She excitedly called to me. The moon had just appeared over the trees, there was a tiny fire going, and in the dim light was the strangest sight I was to see on the island. In addition to six guitarists there were more than twenty of the village young people—covered from head to knee with sheets or blankets—dancing to the crude music. To call it "dancing" is to be charitable, for clearly none of

Mama was young when the first anthropologist came to Ra'ivavae and photographed her as an example of Polynesian beauty

A Remnant of the Past. The daughter of Mama Iē displays an ancient feasting bowl no longer used now that laughing and dancing are considered sinful.

The Daily Bread. Pogi wraps a bundle of poi in leaves for storage until morning

Building a plantation house, the workman uses only a knife and materials supplied by the pandanus tree

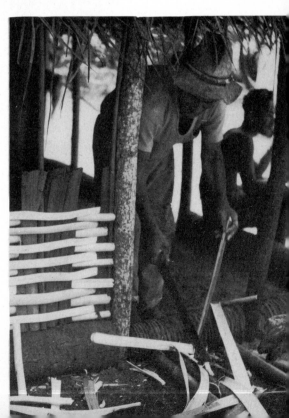

Cave of the Giant Fish—the village of Anatonu

A familiar sight on an early Sunday morning as families from outlying plantations pole their canoes to church

(ABOVE) *The church at Anatonu, constructed of stone from the hills, timber from the valley, and lime from the lagoon, took thirty years to build* (RIGHT) *Women's Service. After the regular Sunday service is over, the women of Anatonu conduct their own period of worship*

them knew the rudiments of either the European or Tahitian dances they were trying to do. Most were merely hopping or jumping like participants in a sack race, in their attempt to keep tune to the music. In a few cases there were two people covered beneath one blanket. It was clear that the sheets and blankets were a deliberate attempt at disguise. Even the voices were altered.

At the beginning of the dance, I later discovered, boys danced with boys, and girls danced with girls. But after a time a boy and a girl would dance under the same blanket. Our neighbor Giggles became so excited at the goings on that she dropped down in a faint, but after resting on the porch a bit she was soon back in the thick of things. While other young people and children stood by as excited spectators, the affair went on at an increasing pace until midnight, when we asked the bacchantes to break off in order to allow us some sleep.

Zenie soon pieced together the history behind this extraordinary scene. Until two years before there had been absolutely no dancing on Ra'ivavae because of the strict church control of all social activity. Then a group of boys and girls were sent to the *motu* to gather sea shells which could be sold to buy a generator for the church. Lying in the damp coolness one night, one of the girls realized that a blanket makes a perfect disguise. As one of the boys strummed his guitar, she started to dance covered by her blanket. Others joined in and a new custom was born. The boys enjoyed it, though they knew no dance steps, because they could bring the girls inside their blankets and talk and be close to them. The girls had no objections because the old deacon and the women who were chaperoning the excursion were so confused that they could not report any individual to the church council or the parents. The impromptu dancing had only taken place a couple of times on the *motu*. But the appearance of newcomers on the island provided an opportunity for the boys and girls to revive the pleasures of these evenings before our house.

Reaction was immediate and violent. Our landlord Toāri'i told us that he was glad to see his daughters have a chance to amuse themselves (under our watchful eye, he implied).

The rest of the men were less temperate. Our friend Tino beat up his daughter and gave her a black eye for daring to go to such an affair. (She was the only girl who did not dance!) His son punished the girl who was living with him and made her leave the house. A man of thirty-eight threw a bottle at Giggles, saying that he had lived for thirty-eight years without learning to dance and wanted to see none of it in his village. Sunday evening saw high tempers in the meetinghouse as the oldsters rose up to condemn the new ways.

But none of this seemed to have much effect on the young people. Every night, in the neutral space before our bungalow, the hooded figures assembled, guitars and all. At times they were as active as the first evening, but there were occasions when their dancing was less spontaneous and they seemed to split up in little groups, at odds with one another. The tension frequently seemed related to the presence of outsiders from other villages. Though I did not encourage the dancers after the first few nights, they showed no sign of stopping. In fact, since no one punished them, the dancers took heart and seemed to increase their nightly efforts. Where formerly only the boys sang to the guitars, now both sexes lustily joined in. After a while there was more singing than dancing, which by this time had degenerated into a form of wrestling between the sexes. The songs became more and more risqué, with the term *navenave* ("to experience the orgasm") playing a prominent role.

Toward the end of our stay on Ra'ivavae, the boys and girls had lost their awe of the visiting anthropologist and his colleagues. We had, after all, indulged them all these weeks by letting them dance before the house. On the final night before we were to leave the boys clustered around Zenie telling her how beautiful she was.

"You smell so nice, not like the girls of Ra'ivavae," one said.

"What do your girls smell like?" I asked.

"Food."

"What food?"

"Fish," was the reply.

Chapter Nine

PIGS IN THE TEMPLE

EVERY time I had my doubts about the quest which had
led me to Ra'ivavae I soothed myself by remembering that
we were living on the site of a great pagan temple. In the
shrewd way of priests everywhere, the first Christian pastor
here had placed the Anatonu church over the remains of the
greatest heathen marae in the district, a gesture symbolizing
the power of the new God who had supplanted the old. Many
of the ancient altar stones were put to use in the foundations
of the church or were buried in place to get them out of the
way. The marae had been a huge intricate affair, and its outer
works extended well beyond our house. Even now, stones from
the ancient temples still peeped out of the earth in our front
yard, and I had the pleasure of showing my friends the remains
of temple walks along the seaside of the open area in front of
the church. Old Piahuru remembered the time when work on
the church had first begun. Over fifty human skeletons had
come from the excavations for the foundation—made right
in the heart of the ancient marae.

The detailed records of scores of different marae made up
the most voluminous part of Frank's Ra'ivavae manuscript.
This was understandable, for the stone temples were the focus
of ancient life, not only as places of religious worship, but in
sexual matters, and in seeking the aid of the gods in agriculture
and fishing. Oddly enough, things had not changed very much,
for the church and its meeting house were now the focus of
virtually all of the social activity in the community. I felt that

I would be quite justified in devoting a major portion of my time to the study of the ancient temples, which I could then compare to the modern church.

Since Anatonu was the center of our study, we set out to make a detailed analysis of the temples of our own district. In a sense, this was an unfortunate choice from the start, for there were no large and well-preserved remains within our boundaries. Before the Europeans arrived the district had been rather poor compared to the others, with their much more extensive and rich taro fields. It had no striking remains such as Te Mahara and Raŋi'ura in Vaiuru or Atoraŋi in Ra'irua. And from the start Piahuru, who was usually so helpful to us, seemed strangely reluctant to work with us on this phase of research. He professed a bland ignorance of temple sites which we knew existed, and he did not seem anxious to visit them.

Yet even in this rather barren district the marae had proliferated. Everywhere we went there were stone remains, some high in the foothills behind the village, but not always the ones we were looking for. One of my first excursions was to look for the "lizard marae," so called because it projected out from the shores into the sea in the general form of a lizard. Hapai had once given an account of it. The marae was said to be just beyond Ruatara, a gigantic boulder resting beside the sea. Many legends were told of this unique rock, but Piahuru merely said that it was dropped there by an evil spirit, Varua'ino. We found no trace of the seaside marae, but we did spot a bed of uplifted coral rock which was almost perpendicular to the beach. An imaginative observer might have taken it for something made by man. Perhaps there had been a "lizard marae," but now it was forever lost, if indeed it had ever existed.

After this disappointment I returned to the borders of Anatonu, where a gigantic landslip has created a natural district barrier, and there began a systematic search for temples.

Piahuru had heard of a marae right on the border and took us in search of it. We climbed a winding route, up past vertical sheets of uplifted coral slabs, *ma'atea*, and moved onto a small plateau. Piahuru could not locate the remains, but an elderly woman working nearby led us directly to them. The temple was exactly where one would expect such a boundary-guarding marae to be, on the very crest of the hill separating Anatonu from the neighboring district of Mahanatoa. It was set on a tiny grassy plain which crowned the summit, and trees were scattered openly through the flatlands behind it. The whole area nestled at the foot of a sheer cliff, which served as a backdrop for hundreds of birds which plunged down in front of it from high above and then soared into the sky again, their white feathers contrasting strikingly with the brilliant blue sky. Looking out over the lagoon to the pass through the barrier reef, with the deep sea visible beyond, this marae was a spot of great beauty. One could easily see why the people of ancient Ra'ivavae were moved to compose odes to the splendors of their homeland.

The altar stones were some five feet high, but the lush ferns and grass had covered the fallen stones and paving so that it was difficult to make out any pattern other than a simple walled rectangle. Many of the temple remains seem to have been used to construct a nearby stone wall, and most of the steles had fallen. A few feet in front of the marae was a huge boulder whose flat top could easily accommodate several people.

Below this striking site was the fishing-village part of Anatonu and there between the houses we found one wall of the altar of Marae Motutua still standing upright. Farther along by the taro stream there were other stone remains, and in the foundations of a few stone houses nearby peeped the telltale squared red border stones of another ancient temple. As we continued on this first systematic tour we came to the remains of Marae Vai-o-igi on the other side of the taro stream, located on land belonging to Piahuru himself. Here he had refused to allow the *toa* trees to be cut, and they still stood sentinel-like on the shore, protecting the land from the sea winds. Although the belt path cut directly through the temple, and the paving stones and steles had been used in the construction of a bridge over a nearby stream, most of the landward altar stones still remained in place. However, the relentless sea had undermined those toward the shore and the huge granite slabs had dropped down to the beach below, exposing the neatly-made square-cut burial boxes below the paving. Reconnoitering the area we not only found great amounts of human skeletal remains below the altar but also a segment of red tufa phallic sculpture. In this one spot there was enough evidence to confirm the theory that the marae had been used as a burial ground.

I was anxious to investigate further and find out what had been buried with the bodies. I had vague hopes of discovering stone implements or ivory ornaments and thought that Piahuru would surely agree to let me dig, since he not only worked for us but had, presumably, cast off the old superstitions when he received a European education. I was disappointed. Piahuru did not refuse my request point-blank, but he did not agree— and by Polynesian custom this is tantamount to a strong refusal. I again realized that Piahuru would be of little help in this delicate business of looking for old marae and I went my way without him after this. Everywhere I looked there were ancient stone remains, thickly clustered in the lowland areas of the island, thinning out in the foothills. Most were marae, but there were also house sites, play platforms, work and teaching sites. It was difficult not to confuse them.

On my first extended expedition around the island I came upon a well-preserved temple near the first extensive area of taro fields. It was set on a slight elevation and obviously served as a place where the gods could be honored so that the sur-

rounding land would be fertile. It was known as Marae Āhe'e, and enough stones still surrounded the well-paved altar area —vertical slabs up to ten feet in height—so that it could be used as a pigpen for several huge animals. Though most of the islanders will not tamper with marae stones for fear of contracting leprosy, they have long used the altar precincts of the smaller temples as ready-made retaining areas in which to fatten their hogs. To judge by the size of these porkers, the old magic still seems to work.

As we went from temple to temple, certain recurrent features became apparent. Not only was the altar area—whose walls ranged from five to ten feet in height—invariably paved with flat stones, but extensive well-paved and complex areas, frequently bordered by upright *ma'atea* slabs, stretched out on the sides and to the rear of this sacred spot. Some of these areas had been built up by cut-and-fill engineering techniques, and often they were set off by alternating vertical slabs of *ma'atea* limestone and slivers of volcanic rock in the typical phallic form. Generally there were one or more seaward gates to the altar area, some two to three feet wide. The huge uprights beside these openings frequently had petroglyphs carved upon them—some with the Ra'ivavaean "sun" motif. The phallic *tara*, on the other hand, invariably seemed to be landward of the enclosed areas. A particularly notable feature of virtually every marae studied was that landward from the altar itself were one or more small connected areas, opening one upon another, which were either walled about or set off by low vertical uprights.

There were also indications that there had been beautifully squared and nicely finished red tufa slabs within the altar areas. These may well have been colorful backdrops for the images. Another feature of most marae was the presence of a single huge *tara*, up to twelve or fourteen feet in length. These either occupied a central position in the altar area itself, or else were placed in the middle of one of the smaller sanctuary areas. An almost invariable auxiliary, though usually in a poor state of repair, was a paved path leading from the sea to the altar portals. This was lined with stone uprights on both sides. In some cases the path led to a paved and slab-bordered courtyard before the altar proper.

Often one of the four altar walls would be a double one, made up of two rows of stone uprights. Sometimes it consisted of alternating pointed *tara* with flat slabs of limestone or tufa. There were interesting indications that a whole series of images had been placed between the successive wall slabs. On some altars huge, curiously shaped stone slabs were set into the

walls. Another fascinating find I made was that near a full-sized temple there might be what could only be described as miniature marae, complete with altar area, red-curbed court-yards, and *tara*. Although coffee plantations covered virtually all the stone remains, it was clear that no one except visiting archaeologists and Tahitian public-works engineers had tampered with them. The great exception to this was the destruction and removal of the great stone images. Most of these had been smashed to bits or defaced in the original conversion period in 1820 or in the later wave of antipaganism which swept the island at the turn of the century. And those that were left vanished into the eager hands of each scientific expedition which came to the island.

One of the most splendid temple sites on Ra'ivavae is the Marae Unurau, set on the far side of the mountain in the Ra'irua district. It is notable not only for the immense size of the altar stones, some of which weigh sixteen or more tons, but for the magnificent, paved road which led straight from the main portal to the sea, some five hundred feet distant. This route, twelve feet wide in places, was bordered by commemorative slabs, two and a half to five feet high. These were set on each side at intervals of two to three feet, and they were joined by a curbing bar of red tufa. Near the end of the road by the ancient sea wall we could still see the bases and fragments of two facing images which had long since disappeared. A half-ton seat of stone stood overlooking the road, halfway to the sea. By the time we commenced our studies, the paved road had been covered with mud, and root pressure and weathering had toppled many of the altar stones, which measured up to twelve and a half feet long. Yet this temple, which is only of moderate size compared to others we saw, was still an impressive affair.

Its altar area was surrounded by a red tufa border and the same materials were used for the steps of the single front portal. The paving within the area and the neat matching of the multitoned upright walling stones was carried off perfectly. The rear altar wall contained three portals, one of which led to a series of successively chambered areas. There were remains of terraces, broken walls, and pavings throughout the area, and the surface of the soil was covered with the red stone remains of the desecrated images.

The sides of the altar stones clearly showed that they had been quarried, and not just picked up. By cutting and filling, the altar area was leveled to an inside dimension of twenty-one by eighty-five feet, plenty of room for ceremonies to be carried on in complete privacy within the high stone walls. The feat of setting up a vertical series of twelve-and-a-half-foot stone slabs, with only a foot dug into the ground, was remarkable considering the lack of any mechanical tools or aids. To the northeast of the altar room was a typical smaller sanctuary room, this one fifteen by twenty-two feet on the inside, set off at a higher level than the altar floor below. This in turn was further extended to the north for forty-one feet of paved flattened slope, terminating in alternating slabs and red stone curbing. Above this was another area, in which we found the pedestals of four stone images.

John Stokes, the great Polynesian scholar, who visited Ra'ivavae almost forty years before, was impressed even then by the massive simplicity and striking color contrasts of the temple. The beautifully leveled floor is black, the neatly squared curbing stones orange-red, and the high stone walls gray-white. Adding to the beauty is the contrast between the elegantly finished horizontal red curbing and the natural upright walling. Stokes was told that the marae was built by Tutini, chief of the Ha'amemene clan, just before the arrival of the first Europeans. Supposedly it was used in preparation for war, and only the king and those whom he invited were allowed to enter the sacred main enclosure.

If Marae Unurau is celebrated for its complex elegance, the Temple Moanaheiata, just a few hundred yards over the hill to the north, is famous for the numerous and immense statues which once filled it. Looking out upon the bay at Ra'irua, this marae contained the two largest statues to survive intact after the waves of image-smashing at the beginning and end of the nineteenth century. The female and largest of the pair, now standing with its mate in Papeete on the grounds of the former museum, was eight feet high and five feet thick. The male was six feet high and three feet thick. For several decades the crews of every major ship that put into Ra'ivavae tried to carry these statues away. But it was only a few years ago that an ingenious engineer named Steve Higgins was finally able to move them to Papeete. He died under tragic circumstances soon after, and Tahitians and Ra'ivavaeans laid his death to the anger of the gods for having moved their images. Since then the mayor of Papeete has seemingly found it impossible to hire local men to move the images to the site of the new museum.

Alvin Seale, who wrote about them first, saw these two images set about twelve feet apart. Some distance away in the underbrush he also found a fallen row of eight other stone images about the size of the male of the pair. Near this group he stumbled on the broken remains of a Janus-headed image some four and a half feet high, sitting near a decayed temple area about a hundred feet long by thirty-five feet wide. Seale describes the two gods as being made of granite, but closer study indicates that they were cut from the red tufa in which their particular district abounds, and which was exported to other parts of the island for similar purposes. By the time we arrived nothing but a few odd stones indicated the great temple that had once stood there.

The most significant stone remains on Ra'ivavae are those of Marae Atorani, but I simply could not get any of the local inhabitants to work in the area. They were afraid that it was a source of leprosy. Stokes told me that he had run into the same problem. But he was so moved by the richness of the archaeological materials before him that he impressed his wife as a laborer for the occasion. Unfortunately his detailed excavation notes from this significant site seem to have disappeared. Jim and I spent considerable time prowling around the remains but attempted no systematic excavation. Nevertheless, in the few minutes that we scratched about, we found the torso of a huge image, together with a number of fragments of other images. There were red stone curbings all around, and several of the huge, beautifully squared red blocks of tufa. Amid the debris of this complex site were altar stones some sixteen feet high. As we rummaged around I remembered Stokes' remark that it was in this marae that he had excavated the clearest evidence of the erotic basis of the ancient religion. In one site he had dug up a large stone image which was obviously an erect male phallus. And on each side of it he also found a full-size statue of a pregnant woman! The meaning of this would be made clear to us later.

Our favorite marae was Raŋi'ura, "Sacred-red-heavens," otherwise known as Pōmoavao. To my mind, it had once been the most beautiful temple on Ra'ivavae. A paved route six feet wide, flanked by small upright slabs placed at wide intervals, led to the marae from the sea a hundred and fifty feet away. In front of the altar enclosure itself was a narrow terrace, set off by a row of alternating curbs, slabs, and images. There were the remains of four images in place, and probably there were more at an earlier period.

The altar area proper was one hundred and twenty-four feet long by thirty feet wide, surrounded by closely set slabs which ranged from five to seven feet in height. The northwest wall was relatively open, and seemed to have been composed of alternating curbs and images. The smashed fragments of the latter covered the area. Within the altar area the floor was paved with matched black slabs, which must have contrasted beautifully with the red curbings that lined the raised walk encircling the inner faces of the altar. (These red stone blocks were later sold to a Chinaman on Tubua'i for use in his bread-baking oven. Presumably he had no fear of leprosy.) Opposite the front portal of the marae was a thin upright stone slab over seven feet high and two and a half feet wide. Behind it was a red stone block. At the base of the stele, inset in the paving, was a stone of the same width upon which the priest was said to have stood when rendering the prayers.

From the northeast corner of the altar area a series of walled-off paved areas led directly north. These ascended the slight slope of the hill against which the temple butts, and were walled in by alternating uprights and curbs. The last room was closed off with a series of immense rectangles of red tufa. It was here that Jim and I, scratching about the surface remains, experienced the wonderful thrill of a real archaeological discovery. In the litter of image fragments I noticed one piece which seemed more rounded than the rest. We worked away at it —gingerly, for the wet tufa was soft enough to crumble in our fingers. Within a few minutes we had exposed the upper portion of a torso, with a huge collar resting upon the tiny exposed triangular breasts. This led to a more intensive search, and a few minutes later—some yards away—we uncovered the lower part of the bust. Gingerly we tried to place the two parts together. They fitted perfectly, and before us stood our "Ra'ivavaean Venus." The figure was particularly notable in that near the base of the well-formed back, just above the buttocks, was a neatly raised series of concentric circles. These strongly indicated an old practice of female tattooing, still a debatable point in anthropological discussions.

Later on we dug up fragments of the limbs of another of these red stone images. Clearly they did not belong to our "Venus," but they were equally important. This image must have been smashed and buried before it had a chance to weather. The original finish still remained, and it was clear that these stone images had been as beautifully and smoothly finished as the wooden spears which so impressed the early explorers that they thought they had been turned on a lathe.

Unless someone has made off with her, my Venus still rests in her old marae. I lost her in the mazes of bureaucracy. The governors of French Oceania have long been concerned with the protection and preservation of local antiquities, and have wisely passed laws prohibiting their export without permit.

Too many treasures have vanished without a trace. When I arrived on High Island I expected to do no archaeology. But soon I changed my mind and determined to dig in Marae Raŋi'ura to find any images I could. To avoid any trouble and to forestall any rumors that we were looters, I decided to go through the full formal process of application to the governor of French Oceania and his council. Unfortunately we left the island before the necessary approval arrived.

Disappointed in not being permitted to do the archaeological work we desired, we were doomed to disappointment in our studies of the marae. For many years I have realized that just as today the Christian church is the focus of all that is important in the social life of the Polynesian, so in ancient times were the marae the focus of all that was significant in pagan life. Indeed, so impressed was I with the importance of the many marae on this exotic island, which was—as Alan phrased it—"sinking beneath the weight of its countless fallen stone temples," that we had made a special tour of the Society and Austral Islands solely to gather comparative marae material before coming to Ra'ivavae. We found much to interest us with respect to the numbers of marae on each island, the differences between types of construction, the varied layouts, and the decor. But despite all efforts, we could not do the one thing which I sought above all else, the one thing which could eventually make the marae studies of significant use: we could not bring to life what had happened upon these ancient stone pavings and what went on inside the stone altar enclosures.

My informants, despite their claims, could not reconstruct in even the most elementary degree the ceremonies which had taken place. Jim could draw for me a composite reconstruction of what the stone remains might have looked like a century and a half before our arrival, but nothing we could do would bring to view the living religious activity of priest and king, commoner and warrior.

13   197

True, the few fragments of stone images we found here, and those I was later to study in museum storerooms, clearly contained the contention that there was an intimate connection between marae decor and sexual activity. But details of the activities which would have led us to a greater knowledge of ancient life and thought could not be brought to life.

Yet I have seen enough of these stone images which once crowded Ra'ivavae to understand their great importance. In all Polynesia the art of this island was unique. The marae not only contained sacred images done in a brilliantly stylized form, but they also sheltered naturalistic images which actually depicted women in childbirth. At first I had refused to credit Hapai's account of such images, saying that it could not be true because "naturalistic images do not fit the Polynesian pattern." But soon I had to eat my words. Within a few days of my arrival Tino came to me saying that he had a *tiki*—a stone image of a god—for me. Since he had previously brought me one of the stone lamps of High Island, I decided to go and see what he had found. The next day we walked several miles along the belt patch, and then suddenly turned off into the taro fields. Here we were in one of the lushest agricultural areas on High Island. Everywhere I looked there were paved remains of dwelling and temple sites amid sections of taro bed. Tino led me along the maze of banks until we came to one belonging to his own family. Beside the ditch from which they had just been pulled, still wet, were two large red stone fragments. One was a "portrait" head, so called because it did not conform to the stylized design of the heavier, more familiar images. The other showed the lower part of a torso and the upper part of a pair of legs. The fragment was clearly from a figure done in a sitting position with the legs spread, displaying a huge genital area. I was certain that this type of figure was unknown anywhere else in Polynesia. Immediately I thought of the sexual-inspection marae which Stimson had written about.

Perhaps the most unbelievable sections of Stimson's Ra'iva-vae manuscript had been those dealing with the religious practices held in connection with clitoral lengthening. Hapai had first given an account of how the clitoris was enlarged by years of rubbing with unguents, tying with cords, and other manipulations by the parents of the girls. This part of the ancient practices could be pretty well substantiated by comparative evidence I had derived from prehistoric wood-carvings and folklore which survived from Easter Island and New Zealand, and by the similar practices which had survived in the Marquesas well into later generations. What was without parallel was Hapai's detailed listing, description, and location out of his memory alone of some sixty marae devoted to the inspection of the lengthened clitoris by the priest. There were stories of disrobing rooms, special stone seats upon which the girl sat to be examined, and even a drawing and description of the rosewood instrument which was used to measure the enlarged clitoris to determine whether it had achieved the size regarded by Ra'ivavaeans as ideal. We had, indeed, located stone remains—never before reported—exactly where Hapai had said that a particular sexual-inspection marae was located, and which still contained a stone bench which would have exactly fitted such inspectional purposes. But how were we to know whether or not this bench-like stone was indeed what Hapai had claimed it to be, and not merely the seat of a high-ranking personage? What evidence could we ever find which could confirm or give the lie to the unique reports of Hapai? The fragments of the images we found were suggestive, but could not be taken as conclusive evidence.

Months later, on my way home from Central Polynesia, I stopped off in Hawaii to discuss these images with Stokes. The elderly anthropologist remarked that he had excavated related ones and told me that Mrs. Stokes, who was formerly a professional nurse, had immediately said when she saw one image,

"Why, that's a reproduction of a woman ready to give birth; the baby has already dropped down into the last position before birth." Following this lead, I searched the museums for torso remains from High Island. Here fragments of stone which no one had been able to identify, suddenly took shape now that I knew what to look for. There was a figure of a woman in the ecstasy of being implanted by a huge penis, the torso section of the curved, swollen belly of mid-pregnancy, and figures of the last stages of pregnancy. Everywhere I looked I found new evidence to reinforce the view that the basis of pre-European religious life on Ra'ivavae centered about the propitiation of the gods so that fertility might be increased. But there was little hope that I could relate this new evidence to Stimson's earlier findings.

Chapter Ten

BY BREAD ALONE

O Sacred origin!
Reveal thyself,
Arise from the ocean deeps!
O Unknowable one!
Creatress of power and authority,
Approach in answer to my entreaty!
O our Sustainer!
Thou art Sovereign of multitudes,
We acclaim thee!

WITHIN a few years after the coming of Christianity to Ra'ivavae in 1819, the island suffered the tragic pestilence which not only decimated the population, but killed the old ways forever. Soon the marae, the temple areas around which the religious, ceremonial, and social life of the people had centered, crumbled away and were buried beneath the lush vegetation which covers the past on all these Pacific islands. In their place the churches were built—for the time and for the place, imposing buildings which dwarfed the native houses. Around them grew the villages, and I have long felt that the only reason for the modern Polynesian town is that the inhabitants can be near the church and can attend the endless round of meetings and services conveniently. For now the churches dominate the community life of Ra'ivavae as thoroughly as the marae of the older religion once did.

Our church, the church in the village of Anatonu, was

named Siona (Zion). The house which we had taken as head-quarters was right beside it, so that if there is anything which I came to know intimately during my stay on Ra'ivavae it was the formal religious life of the people. Compared to everything around it, Siona is immense, looming protectively over the village, its white bulk visible for miles over the water (yet the increasing population of Anatonu now almost fills it of a Sunday).

On the steeple which houses the church bell is the painted face of a clock, whose hands are set at ten-thirty, the hour the church was consecrated. The interior of the limestone building is painted in pastel blues, pinks, and greens; the Victorian fretwork and brass chandeliers for the old-fashioned oil lamps are strangely handsome against the improbable color scheme. But the newly installed wiring and bare bulbs which dangle from the ceiling look out of place against the mellow colors. These lights are only for great occasions, such as the New Year's celebration, while the high pulpit is used only on Communion Sundays, Christmas, and New Years—or by visiting churchmen such as the Rimataran pastor who addressed us one day. The deacons' table on the main floor, and the pastor's regular table, set behind the balustrades below the pulpit, are covered with matching cloths—green and yellow for high occasions, gray for ordinary services. On a supporting column at an angle to the pulpit there is a clock, but it works rarely and even when it does no one pays it much attention. The services are often interminable—though the gracefully simple pews are surprisingly comfortable.

I came to appreciate this comfort, for I spent many hours in the church called Siona, six or seven sessions a week at the least. Not only were they valuable to me as an anthropologist, but I must admit that I felt a peace and a tranquillity during these services which I have rarely experienced. Most Europeans and Americans who live in the islands rarely visit a native service, since they dislike anything that smacks of missionary activity. The islanders appreciated my attendance and treated me as a valued member of the group—a compliment which I returned by taking a role in the most important social activity carried on in their community.

This sense of belonging was greatest during the daybreak services which are held every Wednesday, Friday, and Sunday. Shortly after six o'clock the steeple bell would sound, a sign for me to pull on a suit coat and assume the dignity of an elder of the community. This honor was given to me because I was a European, the titular "father" of our expedition household, and because I made it a point to dress soberly—right down to my shoes. Even the deacons usually went barefoot at these services unless they were leading the service, and the thought of shaving occurred to them rarely.

Often, as I walked down the front steps of the house, I would meet Tino or our landlord, Toāri'i, and we would shake hands, walk along together, and discuss the weather or the shipping news. Outside the church there would be another round of handshaking, with the early arrivals more conversation about the weather, pleasant laughter at my efforts at Tahitian, and usually some form of salacious joke from Uncle Bert or Mama Iē. The women went directly into the church, where they sat in front; the men would generally wait for the pastor or me to make the first move. Then we separated, each carefully wiping his feet on the copra sacks placed in the doorway, and moved to our usual place among the pews. Each member of the congregation first bowed his head in silent prayer, and then all waited motionless for the service to start.

At these early-morning services there were never many of us present; usually six women and eight men—all middle-aged to old. The sex ratio was in contrast to all other churches I have regularly attended, where women always outnumber men. These good folk were typical of the "best elements" of the community. In addition to the pastor and his wife, and the domineering but beautiful widow of the former pastor, there were the heads of the two "best" families—and several other pillars of Anatonu society. The group never changed, it never included any of the younger people, and certainly never the imported Tahitian instructors or any of the more worldly wise.

The deacons took turns at leading the service, but occasionally it was the pastor or one of the young men who had just become a member of the church fellowship. The women were only allowed to preside at their own service, held after the regular Sunday morning one. As the small congregation sat silent in the morning freshness, the leader of the day moved to his seat behind the cloth-covered table below the pulpit, upon which rested a Bible of modest size. After bowing his head in silent prayer for several minutes he might wait for some time until the majority of the congregation was present. There were always late-comers, who tiptoed in ostentatiously and then reached around to shake hands with anyone nearby. Then a few brief announcements concerning church affairs were made.

The real service always began with the high falsetto whine of Toāri'i's wife, the song leader of the first *pupu*, one of the two work groups into which the entire church is divided. Sometimes the pastor's wife would join in the song and do her best to outlast the leader, to the amusement of the rest of the congregation. After a while the other women would sing along in a halfhearted way while the men kept up a nondescript hum. To put it charitably, the singing had a leaden seriousness, an absence of vivacity which is in strong contrast to the music on some of the other Polynesian islands. This first hymn was followed by a Bible lesson, and this by a prayer. The second hymn was always led off by Anni Mervin of the second *pupu*, who was a master of local hymn-singing. The sermon was always brief, though the dynamics were formidable. In the approved local style the speaker always began in a barely audible voice and ended with a roaring bellow which seemed to shake the rafters. The service was closed by a very brief prayer.

It was the ten o'clock service on Sunday morning, however, which revealed the full influence of the church in the affairs of Ra'ivavae. This was the ceremonial focal point of the week, the reason for the existence of the European-style houses of the village, with their stone and timber and iron. While a family might spend the rest of the week living and working happily by its plantation, in a pandanus and coconut-frond shack, on Saturday afternoon or Sunday morning it would load up the necessary food for the weekend and return to the village. Then one could see families being poled along the shore in huge canoes, laden down with green leaf packets of *popoi* pounded out the day before; or two or three young children tied together with a *pareu*, riding fearlessly along on the back of a horse, the father shuffling along behind laden down with a bundle of firewood. Everyone looked forward to Sunday breakfast, a leisurely meal for the whole family. This was made even more agreeable by the carefully hoarded delicacies which had been put aside all week long.

By midmorning, the streets of the village were filled with the howls of children, as their parents scrubbed them clean and forced them into clothes which were never worn at other times in the week. At the village faucet and in the pools which ran off from the taro beds the women washed their bodies and long hair—and often a few clothes as well. Church was in the offing, but no one seemed pressed for time. Time is the most available of Polynesian commodities and when all is ready the villagers amble slowly in the general direction of the church, everyone moving along on his own, the young bucks carrying guitars and the older men stopping now and then to chat.

Remembering as I did the beautiful Sunday dress of the other parts of Polynesia, I was always depressed by the dowdiness of this sabbath spectacle. Except for the babies, the Sunday best of the High Islanders was a poor thing indeed. Although the young girls looked chipper in their white blouses and brightly colored *pareu* skirts, the only thing which redeemed the rest of the women was the small flair with which they wore their hats. The old men looked completely dismal, somber, and awkward in their ill-fitting suits, which had been copied from the clothes of visiting European pastors. The young ones were obtrusively gay in their flamboyant *aloha* shirts.

But the babies were something else again. These poor infants were decked out like pieces of elaborately decorated candy, their long robes and bonnets heavy with embroidery, ribbons, and lace. Up and down the church aisle they went, as the girls and young women tending them carried them in and out of the church during the service. These overdressed babies were a source of diversion, each Sunday morning, only matched by the Tahitian instructress who occasionally put in an appearance in church. She was carefully dressed in a low-cut, sexy, simple black dress, set off by white shoes and a white chiffon handkerchief laid over her reddish hair. Her flashy gold wrist watch, huge gold ear bangles, and a baroque pearl ring may not have been the most appropriate adornments for a Sunday service, but they were well suited to her golden-brown skin. During the service she always left her handbag open so that everyone could see the king-size Chesterfields she carried, for no one else could afford them. Despite this ostentation she was an educated woman and she practiced her skills even during the sermon, cutting her name with a penknife in the pew in front of her.

To the Western eye (and ear) there is a pleasant madness about the Sunday service on Ra'ivavae. People come and go, shaking hands with their neighbors. Some yawn, gossip, or fall asleep, against a constant background of crying babies. I have even seen one of the good deacons reading a paper while a visiting pastor labored in the high pulpit above him. No one ever paid much attention to the words of the preacher, which often could not be heard over the continuous chorus of hacking coughs from the congregation. Fishing and taro farming tend to leave the men with constant colds, while the women probably suffer strained throats from the falsetto singing which is *de rigueur* on Ra'ivavae. To this day I can hear the penetrating whine of our friend Giggles ("the most beautiful voice on High Island") singing "Silent Night, Holy Night" as the warm breezes of the Pacific rustled through the church.

In addition to this buzzing informality which marks the service, two other things are apt to strike the European visitor most strongly: the absence of any collection plate (donations are made annually, by family) and the presence of three male preceptors with long white sticks standing in the aisles. Their job is to maintain order, but no one, as I have pointed out, seems to mind. Occasionally these guardians of the peace would point their rods like an accusing finger at someone or even crack the offender over the head. But to no avail; the buzz of conversation only lessened for a moment. Aiding the wardens was the pastor's wife, who stationed herself among the girls and tried to keep order by glaring at them, batting at them with a rolled-up newspaper, or by pulling at their glossy black braids. Despite her efforts the villagers held that she was "not strict enough with the girls"—who were her responsibility—just as they felt that her husband was not severe enough with them!

Once a month, the most solemn service of all took place and only the well-behaved, married members of the congregation could attend this Holy Communion. Denial of the privilege of taking Communion was one of the few social sanctions which could be invoked here on High Island. I was allowed to be present to view the taking of Communion, but for the first time in my life was not served the ceremonial bread and wine; I was not *Etāretia*, a member of the church fellowship.

Those who were to participate in the Holy Communion remained behind after the church had been cleared. All of the women wore broad-brimmed hats, none of which were colored. There were no young people present, and—as always on solemn occasions—there were more men than women. The wife of the pastor moved up to the bench specially placed to the left front of the Communion table, behind which sat the pastor. Two deacons sat facing the women, and two others in front facing the pastor. Utmost solemnity prevailed. The hymns were special Communion hymns, sung in an unusual fashion. The harmony was the finest I had ever heard on Ra'ivavae, but they had a drone-like quality, similar to that of the bagpipe. Men took a much greater part in the singing than was usual. Following the first song a lengthy sermon was preached, which in turn was supplemented by a very long prayer. After another special hymn the pastor began reading the Communion ritual, and then broke off a piece of bread from the loaf and ceremoniously ate it. He silently prayed to himself, after which the deacons passed among the brethren serving bread. This was taken, eaten individually, and ceremoniously, and followed by personal silent prayer. The same routine was followed with the wine, and another hymn and prayer ended the service. The special significance of the ceremony to all who took part was clearly obvious to an observer.

The ten o'clock service, which lasted from an hour to an hour and a half, was immediately followed by the women's service, except when Communion intervened. The pastor's wife in company with the wife of one of the deacons led the meeting. From her privileged spot by the pulpit, the widow of the old pastor kept a watchful eye on things. This was the only chance the women had to lead a meeting and the opportunity was seriously sought after by the big-hatted elder females.

In the afternoon a two o'clock service duplicated that of the morning, but it was somewhat abbreviated. The major differences between the two were that this one was led by a deacon rather than the pastor, and was generally not attended by the young men, who had piled into the morning meeting toward the end of the sermon. In the afternoon they either stayed in the village and played their guitars, or went off into the bush to drink beer, or played anything from marbles to football. The older people simply rested in preparation for the evening, and only rarely paid a social call upon kinfolk.

On Sunday evenings at eight o'clock the population of High Island really came to life when they gathered in the *fare himene*, the "singing house," which serves the same function as a church meeting house or parish house in the West. The church itself was a place where one was prepared for death and the afterlife, and in keeping with this awesome purpose little vivacity or spirit was allowed to enter the services. The meeting house was completely the contrary. The same young men who avoided the church services flocked to the *fare himene* and took an active part in both discussion and singing. Whereas no one seemed particularly interested in the formal sermons of the great church, the closest attention was given to the informal discussions in the meeting house. Even the singing was different, for where the church services called forth only the most dreary versions of European hymns, the meeting house was the place where the songs which had a flavor of High Island's rich past were sung with verve. As each member of the group waited his turn to talk about the passage from the Bible which had been chosen for discussion, the entire meeting sang and enjoyed itself. It was at this time that the newly developed Polynesian sense of democracy was at its best. If she had something to say, the village whore was listened to with more interest than the *Tavana*, who was an abominably dull speaker for a political figure, and the deacons sat on the floor with the *taure'are'a*. Only the stupid or thick-tongued were listened to with impatience.

There was nothing in ancient Ra'ivavaean religious life to compare with this Sunday evening singing-and-discussion meeting, which is perhaps best compared to our own Christian Endeavor. The closest thing to it in pagan times must have been the social affairs held to celebrate communal achievements, or to mark events of interest to all. But even in these great gatherings of people, the right of dominant sex, of dominant class, of physical and spiritual right, overrode individual worth. The present Sunday evening meetings represent an entirely new force in Polynesian life, for it is only here that one can say a true communal feeling has begun to exist, and only here that the worth of the individual is assessed upon its own merits, regardless of sex, age, social status, or class.

These Sunday evening meetings were the most pleasant part of my stay on Ra'ivavae. After a late meal I would leave Zenie, Alan, and Jim to their conversations, and amble across to the meeting house, frequently in company with Tioti, Tino, or Toāri'i. Along the path would be groups of young fellows sitting around strumming guitars, wrapped in towels and blankets against the insidious cold of night. Occasionally there would be a couple of boys standing silently in the darkness between bushes, waiting for the girl of their choice to pass. Having more important things on their minds, they looked at us coldly, whereas the others shouted good-natured greetings. Almost always a troop of smaller boys and girls, laughing and playing, would form directly behind me, virtually walking on my heels. During the day they usually kept a rather fearful distance, but darkness gave them courage to come up close and comment on the odd behavior of the white man from afar. On the borders of the playing field, across the path from the meeting house, I would occasionally see fifteen or twenty young children lying side by side in a long line, stretched out beneath towels and blankets. They called out greetings as we turned to the "singing house."

Generally I tried to arrive well in advance of the actual session, so that I could catch the unguarded activities during that informal period. The women would be gathered around open kerosene lamps on the floor, gossiping and rocking their children to sleep. Owing to their current economic troubles most of the people were smoking locally grown tobacco wrapped in the outer layers of pandanus leaves, and the open lamps served to cure the tobacco quickly as well as to light the cigarettes. One of my most cherished memories is the sight of two deacons with an open Bible between them sitting beside the lamp, intensely discussing the meaning of a passage. Uncle Bert went over to light his cigarette and listen to their talk, and the three seemed to show the most intense glow of real and deep emotion that I had seen in the islands.

This meetinghouse hour is the only period of the week, so far as I know, in which whole families are active together beneath one roof amid an immense number of bright-eyed and seemingly very happy children. One could feel sociability warm the atmosphere as the infants slept, the younger children played, the youths waited outside the door for the activities to begin, and the elders gossiped together. There was always an ease and freedom here which is rarely found at other times. Somehow, in stepping into his community character for this one time during the week, the High Islander finds a release from the fears and responsibilities which bind him at other times. Even the most familiar gestures and sentiments seemed to take on a special warmth in the singing house. I watched how tenderly grandparents cared for the young children, covering and recovering a sleeping tot with a towel as he stirred in the growing cold. Sleepy children would awake, gaze drowsily around, crawl closer to a favored parent, and then return to sleep. If they were whimpering, the mothers would pick them up and rock them gently back to sleep. Frequently two little girls would share the same towel and after a bit of lively chatter they would doze off, undisturbed by the warm bustle about them.

The leader of these meetings changed from week to week, and occasionally the pastor himself would take charge, bringing to the occasion the same formality and long-winded dullness which he displayed in church. He was the one discouraging note in these Sunday evenings and no one was pleased when he decided to direct the discussion. I was particularly impressed when they invited our Tioti to lead one of the meetings. Though he was a member of a completely different sect and came from the reputedly "savage" Tuamotuan islands, the people listened to him with both interest and respect; and they gave his question a full measure of discussion.

The main part of the singing-house meetings generally began with our friend Giggles launching into her piercing whine on a preliminary hymn which no one took very seriously. Then the leader announced his question, usually extracted from a Biblical quotation, and the responses began. The young people gave their answers first and it was amusing to hear the teenagers start their communal participation by awkwardly reading off the answers which adults had helped them prepare in advance. After this the women began to speak, and to me most of them seemed far more impressive and impassioned speakers than their husbands. A conspicuous exception was Toāri'i's wife, who like the pastor himself usually recited to the accompaniment of yawns and desultory gossip. Many times I have heard Toāri'i clear his throat loudly in an attempt to quell the rising chatter during his wife's lengthy and almost inaudible texts. When he succeeded it was only because a good part of the audience had dozed off or left the room.

But there were memorable speakers too: Mama Iē and the widow of the former pastor to take but two examples. Standing up before her audience, who were seated on mats in a rough semicircle around the speaker's table, Mama Iē was always the

first of the older women to comment on the evening's text and she would inevitably draw a laugh with her comments. The pastor's widow usually followed her, but she was cast in another mold, an impressive, arrow-straight figure draped in a long, loose Mother Hubbard and topped with a vast, broad-brimmed hat. As a deacon whispered *Maniania*, "You are too noisy," to the buzzing audience, the widow would look long at the colored map of Jerusalem on the wall and launch into her speech.

Whatever the question at hand, she would generally take the occasion to prophesy hell and damnation to the younger generation. She was apt to hold forth for long minutes on the evils of the present way of life, and no one seemed to mind her departure from the subject at hand. Everyone feared that she might point her long bony forefinger at them if they strayed from the straight and narrow path. Her air of virtue was not offensive, for it merely suited her person and history. I invariably found her fascinating and admired the lively pleasure with which this ancient yet truly handsome woman lit her cigarette in the open lamp before beginning her discussion.

Exciting, enlightening, amusing as the discussions were at these meetings, they rarely moved me as much as the singing. It was led by Toāri'i's wife, who must have been a talented woman, since the music at the Sunday meetings was completely different from the tiresome hymns at church which she also led. Here the young men sang with enthusiasm, eyes closed, faces red, and bodies bending with their lusty efforts. The rhythm was persistent and pervasive. Indeed the singers sometimes became so entranced with their own efforts that they carried on far beyond the customary period, to the discomfort of the next speakers and the amusement of the rest of the audience. When answers were slow in coming forth, Toāri'i or one of the other deacons usually jumped into the breach with a shouted "Hurry up and sing!" Occasionally both singing and speaking were interrupted as everyone took up the chase after some sad cockroach that had wandered into the lighted area, finally to meet his doom under a young warrior's heel.

After all this excitement, the meeting usually drew to an end with the main speaker giving an answer to his own question. By this time it was ten-thirty or eleven o'clock, time enough for a brief hymn and prayer to close the session. Parents quietly picked up their sleeping children and made their way home. On the way they passed the embers of the small fires built by the *taure'are'a* to warm themselves. A few were still there strumming their guitars around the ashes. Quiet "good nights" and a few handshakes marked the end of one week and the beginning of another.

A few weeks after I arrived in Ra'ivavae, Uncle Bert and Toāri'i began urging me to lead one of the Sunday night meetings. I finally agreed, for this would give me the opportunity to explain to our neighbors what we were doing here on the island. As a text I chose I Thess. 5:21: "Prove all things; hold fast that which is good," and asked our good Tioti to assist me in planning the talk and translating my words.

On the evening of my talk Tioti and I, dressed as formally as we could manage, went to the meetinghouse early in order to make the final arrangements, but already small groups were gathered around the smoking lamps, the women casually searing the green tobacco leaves. Since the pastor was not there on this particular evening, Toāri'i was acting as the chairman and announcer. When all was finally ready, we took our seats at the large speaker's table. The group was unusually quiet. Toāri'i rose and asked the group if they were finished smoking. Then Giggles struck up a hymn and the meeting was under way. I rose and stumblingly announced my question in Tahitian—E aha ia te maita'i no te ha'apoo e te tapea maite? "What is the value of examining well and holding fast?" Tioti followed with a prayer. Toāri'i spoke briefly, welcoming us, and then warned the congregation to be quiet. He finished by announcing the evening's text in more comprehensible Tahitian than mine. Before me I could see the children staring up with their wide eyes, which glistened with life and good humor, jostling and tussling with one another, passing secrets back and forth. There seemed to be more of them than ever before.

That night everyone seemed to have something to say—the young and the old, the men and women. Some held their audience, others wandered on with no one listening to a word. One of the older deacons got up to criticize the dancing that went on before our house every evening, but he was good enough to praise other aspects of our stay. I felt flattered.

Finally, when the evening was long gone, I was called upon to give my talk. Mistakenly I tried to give part of it in Tahitian to the disappointment of the audience, who wanted to hear what I had to say in "sweet English words." I began by repeating the Tahitian words of my text: "Prove all things; hold fast to that which is good"; then, in the same tongue I struggled through the endless formal salutations which were expected: to the pastor and his wife, all the deacons and their wives, the chief, and the policeman, the brethren and sisters of the church membership, the taure'are'a, the children, my friends Tioti, Zenie, and Jim, and "everyone." I apologized for my insufficient knowledge of the language but noted my good fortune in having Tioti to translate. I admitted that I was neither pastor nor deacon, planter nor fisherman. The reason that I spent my time walking about the village, talking with Piahuru and Tauira'i, chatting with my friends Toāri'i and Tino, was that my work consisted in knowing about the life of other people, both as it was lived in the past and as it is lived now. "You may think," I said, "that I refer to European things in my text for tonight"—the beautiful Christian church which now stands in place of the ancient marae, the Western cloth which has freed the womenfolk of the back-breaking daily labor of making bark cloth, the music of guitars, the game of football. True, all of these are good in their own way, but my real message referred to the task of examining and holding fast to the things which were good in the days of Ra'ivavae's great past.

I noted that food cooked in the umu was better than food prepared in any other way and I criticized the modern tendency to boil everything in a pot. I pointed out that the health value of the native taro and bananas was far greater than the newly fashionable white bread and sugar. Then I went on to deplore the destruction of the toa-tree windbreak and its long-range effect upon their taro and coffee crops and upon their health. Warming to my subject, I quoted Deuteronomy—Maha, maha. E'ore te ta'ata e ora i te ma'a anae ra—— "For man shall not live by bread alone." I gave this line a most untheological twist, I am afraid, turning it to a purpose which no good pastor would have approved. My remarks concerned museums and my associations with museums, and how I had seen preserved in museums throughout the world the lovely things from the prehistoric days of High Island. I described the beauty of the carving and the workmanship, and repeated the remarks of Reverend Ellis that Ra'ivavae had been a greater center of art and beauty than Tahiti at one point; and I ended my sermon, for such it turned out to be, with a plea that they should do something to adorn their lives again, just as they paint the outside of their houses with flowers.

Then it was over. Everyone shook my hand warmly, but I never did find out what they thought of my message. It probably meant more to me than to them.

Yet later on, as I reflected on that evening at the singing house, I realized I had not been quite fair. The church itself was an example of the considerable effort which the High Islander can put forth when he must. All the churches on Ra'ivavae were built entirely by local labor and local funds; and for this part of the world they are considerable achievements, with their heavy limestone walls, red-painted, corrugated-iron roofs, and glass windows. Leadership, vision, and communal pride were indispensable in their construction, as well as a long-range tenacity which is unusual in Polynesia.

The church in our village of Anatonu was conceived and pushed through its early stages by the second pastor to preach there. The original design was by a local High Islander who had gone to Tahiti for an education, and then to Moorea where he took a wife and became a district chief. In his last years he returned to Ra'ivavae with his wife and was elected chief of the Anatonu district. Actual construction was carried on by all the men of Anatonu, aided by the men of Vaiuru, who each worked half a day for three months of every year over a period of thirty years. The old pastor directed the work for a year or two, and when he died the chief took over. The walls were built of quarried *ma'atea* from the slopes behind the church. Gradually the work slowed down, for the aged chief was not sure of the proper design of arches for the window. Then the Chinese storekeeper in Anatonu redesigned the arches and undertook to supervise the construction. He was neither a churchgoer nor was he paid for his services, but since he was married to a local woman the work was considered to be one of his social obligations. The pastor who brought the church to completion after thirty years of labor was the last, late pastor, a domineering figure whose widow still has some of his power. It was she who conceived the plan of buying a generator and electrifying the church, a labor carried through entirely by the women of the church.

The Christian church represents to the Ra'ivavaean what the pagan temple must have meant to his ancestors. Physically the church building is the product of his greatest expression of material and aesthetic labor, just as was the marae. Socially the church building and the *fare himene* are the focus of virtually all of his group activities, just as was the marae. And just as the marae once physically dominated all social activities, so does the Christian church in even greater measure dominate all of the Ra'ivavaeans' thinking and behavior.

High Island is also unique in that its effective church pattern and structure was developed entirely by native pastors. Since the earliest days there has never been a resident European missionary and only rarely was the island visited by Tahitian-based missioners or inspectors from Britain. In Anatonu the pastors were long-lived men of force and vision. In close collaboration with their kings and chiefs who were always careful to become deacons, they insured the continuity of the early-established English pattern of formal worship, tinged with survivals from a pagan past. Trained in Ra'iatea to give their parish children a modicum of education, the pastors were more than adequate to their original task.

There are four churches on Ra'ivavae, one for each district and village, and all report directly to the Protestant headquarters in Papeete. (In the last century the London Missionary Society turned responsibility for churches in the French Oceanic area over to the French Protestants.) Despite the four churches there are only two pastors at present, each handling two districts. This is not the best state of affairs since the smaller district usually feels slighted. (Our pastor at Anatonu, who also handles the church at Vaiuru, was involved in a long drawn-out squabble which led the hard-pressed missionary at Tahiti to come down to smooth things over.) In the district and village of Anatonu, the pastor has six deacons to aid him, elected from the two work groups into which the village is divided.

Membership in the church itself is a carefully guarded privilege, restricted to married men and women of good repute. The importance of belonging to the *Etarētia*, as it is called, is constantly stressed during the services and church meetings.

The social restrictions imposed by the requirements for membership in the *Etarētia* were new to Polynesians. Nothing of this kind had existed in their former pagan practices. The priesthood was then restricted to men, and it was generally men who were involved with the temple ceremonies; this fitted in with the church structure and practice introduced by the Christian missionaries. But ideas of joint worship by both sexes in the holy place, of "membership" in the church restricted by democratic admission rather than by right of birth, of the restriction of the Communion to people who abstained from extramarital sexual activities, all were foreign to previous Polynesian ideas.

To my surprise, I learned that the deacons were elected annually, not only by the *Etarētia* but by all people of the village over twenty-one years of age! They are rarely changed, however, unless there is some very important reason. Periodically all of the *Etarētia* meet together in midmorning on a Friday, passing up the usual daybreak service. Dressed in their best clothes, the group considers applicants who want to join its membership, and decides who is to take Communion. These meetings are of great importance. As we have seen, the church (and family) is the center of social life for every High Islander when he grows up. To be barred from the *Etarētia* would be disastrous.

Yet despite the importance of the church, life on Ra'ivavae is becoming more secular. Once no one cooked on Sundays. Now even the deacons and pastor do it. Once the old women danced for religious joy and excitement at the Sunday night meetings. But the young pastors—newly trained in the seminary at Papeete—have put a stop to this. No longer are there intervillage competitions in psalm-singing and at home hardly anyone reads the Bible, sings psalms, or gives morning and evening prayers. There is one day of fasting and prayer in which the Lord is entreated to spare the island from hurricanes. This commemorates the ruinous storm of 1919.

Oddly enough, the High Islander is not entirely happy with modern laxity. There is considerable grumbling against the local pastor, who is considered "too soft." Although he is nearing fifty he has only been a pastor for ten years, following four years in the seminary in Tahiti. He is a Ra'irua man, whose grandfather and father before him were pastors, and he lives on his wife's land in Anatonu. He works hard, for he has seven children—two of them at school in Papeete—and his pastoral salary is but a token pittance. He is a great contrast to his predecessor, who held the community in a grip of iron, and wielded dictatorial powers.

This desire of Ra'ivavaeans for a "strict" pastor, despite the pressure he might put on the everyday pattern of their lives, seems to be a direct clue as to what the Christian church means to the Polynesian. For the Polynesian's Christianity is not the

European's Christianity, with its emphasis on preparation for the afterlife and on adherence to a moral code as a part of this preparation. By every force of his past culture and his present circumstances, by every act of cultural values he has, the Polynesian looks only to the past and to the present; the unknown future is of little concern to him. He is concerned with filling his belly and the bellies of his family today and during the season; let tomorrow and the next season be taken care of when they arrive. His concern with God—either the gods of his ancestors or the present Lord God Jehovah—is primarily with the insurance of bountiful crops, plentiful fish, and many children.

Despite his Protestant belief, the High Islander (and the Polynesian in general) looks to his pastor as the direct intermediary with God. It is the pastor who makes contact with God, and it is the pastor who is blamed for crop failure or a poor season of fishing. Despite their own wishes and shortcomings, the villagers believe that if the pastor sees that they carry out the proper propitiation to God, then they will have the plenty that they desire. If he is less than adamant about their actions, if he does not himself pray sufficiently hard or follow the proper ritual, then God will not grant them proper fructification and multiplication. The pastor is—or, at least, was until the present decade of rapid increase in the temporal powers of the state and the slow decline of religious authority —the substitute for the pagan priest, and to some extent for the pagan king. For the pastor is the ruler and arbiter of village life; the village exists only because of the church, and the pastor is supreme in the church.

Chapter Eleven

CONFESSIONS OF SIN

May death take thee!

May sudden death descend upon thee—
Standing, or moving about!
May death seize thee—
In the hidden retreat, or on the open way!
May death come to thee—
In the darkness, sleeping in the arms of thy beloved!
Even while gazing upon me, in the full light of day—
May death blind thy eyes!
MAY DEATH TAKE THEE!

ONE of the first things that Alan Seabrook told me when we first met was that Ra'ivavae "had a darkness." It was a spiritual or psychic darkness which cast a shadow over the islanders and their relationships with one another. It was a darkness symbolized by the illness and death which had dogged the island for seven generations. As I have mentioned before, something of this strange blight seems to afflict everyone who has worked on Ra'ivavae. We were no exceptions. From the day of our arrival our party had been beset with illness.

Indeed, from the time I had commenced to reread the High Island manuscripts, things went wrong. In Tahiti, working at my place in Paea, I had come down with an unknown throat illness. The day after we came to Anatonu both Alan and Jim became sick and were forced to resort to miracle capsules. Jim was down with the malady for many days. Only Zenie seemed

223

to escape, although her nerves wore thin toward the end of our siege. She felt that our constant tampering with marae and *tiki* might well be the cause of the chronic illness. Before she had left Tahiti her father warned her to leave these alone and not to permit me to handle any image carved with the hand resting upon the stomach. All this had led me to be acutely aware of the place of illness in the life of Ra'ivavae.

When the *Mareva* docked at Ra'irva for its brief stay, I visited the local medical aid man, Taupoa. He was vaguely related to Zenie and we were happy to accept his invitation to visit his "hospital." The bare wardroom contained only one sick patient and his attending family, but the examining room was well supplied with drugs—particularly penicillin. Later on, Taupoa proved to be of considerable assistance to us. In addition to his medical qualifications our friend was both an excellent fisherman and a good cook.

Only a day after this I was plunged into the medical problems which beset the natives of High Island. I had just returned from church, and found our landlord Toāri'i waiting at the house for me. No doubt he had heard me addressed as *Tāote* (Doctor) and had assumed that I practiced medicine. He wanted me to attend his fourteen-year-old sick daughter. I immediately referred him to Taupoa but he told me that the aid man "never came out to the villages—sick people must always go in and see him." I also carefully explained that I was a "*Tāote Puta*," a doctor of books—not of human ills. Toāri'i still insisted. Since I knew a good deal about sickness from my military service and my other expeditions, I felt that I knew enough not to do any harm, and agreed to look at the girl. I found her huddled on one of the few beds in the little house to which the family had moved. Her fever was 104 degrees. After giving her some aspirin to lower the fever I insisted that the family call the aid man, telling them to use my name if necessary. It was then that they confessed that the reason they did not want to call him was that he had tended her before, and warned them not to let her get chilled again.

Taupoa, however, came along in a surprisingly short time and gave her the modern panacea for all island ills—50,000 units of penicillin. He was not sure just what was wrong. But he thought that it might be the onset of menstruation, accompanied by a chill, or even another bout of the typhoid fever which the girl and her sister had had before. Typhoid was new to Ra'ivavae. After treating the girl he told us more about the medical problems here.

Last year he had handled a case of polio. The boy had recovered, and despite a withered leg manages to hobble around with his age mates. There were broken limbs resulting from falls from trees, horses, or mountain sides—even from the rough waves which sneak upon the reef. Tuberculosis was his most serious problem, and perhaps the most frequent killer. Gonorrhea is an easily treated and frequent complaint, though fortunately there is little syphilis. Tetanus takes its toll, and there are local poisons, some of which come from the deadly scorpion fish or balloon fish—all this seemed fairly commonplace in a clinical sort of way, but it did not tell me much about the deeper relationships between mind and body, a subject which interested me deeply. Nor did a visit by a member of the Colonial Health Service which followed a few days later. He arrived in a passing schooner and spent several pleasant hours with us telling about his work in Africa and the Marquesas. His most important remark was that he usually had little work to do on Ra'ivavae because the people fear European doctors.

I seemed to be in greater favor, however. The next patient to require treatment was Toāri'i himself. A few days after our arrival he sent for me again. I found him lying on a mat in the corner of his little home, wrapped up in the usual blanket, curing the green tobacco he used on an open kerosene lamp.

His symptoms seemed to be the same as those Alan had when he was suffering from a filarial attack. I could do nothing except prescribe the usual aspirin and warmer covers. From time to time I sent over a small toddy of rum. Toāri'i was soon up and about.

But all treatments were not as easy as this. One day a family who had once befriended Alan brought to me a beautiful little boy whose leg was covered with a frightful, scabrous disease. There was absolutely nothing I could do for him, for I had seen the condition of the home and yard in which he lived. I insisted that they take him to Taupoa, but they kept saying that they were afraid that he would be given an injection. I met this unreasonable fear of the hypodermic needle on several occasions.

Another treatment I was called upon to give from time to time was the bandaging of stumps of fingers bitten off by moray eels. This was a common accident to the young men who grope-fished among the coral heads of the reef and channel. Taupoa wasted little time and less medicine on these fellows, but I could not bear to turn them away without washing and bandaging the stump and giving them codeine and aspirin to ease the pain. Indeed, I much preferred these moments to the stormy business of giving an enema to a young child who had not passed in several days. On one occasion, in the dim light of a flickering lamp I did my best for a two-year-old child, screaming with fear at the strange European with the ominous equipment.

Taupoa and I, however, were not the only dispensers of medicines. There were local experts who spent their time massaging friends with a "sick back" or "sick belly." Other local "doctors" made medicines of everything from hibiscus flower petals to sandalwood. Some of Zenie's female friends even presented her with a favorite local concoction to make the menses flow more rapidly and freely. It was made from the juice of a special variety of coconut, to which lime juice, guava leaves, and other local herbal ingredients were added. One had to drink a full bottle of the product for three successive days to make it work.

The people of Ra'ivavae were quite stoical about minor ills of the body—the missing finger tips, the aches and pains, the colds and fevers. What they really feared were the *tupapa'u*, the malcontent spirits of the dead. Death itself caused no great concern, but the unearthly beings who wandered in the dark of night terrified them. These beings had the power to interfere with man's activities when they chose, and this made them doubly frightening. Alan was told by Toāri'i that the patient in Taupoa's hospital bed had his swollen stomach as the result of a *tupapa'u*. It puzzled me that our landlord, a deacon, a true believer, should give any credence to pagan ideas. Finally we came to understand that the people believed that these unearthly beings were instruments of God's will.

There were *tupapa'u* which served "the new God" Jehovah, and others which still served the ancient gods. Alan, for example, hoped that the people would not notice his legs when he returned to Ra'ivavae. Since his last trip he had been afflicted with elephantiasis, a disease which he contracted during his long stay in the outer Tahitian valleys. But he remembered that years before he had been warned that his marae explorations on High Island would bring down the wrath of the sleeping ancient gods in the form of elephantiasis. Other foreigners have tampered with the marae, and all seem to have met later with ill luck. The few local people who have dared usually had disastrous things happen to them. One neighbor of Mama Iē's pulled down the altar walls of the small ancestral temple on his own property in Anatonu village in order to provide materials to build his new house. No sooner was the foundation laid than he became fatally ill. On his deathbed he called together the family and explained that he was dying because he had broken the *tapu* against tampering with marae, and that his children must tear down the structure and learn from this experience. Such tales travel widely and help account for the fact that most of the off-trail marae have been left undisturbed.

Though they do not fear it, death has always been a momentous event for the Polynesians, and at one time they surrounded it with great rites and ceremonies. When royalty flourished on High Island, death was a grand spectacle. At the first announcement that death was imminent, the specialist dirge-singers and mourners gathered near the home of the dying one to weep and to sing laments. Relatives brought gifts of food and fine tapa cloth. At the moment the soul commenced the long voyage to the underworld the womenfolk—mothers, wives, sisters—mutilated themselves with the jagged edges of sharks' teeth, and a general wailing and chanting over the corpse began. If the dead was of high enough rank, the body might be rubbed with perfumed oils and wrapped in special tapa cloths. Indeed, if the person were of great rank the corpse might even be preserved for long periods by a form of dessication and oiling. On the other hand, the body of an ordinary soul would be exposed to the action of the elements so that the flesh might be separated from the bones, for only the bones were interred. Great personages were buried within the area of the marae itself, others nearby or in their home areas. But it was the skull and bones of the kings and the adult males which were matters of greatest concern, for in these rested the power, mana, flowing down from ages past. Since enemy tribes were anxious to seize these bones and defame their power by splitting them into fishhooks or other common objects, the remains were hidden with the greatest secrecy.

When the soul reached the underworld it was received, given another body, and set loose to a perpetual existence. From time to time, if called upon or provoked in some way, it might visit the World of Light again as a *tupapa'u*. During such a visit it

The Sage. The problem informant, Hapai. PHOTO BY IGOR A. ALLAN.

Children's clothing reflects the economic status of their parents. Here we see young boys at play who represent three distinct income groups

Witch? We were called upon to cure the baby this great-grandmother was said to have cursed

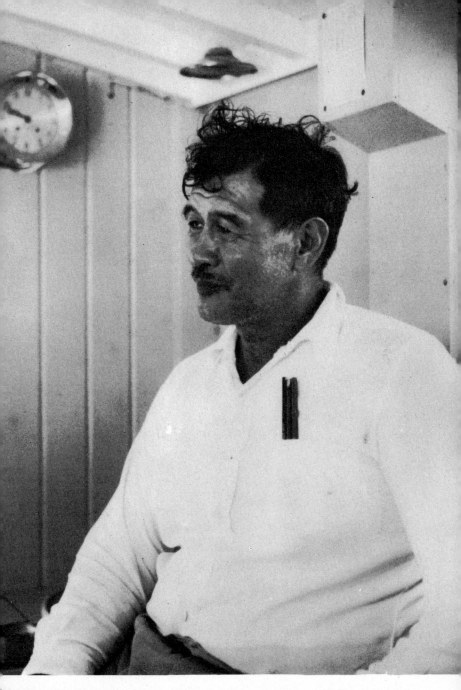

The Fox. Tauira'i, our chief source of information about Ra'ivavae's past

'Ami. Wise in the ways of the past, this most valued informant was at first suspicious, then surprised at our knowledge of her ancestors, and finally she told us of her recollections and beliefs.

could either aid or harm its descendants. It was these visits which the people of Ra'ivavae still feared as they had always done. Perhaps it was for this reason that the dead were buried with many of their prized possessions—clothes, jewelry, watches; even bicycles, huge mirrors, dressing tables, and sewing machines. This was a way of placating the late departed. But many islanders turn the tables when they know they are dying. They give away most of their possessions in their last days, right down to tins of tea and coffee. In return the family provides a suitable tomb, which may even be a complete miniature stone-and-iron house over the grave. In every case, however, the corpse immediately is weighted down with roofing iron and heavy stone and later by a huge block of lime and stone, for no one likes to take chances.

This is the background to our first major insight into the relationship between life, sickness, and death on High Island. Zenie and I were out on our usual afternoon village rounds when we heard shrieks and screams coming from a cookshed to our left. I presumed some errant wife was being beaten by her husband, and both my military training and my New England background told me to keep going and not meddle in another person's domestic affairs. Zenie, however, insisted on knowing what was going on and pushed me forward through the opening in the coconut-frond thatched wall. I found myself in the midst of a crowd of men, women, and children of all ages—all jostling around an obviously sick baby. The faces of the women were red from long crying, and tears still ran down their cheeks. Other women kept arriving, each crying out loudly before she entered the door. In the unhappy group we saw the pastor and his wife.

Emboldened by Zenie's presence, I pushed aside the crowd and took up the infant in order to give it a little air. It turned out to be the same baby that had been carried past our headquarters a half hour before, on the way back from Taupoa's place in Ra'irua. After much questioning I learned that the aid man had told them, perhaps in jest, that the baby needed to have its gums cut so that the teeth could push through "or it would die." He had told them that he could not do this, therefore they should seek a local expert. The whole group was carrying on as though the infant were already dead.

I sent for my medical kit and thoroughly checked the child. Her temperature was only 102.5 degrees, and despite a slight diarrhea she was bright-eyed, intelligent, and co-operative. I dissolved a half tablet of aspirin and a quarter tablet of codeine in a bit of water, and from the greedy way the poor baby sucked up the bitter mixture one could easily see it suffered from thirst as well as illness. From there I took the baby into the main sleeping house, giving orders that no one else except the mother could come into the room with it. Although the air was rather dank in this shuttered limestone room, I felt that anything would be better for the child than the pandemonium in the filthy kitchen shack. People seemed to take my instructions in good grace. They had more confidence in my medical ability than I did. However, since the baby had already been given up for dead I could hardly do much further harm.

Later that afternoon we again visited the child, carrying a type of rice-water mixture that Zenie makes for the sick. We found an even larger crowd of relatives gathered out in back of the house. In front many children were happily playing and we were greeted with smiles by the adults. The pastor's wife seemed to be in charge of things, and the tot—named Etetā-te-Pōāri'i—was in fairly good shape. A neighbor had successfully cut her gums.

The next day Zenie spent much of her time with the sick child while the rest of us were away working on marae. She discovered that the real reason everyone was so upset was that the family believed the illness was due to witchcraft. It seemed that the baby's grandmother was a widow, still full of earthy desires. She had been discovered sleeping with the brother of her daughter's husband. This was a form of incest according to Ra'ivavae custom. To make things worse, the offender was one of the staunchest members of the church, a sort of un-official "deaconess." She was supposed to think only of her children, not of copulating with new men. The incident had caused bad feeling within the family, and it was widely be-lieved that because she had not been penitent, her own mother had called down the wrath of their ancestors. The form in which this vengeance was to occur was the death of the baby, the youngest member of the family, beloved by both grand-mother and great-grandmother. This is a typically Polynesian pattern. In other islands I heard of mothers who had been known to starve their own babies to death in order to avenge themselves upon the father they believed had copulated with another woman.

There has to be some mechanism for stopping this terrible exercise of bad will, for it cannot go on indefinitely. Thus the islanders have an institution called *tatara te hara*, something I was familiar with from my work on the island of Mangaia. These ancient words, which may well stem back to the proto-Polynesian, may best be translated as "confessions of sin." Just as the Western world has long understood the therapeutic value of confession, so the Polynesian finds that the cure for witchcraft lies in group confession. When bad feeling occurs within the family, the place where witchcraft is invariably prac-ticed, the only way of restoring a normal situation lies in calling a family meeting with everyone present under the direction of the pastor. If this can be arranged, each person confesses any bad feelings he may hold, arguments are made public, the whole affair is talked out, and the pastor offers up a final heal-ing prayer.

In the case of the sick baby, who had suffered recurrent ill-nesses, there were difficulties in arranging a confessional meeting. The pastor was loath to preside because of the position of the grandmother in the church hierarchy. Moreover, the family believed that the pastor, only recently trained at the seminary in Tahiti, was "not very good at that sort of work." There was some suspicion that he did not believe in this local version of the confessional. It was only when Zenie threatened to report the pastor to her father in Tahiti, who was a well-known deacon, that he reluctantly agreed to preside and to make the appropriate prayers.

At a series of family meetings, a string of grievances were aired. It turned out that the affair between the grandmother and the young man was only one of them. There had been friction between the grandmother and the mother of the baby, there were quarrels over animals and land. These are common sources of family friction on Ra'ivavae and explain why the practice of witchcraft is usually restricted to those who are related. Within a short time, however, the troubles in this family seemed to have been straightened out. We received a basket of limes, *popoi*, and neatly peeled coconuts from the relatives of the sick baby—a Polynesian thank-you note which indicated that all was well.

In time, we came to know more about the patterns of black magic, *mōkī*, and *tatara te hara* and found the belief in them was practically universal on Ra'ivavae. Almost all serious illness, in fact, was attributed to bad feeling within the family. This turned out to be the "real reason" why people were hesitant to utilize the services of the European physicians. Zenie thought that Toāri'i was an exception, for both his daughters had been down with typhoid fever and *tatara te hara* had not helped. The mother had insisted that they be taken to the hospital, where they were eventually cured. The father now claimed that he no longer believed in witchcraft, but he was not above saying that it was a spirit of the dead who caused the bad stomach of his enemy in the hospital.

When it became obvious that I already knew a good deal about the custom of confessional and the presence of witchcraft on the island, Piahuru, who had been very reticent before, decided to give me more details about the matter. He stated that when a person is ill and local medicines or massages do not affect a cure, the patient begins to talk about his illness and his relationship with others within the family. Someone says, "Isn't this a case of *ma'itāpiri?*" i.e., a *tupapa'u* snuggling up against the ill person. With this, either the sick person himself or someone else within the family brings up the subject of witchcraft and blames someone for invoking the spirit of the dead. The suspected person is asked if it is he who has caused the illness. Generally he admits it, telling how he went to the grave of an ancestor and called upon the *tupapa'u* to injure his enemy. By this time other members of the family have usually tried to ward off the spell by chanting a counter-spell or by sweeping away the evil spirit with the magical *ti* leaf. If this is not successful, the suspect is asked to give up his enmity and effect a reconciliation with his victim. In all this the pastor plays a large role, not only presiding at the confessional but occasionally giving medicines to counteract witchcraft. The present pastor at Ra'irua is famous for this "white magic," while the former one at Anatonu seems to have dabbled in "black magic." Yet despite the intervention of pastors, there are cases where the offended person will not be reconciled with the sufferer. Often the result is a slow death for the man he has cursed.

Just before I left Ra'ivavae I had another strange experience which confirmed my view that witchcraft was a profound sociological and psychological force on this island. I had gone to spend some time with Ta'oto, and as we sat chatting in her little shack, rain beating on the iron roof, the Widow-in-brown came in. Shortly afterward a naked little girl with an attractive and vivacious face passed by the open doorway carrying a basket of food. I asked who she was and was told that she was the daughter of a woman who had been sent to Tahiti when she contracted leprosy. Since she had never been in contact with a leprous person, the villagers claimed that she had tampered with Marae Atoraŋi. The little girl now lived with relatives. From this simple story the widow went on to other aspects of witchcraft. A few years before we arrived, she said, one of the girls of the village developed a swollen leg which rapidly grew to immense size. She was taken to various practitioners who vainly tried massages, poultices of various leaves and flowers, and other types of native medicine. Then the medical aid man in Ra'irua was asked to help, without success, and after that the European doctors in Papeete. No one could diagnose her trouble other than to say that it must be a "Tahitian trouble," a *tupapa'u*. Then one evening the girl ran to her mother, screaming in terror that she was "afraid of the wind." The next day she was dead.

A short while afterward another little girl and the widow's one-armed son fell victim to the same affliction. The widow, noted in the village for her piety and her fearlessness, immediately went to the pastor. She had him conduct a full day of fasting and prayer, a ceremony which disposed of the *tupapa'u* without further harm to the youngsters.

When the widow told this experience to her sewing work group, one of the old women remarked that she knew who was at fault. She said that the sorcerer was an old man who lived with his wife near the marae in the middle of the village which belonged to Piahuru. She claimed that he trapped young people by going to the marae and summoning up the spirits by stamping three times on the ground with his foot. These *tupapa'u* in turn brought down "the wind" to assist them in their evil work.

The widow told us that she had then repeated this story to her Anatonu pastor, who in turn relayed the information to the pastor at Ra'irua. Before long the whole island population knew of it. Naturally enough, this made the old man angry, and he promptly got the native policeman to bring the widow before the chief for defaming his character. The chief, who avoided responsibility when he could, asked Tahiti to send down a doctor and a judge to hear the case. They came, but wanted to finish the hearings in Papeete, free from the passions of High Island. When the widow returned from her appearance before the tribunal in Tahiti, she found that both the old man and his wife had died "without cause" in their home within a few days of each other.

I was surprised that such a good Christian as our friend the widow could believe in the pagan *tupapa'u*, yet as I reflected on the matter the reasons seemed clear. For one, the Bible, particularly in the unsatisfactory Polynesian translations, contains many accounts in which "ghosts" and *tupapa'u* seem to figure. But more important was the peculiar relation between Christianity and disease as the Polynesians must have sensed it when Europeans first arrived in these islands. The arrival of the Bible was accompanied by a dozen new and deadly diseases which the islanders had never known—smallpox, tuberculosis, gonorrhea, syphilis, even that great curse of mankind, the common cold. In the early years the natives died in great numbers. On Ra'ivavae also, the population dropped to a fortieth of its original size. The Polynesians had no doctors, no medicines, and no natural immunities with which to fight these unknown maladies. They did not even understand them. Even today, every schooner which touches an outer island seems to spur a new outbreak of disease.

The intimacy of family life, which was such a basic characteristic of Ra'ivavaean (and all Polynesian) culture, in itself turned out to be a deadly boomerang which led to destruction of the people, for in the thatched houses people slept side by side in long rows, closed in against the cold of the island nights.

Anything more conducive to the transmission of disease could hardly be devised. And the free and easy sex life of the adolescents and young people provided a channel which rapidly transmitted disease from one family to the next.

Until recently, the march of Christianity across the Polynesian islands was not accompanied by any corresponding advance in medical aid to the native peoples. Christianity, after all, does not entail a system of medicine. Thus it is not surprising that the Polynesians, particularly those of the outer islands, should have retained their old beliefs in evil spirits, in the confession of sin, and in other supernatural things. These answer perennial social and biological needs.

The old gods, as I discovered, are not dead. They are merely sleeping in the presence of the new God. The Christian religion lacks a formal dogma which deals with illness and death, and the Polynesians need such explanations to sustain them. They see a continuity between their ancestors and themselves, and many profess to commune regularly with their forefathers, who advise them, warn them of what is to come, and intercede with God for them. Despite the power of the church on Ra'ivavae, Christianity as a system of morality is less important than it seems.

Chapter Twelve

OF PRIDE AND PLEASURE

Here he was born,
Here he passed his days of love-making;
Here he grew old—
His powers waning, dying a natural death.

TO THE Polynesian, sex is life itself: the entire cycle of
birth, love-making, death—and then eternal life through
one's seed. It is all-embracing, like the weather or the sea, and
it is talked about as freely. Even the small children on Ra'ivavae know that *navenave* means to experience the orgasm,
and they further understand that both men and women are
capable of it. Both sexes know from infancy that the clitoris,
tira, is the seat of female pleasure, as is the penis, *ure*, of the
male. Throughout these islands sex is looked upon as an ap-
petite to be relieved as naturally (and almost as frequently)
as eating. Yet at the same time it is considered a force important enough to be carefully cultivated and trained, turned into
an art so that sexual pleasure can be heightened.

For the Polynesian sex is more earthy, more natural, more
frequent, and more satisfying than it is in the Western world.
But since it is less related to the idea of love, it does not have
that peculiar beauty which accompanies it in our own civilization.

We know about the sex life of the ancient Polynesians from
the splendid carvings that have survived the rigors of time, and
from the few chants and stories which have been handed down

to this day. When Christianity came to the islands most of the public displays of sexuality were inhibited, but in private, I am convinced, the Polynesians still behave much as they did two hundred years ago.

Yet discovering the truth about this matter on Ra'ivavae was a difficult and complex affair. On the surface the island had a puritanical atmosphere reminiscent of my own New England upbringing. This was in marked contrast to most of the other Polynesian islands, and I was surprised to find it, for I was certain that the ancient religion had been erotic in nature and there should have been some traces left. After all, despite the endless round of church activity, High Island had historically been subjected to far less missionary pressure than many other places in Polynesia. What then had wrought this dour change? Was it only superficial? Did any of the pre-European customs —such as artificially lengthening the clitoris—still exist?

The Polynesians, normally so vocal among themselves about sexual matters, are unwilling to talk at length with a European about erotica. This *ad hoc* modesty can also be seen in the behavior of some older women who cover their breasts when the European doctor arrives, although they usually go about without any upper garment. Hence it was one of Zenie's chores —as a fellow Polynesian—to gather sexual data, particularly from the women. Her task was difficult and frustrating. Moreover, she had a tendency to generalize from one or two notable cases without further testing the conclusions. Finally we made some progress, organizing our data within the framework of the life cycle—the activities of a person from birth to death, with particular emphasis upon the "rites of passage" which lead a person from one status to another—boy to adolescent, unmarried *taure'are'a* to married *Etarētia*.

The Ra'ivavaean is born, as he lives, in the close-knit web of his family. In addition to the midwife specialist who is called in to direct the accouchement, the father assists a new mother in her labor, holding her, massaging her, encouraging her efforts. Around the striving trio are the rest of the family, male and female, young and old. The High Islander, like the other Eastern Polynesians, is strongly conscious of the virtues of natural childbirth. Despite the loss of ceremony and color, birth practices still follow ancient customs. When the new child is born, the naval cord is cut with a freshly split sliver of bamboo. The cord and placenta are carefully washed and then buried on the family lands (the word for placenta is derived from the word for land) and then the mother is taken and washed in the healing sea. The new infant is bathed, rubbed with coconut oil, *monoi*, dressed in clothes which have been prepared for it, and then given sweet water to suck from a clean cloth.

Today there are no parties given to celebrate birth, or even birthdays for that matter, although this event once was the occasion for great celebrations. In the past, the birth of the first male in a family was marked by a joyous festival. Rank was recognized from birth, and on the eighth day after arrival a baby might be acclaimed the new leader of the clan. One ancient tale tells of a traditional ceremony which took place during this period. The newborn babe was left for a night on a smooth bed of wild taro leaves. The number of leaves he broke up as he twisted and turned during the night was a portent of his ability as a leader and a warrior. He was then given a title name handed down through generations of authority. Gifts from relatives were brought, and the old women danced, naming the past generations of the family and the famous historical incidents in which they had participated. But all this is no more. Most family history is forgotten. The baby rests in a corner, a marvel only to its parents and the close family. Although the grandparents may give the child an ancestral name, it is the medical aid man who thinks up a French name to put down in the official birth register.

Babies on High Island may suckle until they are three or four years old, though most do not regularly depend upon the mother's breast after the first year. For a short weaning period the infant may be given specially mashed and prepared mixtures of taro, fish, and coconut milk, or else boiled bananas or *popoi*. Milkless mothers may use powdered or liquid tinned milk purchased from the Chinese storekeeper. If the family does not have the money to buy milk it tries to find a goat. Cows have been raised on Ra'ivavae for a generation, but milk from them is only drunk by foreigners.

Contrary to the statements of Piahuru, we found that adoption was common on Ra'ivavae. Just as in other Polynesian communities which I have studied, the practice of shifting feeding children around remains a major means of cementing kinship ties. Children are taken by grandparents or by close friends, given to the chief or to important families, and sometimes even offered to visiting anthropologists. Anyone who has seen the deep and open affection of a father for his children on High Island will understand that there is nothing heartless about this practice. Parents love their children as devotedly and unselfishly as Europeans. But the love of children can also cement interfamilial relationships. Young ones give company and aid to old grandparents, and it does no harm to have one's own children raised by the chief of the island. Love on Ra'ivavae is practical as well as deeply emotional, and the child's future as well as the future of the family is always considered. Despite an occasional exception, adoption is generally restricted to kinfolk, and the real father continues to provide some food for the child until he is about ten years of age. Though he has been given away, the child knows his blood parents, and they do not lose sight of their offspring.

The Ra'ivavaean child is a happy child whose duties are few. To be sure, he now has to conform to the schedule of the French-type school which has recently been established, and

he is always home for meals. But the rest of his time is spent in playing games and imitating the adults as they go about their daily work. Most learning is by doing, with some conscious effort at instruction on the part of the grandparents. In particular contrast to the European child, the Ra'ivavaean boy or girl is always around, seldom shunted away from the facts of life. Nothing misses his watchful eye. Every scene of the life cycle from birth to death—copulation and marriage, happiness and sorrow, church service and drunken brawl—all are played out within a circle of wide-eyed children who store away this knowledge of life and its stages.

I spent a good deal of time looking for a "philosophy of expectable childhood behavior," and "a system of childhood training," to use two phrases of the moment. But only after I had visited and studied seven Polynesian islands did I finally realize that there is *no* philosophy or system. To a far greater degree than in the most progressive American family, the Polynesian child is a product of self-demand. The discipline of his age mates is far stricter than that of his parents and family.

An adult never raises his hand to an island child unless his patience is tried to the breaking point. When this happens retribution is savage, and a clenched fist may even draw blood. In the main the child is fully as independent as the adult, and far less conscious of family or communal duties and responsibilities. Even the danger of playing with matches or with large sharp knives is not a matter of concern to the adult. If the child wishes to take such risks, then it is his own responsibility. The same is true in arguments between children. Zenie was interviewing in one of the cookhouses one day and witnessed an argument between two small boys. They were dirty, with horrid skin sores and the tiny curled-up penises of small boys here. One wanted a piece of glass marble the other had. The owner put the fragment in his mouth and his playmate tried to wrench it out by pure force. After this they got down to fighting in earnest. Even when they drew blood, the circle of people around urged them on to further action with cries of *E moto! E moto!* "Strike! Strike!" No one even interfered when one picked up a rock, but Zenie finally got them to stop fighting by promising to give them each a new marble.

The passage from childhood is roughly at the commencement of menstruation for the girl and time of superincision for the boy—roughly, in that copulation could well have taken place before this. At the age of twelve or thirteen the girl begins to have her period. When this happens she may use an old rag or nothing at all. Menstruating women were once restricted in their activities and not allowed to cook for the family, but today such prohibitions are no longer observed. As far as we could determine, the Ra'ivavaean women vary in temperament as do the women of the West—some are ill-tempered at the approach of the menses, some are not.

The boys' entrance to young manhood is less sharply distinguished than the girls. Not only is male puberty less easily recognized than the onset of the feminine stage, but the point

246

of meaningful change is cultural rather than biological. The boy becomes a "young man" only when he is superincised, not before—regardless of age or physiological change in appearance. While he may have commenced adult work (in the *pupu* or for himself) at the age of fourteen, the distinguishing operation may have been made long before this. Some boys may wait until long after so that they can summon up courage to face the ordeal. The moment of superincision depends both upon the character and bravery of the youth, though even a timid one may be driven into it by the taunts of age mates or the local belles.

Ra'ivavaean males undergo much the same operation as those on other islands. The purpose of the cut is the same as that of the Jewish circumcision, free exposure of the glans of the penis. Polynesians detest the odor and sight of smegma. To use the term for it, *taioro*, is the deadliest of insults. Although the superincision is clearly a health measure, there is a persistent rumor among both sexes that it also increases the measure of enjoyment of both partners in the sexual act.

Possibly the permanent exposure of the glans lessens the sensitivity of the organ, enabling a more prolonged engagement in the actual coupling of partners—the most desired aspect of present-day Polynesian copulation. But the custom itself stems from time immemorial in Oceania, the original discovery or reason for it long since forgotten. The operation itself, and the social complexities involved are not subject to the reasoning of "should" or "shouldn't." The cut must be made to satisfy the overriding demand of ancient custom. "What the forefathers do, so likewise do we."

Once there were definite specialists for such operations, but now almost any male can and does make the cut. Slivers of bamboo are still used as knives, for iron blades are thought to be too infectious. The person who has raised sufficient courage to undergo the ordeal finds another who knows how to make the cut, and provides a quantity of cloth for the bandaging. A piece of coconut shell is then cut in the shape of a convex truncated wedge in preparation for the event.

On the day of the ordeal the youth and the person who will do the operation go to a secluded place, usually away in the hills, near running water. The wedge of coconut shell which is to act as an anvil (and also serves to protect the sensitive glans) is laid under the penis, and the foreskin stretched out upon it. A careful study of the veins is made by the operator, and a charcoal line is drawn to indicate where the cut should be made in order to avoid the major sources of blood supply. The bamboo knife is then used to make a long cut through the tough white tissue underlying the skin. After washing the organ it is then sprinkled with a drying or clotting agent made from the fuzz of the stem of the mountain fern or the base of the coconut frond. Certain leaves then are used to envelop the organ, and it is bandaged. The newly cut youth is instructed to avoid "hot foods," and is also forbidden to eat such foods as the *pahua* oyster, octopus, or seaweeds. The entire purpose of the cut is to raise scar tissue in such a fashion as to fully pull back the foreskin of the penis, leaving the glans fully exposed.

The most important part of the operation is yet to come, for psychologically and sociologically the supreme moment comes with the removal of the scab resulting from the cut. Some informants have claimed that this is done by softening the hard tissue with unguents. This is not true. The caked mass must be removed by actual sexual intercourse with a woman. It is this fact—a universal phenomenon in the many Polynesian islands with which I am familiar—which has escaped the pastors who have endeavored to implant the Western concepts of sexual behavior upon the Polynesian. How can a youth be taught the virtues of celibacy when he has already experienced the joys of the flesh?

The anxious boy must *not* search out an inexperienced and frightened maiden to assist him, but an older woman who has already borne children. The excuse is that this will allow the scab to come off "more easily," and it is further justified as giving a "more beautiful appearance" to the organ. Although his operator has already given him some instruction in sexual behavior, it is the older woman partner who really introduces the boy to sex. Thenceforth the youth is *taure'are'a*, a member of the age group whose chief aim in life is to seek physical pleasure of the senses—sexual, musical, recreational. From now on and for years to come his nightly goal will be to win his way—by charm or by force—into the embrace of some partner, either in the bush, by the pathside, or in the very home of the girl herself.

We were not in the least surprised at the pattern of super-incision for the boys, for I have recorded the same type of ceremony for all of the other Polynesian islands upon which I have worked. We were much more concerned with investigating the possibility of a comparable ceremony for the maidens, for it was the manipulation of the clitoris which seemed to have been the unique practice of pre-European Ra'ivavae. The answers to our questions were confusing, to say the least. Everyone had heard of the Marquesan custom in which grandparents rub the clitoris with scented coconut oil, pulling at it daily until it became long enough so that it "had to be lifted up in order for the man to gain entry below." Indeed, within living memory, the Marquesan belles had held "beauty shows" in which the length of their favored organs were publicly compared.

I knew from the literature that in Micronesia clitoris enlarging by labial manipulation was known and that on Easter Island there were complex customs in regard to the clitoris. There it was teased out by the priest until he could fasten a cord to it. From this dangled a weight which stretched the organ to a length of two to three inches. Moreover, both Zenie and the visiting French doctor had seen comparable practices in Africa. The doctor had ministered to a tribe where the grandfathers had cut the clitoris with a stone and so manipulated it that it grew to half a thumb's size. Zenie had been with her husband when he administered a tribe where the women "beautified" themselves by not only pulling at their breasts to elongate them but attached a cord to the clitoris. The loose end was pulled up under a belt and hung over it with a button at the end. This button, colored according to the female age group, also served the purpose of "driving flies away." The clitoris would sometimes grow to the length of half a finger.

Despite the detailed information of Hapai, our informant Tauira'i denied ever having heard of Ra'ivavaean clitoral manipulation. (Indeed, neither he nor Alan admitted to knowledge of the Tahitian or other Polynesian words for clitoris.) He did note, however, that there were "houses of joy" for the young male *taure'are'a* in Ra'ivavae though "not for the young girls." But he confirmed previous reports that young girls were confined in the typical Polynesian "bleaching and fattening houses"—one for each tribe. Old Piahuru was slightly more informative. He told of the *hare ha'apori* ("fattening house") where girls were fattened and their skin kept fair, a confinement which also "saved them" from spreading their favors around. There was one of these houses of beauty for each tribe, as well as a tribal copulating house for men. Many songs of praise had been composed to extol the beauty and chastity of the confined girls. But Piahuru had only "heard a little bit" about the ancient custom of clitoris lengthening here on Ra'ivavae. He believed that the work of manipulating the organ had been done by the mother, but he much preferred to discuss the Marquesans, whom he said "liked this a lot." He had no idea why the custom was practiced.

Zenie had also learned from Mama Iē that such a custom

existed but could obtain no further details. Her friend Ta'oto, however, was more explicit. She had heard that the grandfathers, using scented coconut oil and finger manipulation, worked over the genitals of the girls from infancy until the verge of adulthood. Her explanation of why this was done was highly unlikely. She claimed that "this was done to protect the virginity of the girls, as the clitoris covered the vaginal opening and prevented the boy's organ from making entry. When the girl was ready for marriage, the mother explained to the girl how to raise the clitoris in order to allow the boy to gain entry." In any case, there was absolutely no indication that clitoris lengthening was practiced today. Moreover, despite the fact that we had discovered a sexual-inspection marae described by Hapai, complete with its stone "inspection seat," I could not confirm any details about the religious aspects of this ancient custom. All I could be sure of was that some form of genital manipulation had once been carried out on both boys and girls, but only the male rites still survived.

Indeed, not only was there no longer vaginal manipulation for the young girls, but to our intense surprise we discovered that there were probably several virgins in the village of Anatonu. The concept of a virgin—even one in her teens—is foreign to the Polynesian in other than a ceremonial sense. In Central Polynesia the arrival of pubescence in a girl is virtually synonymous with the commencement of frequent sexual intercourse.

Yet, we had every reason to believe, after long and careful investigation by Zenie in a community where there are no secrets, that our maid Pogi, her sister Tara, and our neighbor Giggles—all in their early or mid-twenties—were virginal. This was even more surprising since they were attractive and obviously the village boys had done their best to change the situation. Besides, all three wished to get married. But oddly enough the virtues of chastity were appreciated by both the girls and their parents. In part this attitude stemmed from the girls dislike of *motoro* customs and of their fear that they might be taken by an unattractive male. In part it seemed to stem from the fact that a girl was better off at home sharing the good food and the house of her parents, and taking part in the division of coffee money, than being with an improvident youth. The church, too, as the girls admitted, was also a factor. Once a girl had a man she no longer went as regularly to church services. After two Sundays of unexplained absence she could be sure that the wraithlike widow of the former pastor would rise up in the singing house, terrible in her cold storm, and point her bony forefinger at the offender, calling down the wrath of the Lord.

As a balance to the three wise virgins, Anatonu had a woman who could only be described as the village harlot, besides several other women who were completely promiscuous. One of these was a young girl at the end of our village who was noted for her huge privates. She had aborted many children, and from time to time our virgins would visit her to watch her thrust a huge wooden "baby breaker," as she called it, into the depths of her womb. Zenie said that she was merely "simple," and since her family neglected her and the men took advantage of her, she had virtually no chance for a marriage.

Though our virgins were pure in the physical sense, they had the usual competent knowledge of life and its ways. From time to time they put on male clothing and sallied forth after dark to crouch by the whore's house and listen to her carrying on with the sundry males. They frequently discussed the clitoris (which they nicknamed "the mast") and mentioned its ability to become rigid and how this could bring ecstasy. Zenie reported that they continuously discussed the possibility of being "attacked"—almost with a longing, it seemed to her—and that they knew and used more dirty words than she imagined existed. Indeed, the only time I ever saw Jim get angry was when Giggles, abetted by Pogi, attempted to get him to use dirty words under the guise of teaching him to speak Tahitian. Sex was a constant joke to them, as it was to most women. In fact, Zenie found that the reason she had such trouble getting serious sexual information was that the women had such fun when they spoke of sex.

To the High Islander there is little of sex that is sacred or prohibited to discussion. Good old Uncle Bert, staunch pillar of the church, joked with a young boy in front of Zenie about his orgasms. Even the hell-fire and damnation widow of the former pastor joked with her in front of the church women about virginity and sexual matters. Dear old Mama Iē, passing our house on the way home from a church meeting with the pastor's wife and a flock of young girls, called to an embarrassed Jim, "Come to my house tonight for a round of fun." When he did not answer she remarked, to the delighted shrieks of the girls, "I know I'm too old, but my vagina is clean and you need only to look at that."

Obviously, our young neighborhood virgins were unusual, even for Ra'ivavae. Though I am a believer in much of our own Western idealized pattern of chastity and monogamy, I was not convinced that the path they had chosen was adequate for High Island. A pattern of chastity and monogamy needs some reasonable tradition of close acquaintanceship and courtship which can lead to satisfactory marriage. Here on Ra'ivavae, as elsewhere in Polynesia, separation of the sexes is so strong that the only means of courtship is *motoro*—a custom which the three girls and their families disliked. For them the only possibility of marriage was a planned "rape" and eventual family permission to marry the "rapist." This, of course, would have been in complete contrast to the European law which was now beginning to be enforced upon the island.

From time immemorial High Island custom has given free license to the idle, night-roaming bands of *taure'are'a*. Parents did not chide the young man who slept in the day and roamed at night, for this was the pattern that they themselves had followed when young, and the time for work would come later on. Ra'ivavaean folklore tells of the complete destruction of the Teia tribe by the other tribes of the island because they dared to kill a band of these youths who had trespassed upon their territory one night in search of adventure.

Because there is absolutely no acceptable way to meet or talk with a girl socially, the young men must resort to one of two methods, either surprise and secrecy or violence. Good-looking young Europeans who arrive here from other islands —where they have themselves been sought out by the local girls—consider Ra'ivavaeans "queer," for they cannot obtain a girl here. As one of the more experienced islanders (who had had some experience abroad) said, "It does no good to sweet talk a girl here; they are like savages. If you want her, you must grab her and take her into the bushes. Once you have had her, she will then come to you when called." On the other hand, the same informant was quick to say that the High Island girls "know nothing of *amour*; neither these girls nor those of Tahiti know the emotional aspects of sex as do those of France. It is only a bodily release. They do not like or understand lip-kissing, or the caressing of the breasts or genitals—but they can be taught!"

Such violent initiation was formerly the customary practice. The women and girls told Zenie that men would drink orange, banana, or coconut beer in the hills to raise their courage and then descend at night in search of women. They waited along paths and by the bathing pools for a particular girl. During the previous day they may have tried to warn her of what was to come by staring at her or giving her some other sly sign.

Today a more adventurous form of *motoro* is the main means of courtship. When a young man has picked out a suitable girl, he will try to tell her by a flick of the eyes—or perhaps through a trusted intermediary—that he will be calling upon her. Waiting until the household is asleep (the Polynesians sleep the sleep of the dead), the youth will carefully ease open the door or slip in through a window, and find his way to the girl's bed. There the adventurer slips his arm around the girl, places a precautionary hand over her mouth, and warns her not to call out. As one might expect, there are many amusing tales about the ludicrous mistakes which occur if the adventurer finds his way to the wrong bed. But if he is right, the boy then attempts to talk to the frightened lass, telling her of his desire for her and praising her charms. Several nights may pass before he tries a sexual connection, either in the house or outside. The young men offer several reasons for this delay. The first is that the boy is trying to find out whether or not the girl is a virgin. (Ra'ivavae seems to be the only Polynesian island where such a factor appears socially significant.) In addition, these nightly talks not only give the couple a chance to talk and get acquainted, but it allows an adventurous youth his only real chance to prove his bravery in these dull times. And even then he may think he is more daring than he really is, for often the parents may be lying awake, waiting for the laughter of their daughter that will tell them that she will be happy with this youth. This is understandable, for the *motoro* is the normal way to get a mate. A very tiny fraction of the population get engaged and then married by arrangement between parties, but such marriages are looked upon with contempt by most of the population. Most of our case histories involved *motoro* in one form or another. Indeed, it was generally believed that once a boy succeeded in implanting a girl, she would leave her house to go to his. The boys seemed to prefer a steady partner to the business of creeping around from house to house.

Forcing a girl to copulate is common on Ra'ivavae, but the action has several meanings. Throughout Polynesia, mass rape by eight to fifteen village youths is a well-known occurrence. It serves as a way for young men to keep women—particularly those of the lower socio-economic classes—in their proper place. A girl who unnecessarily insults one of the young men, or seems to be putting on airs, is likely to be waylaid and successively taken by the entire band of *taure'are'a*. In Ra'ivavae this custom has a special sanction because of the folklore of the past which enjoins women not to refuse their favors to men. More frequently, however, it is a means of acquiring a girl as a mate who cannot be obtained by either *motoro* or by family agreement. When our landlord Toāri'i rebuffed the suitors of two of his daughters, they deliberately raped the girls—and then asked again. He was obliged to accept the two as sons-in-law, because, by a neat transformation, the daughters suddenly "were no longer young girls." The marriages, it might be added, seem to be working out admirably.

When the youth has succeeded in his *motoro* and has brought a girl home to live with him (or has gone to live with her at her parents' home), pregnancy soon follows. The girl who is not content with her lover is apt to try to lose the child. Despite the contention of Piahuru that there was no birth control or abortion on Ra'ivavae, we discovered that this was not so. A man who is a specialist in inducing abortion told us that he gives the girl a decoction of very young green pineapple or *hotu* fruit to drink, and then walks on her back as she lies belly down on a flat rock in an effort to expel the unwanted fetus. The girl who wants her child is treated well, given good food and new clothes, and kept from working too hard.

After one or more children have been born the couple usually thinks of marriage. By this time, the undisciplined youth who has been content to fish or farm a little as his contribution to home life has found a new sense of responsibility. The children make him see the need for assuming a new dual role in life—that of properly married husband and member of the *Etarētia*, the formal community of the Christian church. Despite Piahuru's generalization that "most people get married before they start living together," a simple check of the civil records against the known history of the people involved indicated that of thirty-one civil marriages, twenty-nine of the couples had lived together for substantial periods before marriage. This, I might note, is true throughout most of modern Christian Polynesia, as well as in some parts of present-day rural Sweden, where couples do not get married until the girl has been made pregnant by the suitor, who has crawled in through her window.

When couples on Ra'ivavae do get married, the union is apt to be a permanent one. There is no divorce and little playing around. The only cases we could discover of persons who have been dissatisfied with their partners were Piahuru himself and the present village policeman. The latter, married to a known shrew who was ten years older than he was, finally tired of her sharp tongue and publicly took up with a young girl. The only penalty seems to be that he is no longer allowed to be a member of the church. Otherwise, all married people in Anatonu are living with their first legal partner, and all are members of the church.

Periodically, at intervals of about two years, the pastor makes a survey of the villages, noting all the young couples who seem to be reasonably content but are not yet married. He suggests that it might be about time for the couple to assume the responsibilities of marriage and church membership. Those who agree must undergo the joint rites of civil and religious ceremonies. This is usually followed by one of the few occasions of feasting on present-day Ra'ivavae. The chief, any *fonctionaires* who may be present, and the Chinese merchants ("they give presents") are invited to the ceremony. Chickens, corned beef, *popoi*, *po'e*, and other delicacies are served, but the most important aspect of a successful feast is the number of pigs which are killed. Eating is the only form of entertainment at these celebrations and a master of ceremonies ceremoniously chants out the number of pigs which have been killed and the other food which has been donated to the feast.

Despite the lack of social companionship between sexes, lasting love and affection does spring up between man and wife. Witness the lament of the pre-European wife:

Long have you been lost to me—
 O my husband!
Pierced by the spears of hidden raiders
 in the dark of night;
No longer does your vigorous body warm the bark-cloth coverlet
 lying cold upon my useless feet,—
For you rest in the dwelling-place of the worm.

Weeping, I lament you,
 day after long joyless day,—
My voice like the mournful cry of the wild pigeon.
And when, in the early dawn,
 I gaze upon the rising sun,
I long for you.

  Oh, hopeless sorrow!

Oddly enough, there is plenty of sexual jealousy on High Island, often expressed by physical violence on the part of the husband and shrewish words from the wife. A woman who is married or living with a man may not even talk to an unmarried man if her husband is not about, and rumor of this is cause for a severe beating. We saw many a black eye and heard many a wail during our stay on the island.

The native pastors talk little of sex, save to repeat the Biblical injunction against adultery. Incest is viewed with complete abhorrence. Indeed, a brother may not drink alcohol in front of his sister, or tell her salacious stories, or even dance with her. While there is little extramarital fornication, even

258

self-righteous Piahuru considers a life of celibacy abnormal for either the married or unmarried. He doubts that any man can remain long without having a woman, whether or not he marries. "A man must have a woman. Why rest without a woman?"

The menopause for the women of Ra'ivavae may occur at any time between forty and fifty years of age, and the reactions to it vary from woman to woman. But long after this most women carry on an active sexual life, well into their declining years. But this ceases to be a major concern and more and more the old folks become concerned with the instruction of the young grandchildren—yet the elderly try to avoid a completely sedentary state and even at seventy they can be seen doing light work.

When death finally comes, the corpse is washed and dressed by the members of the family of the same sex. The body is made as attractive as possible and then placed on a bed. Someone in the family makes a coffin. It is covered with white cloth and then decked with flowers. The next morning a religious ceremony and extensive singing takes place in the house of the deceased, and the remains are interred near the home. The final ceremony is a small dinner held for the relatives.

Chapter Thirteen

VOICES FROM THE PAST

HAPAI, the fountainhead of Stimson's knowledge, the great sage who had furnished him with so much information about the past, haunted us throughout our expedition. He was dead, but the question of whether he had been telling the truth was very much alive. In fact, the larger question of how we could ever learn the truth about the past of Ra'ivavae troubled us more and more as the time for our departure drew closer.

Alan, who had discovered Hapai, had worked with him in person for over two years. He saw no reason at all to question the old man's data on fishing, turtle-hunting, and the like. He believed that Hapai had a great deal of knowledge about the old days and a general knowledge of Ra'ivavaean culture, joined with a gift of expression which enabled him to set such material down in writing. In addition, he may very well have had certain "*parau tupuna,*" books which helped him with a knowledge of the past. On the other hand, Alan objected to the idea that Hapai had "sat at the feet of some old master," and he also believed that Hapai could be stimulated to "creative writing." There were certain accounts, such as Hapai's description of how stone for adzes was quarried, that he wished to delete from his joint work with Stimson. Moreover, he was ambiguous in his judgments of Stimson's own work. He believed that Frank had a superior grasp of Polynesian language, but he also felt that he was capable of overly vivid translation, and he related this to what he considered Stimson's abnormal interest in sex. He also believed that Frank used the questionable technique of "leading questions."

I was continuously troubled by the problem of the validity of Hapai's materials. On the one hand I knew from comparative studies that much of the material to which Alan took exception was soundly based; on the other hand, I too was skeptical of certain things which had been set down—particularly those relating to sex and religion. Of special concern to me was what seemed to be an impossibly detailed account of Hapai's training in the school of Ha'uti. There was too much exactitude to fit in with my understanding of the Polynesian time sense. With Alan I believed that the actual chronology of time was unimportant to the islander. Past and present were so intermingled that in the Polynesian mind there was little clear distinction between the period of the post-European Pomare affair and the episodes of the ancient culture hero Tangaroa.

In Stimson's original manuscript it had been written that Hapai was born in 1876 and that Ha'uti had died in 1890, with Hapai being instructed from his eighth to eleventh year; later this had been lined out and the sixteenth through nineteenth year substituted. In yet another place Hapai specified that he was born on December 10, 1876, and had studied from July 6, 1893, through 1895. But in a third account of his instruction it was recorded that he had been born in 1877, that Ha'uti started teaching in 1893 and later died in 1895.

Hapai claimed to be descended from Tangaroa-i-Mahara, through his father Te Ari'i Hei'ura, otherwise called Fare Pei. Shortly after our arrival on Ra'ivavae we found that Hapai was indeed the *matahiapo*, or first-born child of the former Ariki descendant of his district. Consequently he did have a definite right by virtue of his descent to the knowledge he claimed. Moreover, he was obviously interested in things past. It was a matter of record that Ha'uti had been the first pastor on Ra'ivavae and an eminent man; on the other hand old Haramū seemed to have the reputation of being "just an old man" of Mahanatoa, according to Piahuru and Tauira'i; indeed Tauira'i said that Haramū (who had lived before the youngish informant's own time) had the reputation of being a "drunkard." Curiously enough, however, his drink was said to have been the ancient 'ava—which is known to be nonintoxicating.

My confidence in Hapai's knowledge was not increased by the fact that from the very first both Piahuru and Tauira'i spoke of him with contempt. During our first session Piahuru called him "a liar, a jokester, a person with no right to knowledge. He may have listened to others and then written things down, but he had no book." Both Piahuru and Tauira'i had been to Papeete in 1952, the last year of Hapai's work with Stimson, but during our second meeting Piahuru again referred to him as "a liar, a jokester." He said, "Tauira'i knows because he has a book, but Hapai could only have gotten his knowledge by listening to others." In speaking of Hapai's history Piahuru stated that during his youth the sage was a *taure'are'a* just the same as the rest of the Ra'ivavae men; he had had a concubine and had given her a child. Yet he had no reputation for being overly interested in sex. He followed the normal pattern. Later on he legally married, but went to Rimatara for the ceremony in order to avoid the expense of a local wedding. Following the First World War, he became a deacon and a very responsible local citizen. Later Hapai had taken his two adopted children to Tahiti in order to give them the advantages of an education. He had only periodically returned to High Island for brief visits since that time.

This type of comment was given during the first half of our stay. At the same time, from other local people, I determined that Hapai had been considered a quite decent, hard-working, upright local citizen. He had been known for his oratorical ability as a church deacon and had frequently been called upon to expound at social gatherings. Knowing by this time Piahuru's proclivity for running down the members of other families with whom he was at odds, I determined on a final test. During all of this time I had kept the Stimson-Seabrook documents out of sight. After I got all possible data from both Piahuru and Tauira'i as to Hapai's knowledge and character, I decided to show them both the accounts of his training and his most lurid work, fully expecting an outraged denial of its accuracy and propriety.

To my surprise both informants individually read the accounts with increasing absorption. Stunningly they flatly stated that they now believed both in Hapai's knowledge, his training, and the accuracy of his accounts. "I have never seen these things before, or heard of them, but now I believe this to be true. It is beautifully written and it is old." This was not in itself enough to give me confidence in the data; but it certainly corroborated Stimson's high opinion of Hapai and gave me pause for thought.

Yet my thoughts were even more provoked by the developments of the next few days. Piahuru had been digging out vital statistics for me. A few days after newly professing his belief in the Hapai accounts he quietly brought in the musty island record books and pointed out certain dates: Ha'uti, the Protestant pastor—Hapai's supposed teacher of the ancient lore—died on July 16, 1890, at the age of eighty-six; Haramū, planter, born 1819 and died 1901; Hapai—known officially as Taniau, born November 8, 1879, died 1952.

Our informant was only ten years and eight months old when Ha'uti died! Surely he could have gotten his knowledge of erotica from old Haramū, who had lived until Hapai was twenty-two—but how much of his proclaimed knowledge could he have absorbed from an eighty-five-year-old pastor when he was only ten years old?

Since Hapai's veracity was central to my whole problem, I had worried about it throughout my stay on Ra'ivavae. But now our departure date loomed ahead, and it seemed that there was nothing I could do. We became increasingly preoccupied with carrying out final study trips to distant marae, gathering further data as to the daily life of the people, and drawing from aged informants final bits of information. Thus I was in no mood to react enthusiastically to Zenie's sudden plea that we take a holiday *promenade* on the other side of the island. All I could do was agree halfheartedly. I said I had work to do and would meet her later at the village of Vaiuru. When she and Giggles started off on horseback carrying a *panier* containing their picnic lunch and a bottle of wine, I had my misgivings. Wine and horses do not mix very well.

I finished the morning's field work up on the ridges of Ra'ivavae and then went to our rendezvous. The two never showed up, so I made my way around the island back to our headquarters and awaited their return, quite annoyed. Finally, as the sun neared the horizon, the two girls arrived—exhausted, temperamental, triumphant. All Zenie would tell me at the moment was that her horse had run away and that this had delayed their return.

Later that evening, tempers soothed by Tioti's simple meal of lentil soup, Zenie excitedly revealed her discovery. On the far side of the island was an aged woman with knowledge of the past. 'Ami was her common name, Mere Te Mara her designation of birth. Zenie had talked with her about the past, and found that she was not only related to Hapai, Stimson's great informant, she had herself learned something of the ancient days from Hapai's mentor Haramū. 'Ami claimed that she personally had seen tattooed women and that her own great-grandmother had possessed a mast-like clitoris. She also knew of these old customs in which women had displayed themselves in their quest for suitable husbands. Even in the short time that Zenie spoke with her she poured out information and deprecated the reputation of the present-day "sage," Tauira'i, saying that he knew only what was in "the book"—a book which represented real knowledge, but knowledge which he cribbed or cadged from other people.

This discovery of Zenie's was strikingly important. We decided to pay a visit to 'Ami even though other matters had to be left undone. Unfortunately the discovery led to a final intellectual breach between Alan and myself. For weeks now, we had been drawing apart, our friendship foundering on the rock of sex. Alan approved of my interest in the economic aspects of life, past and present; he encouraged my inquiries into folklore and history; he rejoiced with me at my linguistic discoveries. But he objected more and more to my inquiries into the mysteries of sex, particularly my attempts to ascertain the accuracy of Frank's information about erotic ceremonies and the unique Ra'ivavaean manipulation of female genitalia. He believed I was opening forbidden doors. Quietly but firmly he withdrew from the projected visit to 'Ami, leaving to me all responsibility for what he termed a "clitoris-hunting expedition." He felt that our headquarters had become the type of house in which he had lived with Stimson fifteen years before —a place in which an unhealthy interest in sex was evident, a place "redolent with the odor of female genitalia." He had quit collaborating with Frank for the same reason.

I did not attempt to argue with Alan, though I was disturbed by the rift. I needed his control of the Tahitian language and his ironclad integrity to serve as a check on my interview with 'Ami. I wanted the restraint of Alan's completely intellectual approach to major problems. Emotionally I was thoroughly upset at the disapproval of a man whom I had admired for so many years. Yet there was nothing to be done, for I thought he was wrong. I decided to go without him.

We were up before dawn to the sound of Tioti grinding coffee. For breakfast that morning there was a good omelette, for the *Mareva* had just arrived, bringing eggs from Tahiti. Soon we were on our way.

We took the pathway around the end of the island, past the twin-breasted heights of the islet Hotu Atua. Before six o'clock we passed three young boys seated along the path, two of them strumming contentedly on guitars. Soon, as the sun rose, we met other youngsters bound for the taro patches, digging-stick and burlap sack over their shoulder. I insisted upon a detour to make up for the work I had planned to carry out with Zenie the afternoon before—interviewing and photographing one of Stokes' subjects, an ancient crone named Tāne Puaivi. We went inland, much farther than I had expected, mounting well up into the foothills before we found the small plantation house in which Tāne lived with her descendants. She could no longer straighten her back, but despite her eighty-seven years was in fine health and humor. Puari'i, as she is now known, remembered Stokes, and we exchanged reminiscences of this fine anthropologist. After taking her photograph I briefly examined the cookhouse and the flowers scattered around and mentally checked again the significance of the plantation to the daily life of these people.

Descending to the belt path we continued on our way, fording swollen streams, riding past the taro fields. We passed children on their way to school with a handful of bananas or drinking-coconuts for the midday meal, and then went on by the schoolyard itself, where the instructress was lining up some of the children for formal entry while others made the playgrounds tidy. In the plantations beyond the village the young men were weeding taro. I noted for the first time how many ducks are kept on this southern side of the island.

We also called in at Marae Te Mahara, for I wished to check certain of my notes on Ra'ivavae's second most important ceremonial center. The tide was exceptionally low on this bright morning, and on the mud flats of the fringing reef I could see huge blocks of basaltic rock—raw material for the pagan altars which had been dropped there when some accident befell the prehistoric craft which carried them.

On our way we stopped to visit the ex-chief of the island. I wanted to photograph him, as he had also been one of Stokes' subjects. In talking about our prospective session with 'Ami, he noted that while he could not say whether or not she herself had "knowledge," surely Hapai knew the ancient days. He was certain of this, he asserted, "because Hapai had a book." (Again and again I have recorded this typical Polynesian correlation of "knowledge" with "a book"; equally frequent is the assumption that age in itself begets knowledge!)

Finally, two thirds of the way around the island, we came to the area where 'Ami lived. Zenie nudged me as we neared a large concrete house. There was a woman lumbering through the woods behind it. She was huge, not so much from fat as from some form of aberrant growth which had turned her limbs into monstrous sausage-like links of flesh. Through the trees came her voice, a bellowing bass: *"Haege mai, haege mai 'orua 'i to'u fare. '-Ua pē te fare."* (Come hither, come hither, you two—come to my home—it is a poor house indeed—but come anyway, come and talk with me.) Her welcome echoed on as she disappeared into a coconut-frond-thatched shack to the rear of the concrete house. We tied up Zenie's horse and approached. The big house was for the young people. 'Ami, aging and infirm, seldom stirring now, lived in the tiny cooking shed to the rear.

But her physical infirmities did not interfere with her tongue. As we neared her hut, 'Ami's masculine voice rolled on welcoming us, apologizing for her home, her infirmities, her lack of gifts to receive us in true Polynesian fashion. I stooped low to enter, and then waited by the door as the naked children of the family ran to haul up the fresh guest mat that 'Ami insisted I sit upon.

As Zenie moved toward 'Ami for the caressing Polynesian greeting and went through the formalities of preliminary small talk, I looked over the setting in which this living repository of ancient lore lived. Small it was, and mean by any standards, a scraggly nest built around the vast body of 'Ami. For her infirmities made it necessary for our friend to live out her days here, seated by the fire with which she made her simple meals. Within reach were the pots and pans, the bottles of sauce, the tea kettle, the faggots of wood brought to her by young kinfolk. Above in the rafters were leaf packets of fish and other remainders of food from last night's meal. By her side were two familiar Polynesian possessions: a locked sea chest and a well-thumbed Bible. The hut was dark at first, for there were no windows, but I soon saw there was no need for them. Through the interstices of the woven palm-leaf siding, through gaping openings in the rotted thatch roof, seeped more than enough light for me to see, write, and photograph.

'Ami transcended the squalor of her shack. Her bulbous body

sat still in its accustomed position on the leaf-matted floor. But her face had the most extraordinarily mobile features that I have seen. A mole quivered alongside her nose, but it was easily overlooked as one became fascinated with the expressiveness of her lips. This was matched by the flexible range of her voice as she alternately rejoiced in a low rumble at our arrival and then shrilly cried pardon for her own poverty. To soothe her feelings I ate some of the cooked bananas and Zenie forced down a bit of the fish from the packets above us. I lay back at rest, wishing to watch her face and listen to her words—I had to be suspicious.

But 'Ami, raucous and earthy, seemed more naturally honest than any Polynesian with whom I have worked. She told us of her schooling in Mahanatoa when she studied with the wife of Daniel, the French gendarme of that period. The woman was named Mary, and they called her Marie Antoinette. Afterward 'Ami had continued her studies with the wife of the succeeding gendarme. To demonstrate her powers of memory she sang us a rip-roaring version of the "Marseillaise" and then recited her multiplication tables. She was particularly proud of her knowledge that "the earth is round—like a ball." Periodically she assumed a dignified role, setting a pair of ancient eyeglasses (minus ear pieces) well down on her nose so as not to interfere with her vision, and told of her ancestors—and then of her own knowledge.

A wistful daughter squatted silently in the corner, smoking one of Zenie's cigarettes with appreciation, and the naked children of the family crowded in the doorway periodically. They scattered at 'Ami's exasperated wave of the hand—only to return within seconds. 'Ami deprecated the type of knowledge exhibited by Tauira'i, asserting that it was "obtained from books rather than by right of association with knowledgeable ancestors." In turn, she boasted of her own learning, the knowledge which she had obtained from the *tupuna*, the ancient forefathers. As she put it, she "guards it in the stomach." (Polynesians conceive of the stomach, not the head, as the seat of sensation and emotion.) 'Ami told us that she began learning the ancient lore at the age of eight and continued until her grandmother died when she was fifteen. To prove her ability she began chanting, rolling out lines as they must have been rendered upon the ancestral temples. Then she told of the spears and other weapons which she had once seen, now burned or given as presents to passing Europeans. She told of Tehaupā'ige, the great-great-grandmother of her father. Aneane, her mother of birth (Tūahu) died at age eighty-four and was the sister of Mōutoa, mother of our venerable Hapai.

Zenie, hair awry from her ride, was nervously translating. I strained to check her French and English words against my poor speaking knowledge of Tahitian and Ra'ivavaean. It was at this point that I commenced probing with questions. 'Ami told me of Hapai, and how he had "always been looking for old people to talk with about the old days and about ancient speech." He had begun to learn from Pastor Ha'uti, but the latter had died by the time Hapai was ten years old. "The real school for ancient lore was conducted by the chief Te Ehu —it was Te Ehu [deceased in 1903] who had committed things to a book." But Hapai did not *really* begin to have knowledge until he was some fifteen years old. Hapai's important learning came from old Haramū. Not only had 'Ami actually heard Hapai talking with Haramū, but she had herself learned things from this same sage. Our informant was not sure of her exact date of birth, but she explained that she was ten years old when Haramū died; at this time Piahuru was in school at Papeete, studying to be an instructor. She also told of learning about the old days from the ancient crone Terāpu'atea—a woman "so old that her navel had reverted to her backside." (She was born in 1824 and died in 1901.)

It was this ancestress, Terāpu'atea who was tattooed. 'Ami

said that she had pierced ears and was tattooed upon the outside of the thighs. This tattooing was a social necessity. The old woman had explained to her, "We have to have this—if we had not done so the men would not like us." When I asked her what the designs were like she smoothed a place in the sand by the fire. With a faggot she carefully drew a picture that I immediately recognized as the ancient Austral Island "sun" motif, a pattern which to the best of my knowledge had not been seen on High Island other than on the forbidden marae, in generations! There were, she said, three or four of these designs tattooed upon each limb. Men were also tattooed upon the arms.

An uproar of children's voices in the background and the shouts of men in the big house told us that a passing stallion had frightened Zenie's grazing mare, causing it to break its bonds and run away. 'Ami was now giving me answers as rapidly and as convincingly as Hapai once must have given them to Stimson. This was in itself a danger signal to my overly cautious mind. As she poured out more and more information I kept pressing her for specifications as to names, dates, sexual practices, terminology, and the like.

Our elderly informant told us of the modern practice of 'amurepo, the French soixante neuf, and of the ancient practice of cunnilingus, hoŋehoŋe. She then repeated what she had originally told Zenie. She had herself seen the lengthy clitoris of her grandmother, an organ as long as the first two joints of her little finger. She had been told that under the supervision of grandparents the mother mouthed the organ (just as she also continually pulled at the penis of the boy children "in order to make it long") and then tied it with a cord made of the inner bark of the hibiscus tree, prepared by soaking it in the sea. Although 'Ami herself made a wry face and said that it was "disgusting," she repeated that in those days a woman had to endure this treatment in order to prepare her for a suitable marriage. This was, she said, related to the desire of men. One must make attractive "what a man sees all the time!"

According to 'Ami, it was the king who examined the clitoris of women to see whether or not they were ready for marriage. He "used his eyes"—not an instrument; if the organ was not properly prepared he would show the parents how to make it right. It was after this inspection that the girls displayed their genitals upon the marae in order that young men might see their beauty. In contrast with Hapai, however, 'Ami insisted that there was only one "sexual-inspection marae," that of Atoraŋi. This, she said, was "the greatest marae."

I then produced the list I had made of words from Stimson's erotic glossary; these I had translated for no one. Yet from 'Ami's somewhat shamed lips tumbled the translations of these terms for the immensely varied outlets for man's sexual desires. She explained that her knowledge of these words derived from stories about Tage, one of the ancestral beings in her own kin line. "These are the ancient histories of an evil spirit who loved women and was always changing them. He invented these words for positions he used with them long ago." She had heard these stories from old Terāpu'atea, as well as from old man Tehaupā'igi. Even the 'a'o vao medicine used to aid pregnant woman was told in a "story of Tage."

'Ami then went on to the sphere of religion. She believed that the great stone images, the tiki, were themselves "the gods," and that Tauira'i's "supreme God," Iaha, was only one of the tiki on Marae Unurau—an image now smashed into fragments. But, she insisted, each person had his own God; the belief system varied from person to person. Again 'Ami noted that the first and foremost marae was that of Atoraŋi. The name Io to her signified "a guardian, not a god, of Marae Huānja." The details of worship upon the marae were not completely known to her. What she did know was difficult to

obtain, since it was quite erotic. She said that when men had
finished praying to god upon the marae, and the paraphernalia (or the god) was carefully wrapped up and put away,
they were then sexually excited. Copulation took place in the
temple. The positions were varied, and such acts as cunnilingus
performed. After intercourse the human sperm was smeared
upon the face and in the hair as a kind of *mono'i* (the Polynesian unguent, a perfumed coconut oil).

'Ami would not say much more, and soon we took our leave.
On the way home we stopped to talk with Mama Iē and her
cousin. All during our stay I had attempted to avoid leading
questions, but now it seemed important to check directly with
these aged women who had proved to be so patient and so
human. From them I confirmed the facts of 'Ami's kinship.
I learned, too, that they also had seen the tattooing on old
men and women and viewed the large clitoris of 'Ami's ancestress when she bathed. The ancestress had been a resident
of Anatonu in the household of Hapai. During her senility,
when from time to time she paraded nakedly upon the street,
there had been every opportunity to witness the remnant of
pagan days. They also had heard of the erotic marae ceremonies, and of the practice of smearing sperm upon the face after
temple copulation.

From a discussion of these facts we went on to Hapai, who
was also, I found, a kinsman of theirs. They felt that he had
"learned from a book." Although he had never personally told
them of the old days, at marriages, funerals, and ceremonies of
all kinds he was apt to give "a great talk, from the book, just
as does Tauira'i now from the books of his grandmother—and
Piahuru from the books of Tauira'i." He "gave his speeches
in the old Ra'ivavae language." The ancient women from
whom 'Ami had learned died when Mama and her cousin
were in their mid-teens.

Equally important, Mama revealed that Piahuru had been

deliberately concealing sexual information from me, since it was "dirty," as well as other data. The day I had left him in Mama's house while I went inland to check the marae he preferred not to visit, he had discussed with her the very words which I had read off to 'Ami that morning, and which she had (albeit somewhat shamed by) defined for me in a manner which indicated that Stimson's definitions were correct. Piahuru had previously denied ever having heard of these, when I read off the same list to him, yet he had repeated words and definitions such as these to my aged friend:

Haŋi—"To stimulate the genitals with the mouth"
Pa-kika—"For a female with an enlarged clitoris to mount
    another female"
Tā-amu—"To work upon the penis with the mouth"
Tiki-roa—"The penis"
Tiki-poto—"The clitoris"
Huripopo—"Public sodomy"

He had denied that there was any connection between sex and the temple—yet even in the marae which he owned we had found a segment of a phallic image. When asking about marriage customs in the village he had said that "most people get married before sleeping together"; yet when I made a family-by-family check with him, we found that of the thirty-one marriages studied, twenty-nine of the couples had lived together before marriage—and the two exceptions he still claimed were his own kinsmen. I was forced to conclude that in some subjects a European-inspired sense of modesty overcame Piahuru's natural sense of truth.

The day's events left me in a quandary. With the discovery of this new informant my immediate reaction was to stay on at Ra'ivavae and explore 'Ami's knowledge to the full. Yet this was impossible. The Mareva had returned for us and we were to sail within twenty-four hours. Not only was the schedule rigidly made out, but the operating costs of holding her here would be prohibitive (we had already badly overstretched the original budget). Although I had no funds to hold the ship, I did toy with the idea of sending all the others back on the *Mareva* and remaining by myself to work with 'Ami. But, in all truth, I saw no reason for this. I had completed my own ethnological studies within self-imposed limitations, and to gather more significant data would require a lengthy additional stay and an entirely different method of approach. And I was convinced, too, that any further information from 'Ami would not really be pertinent to the major purposes for which I had come to Ra'ivavae: the task of drawing my own picture of life as it is lived today and evaluating the validity of Frank Stimson's picture of former life, and then determining from these data what universal truths lay beneath the interplay of sexual and religious factors.

For after listening carefully to 'Ami and comparing what she had to say with what I knew of life in Polynesia in ancient days, the concepts which had slowly been forming in my mind over the past months had now crystallized. I was absolutely sure that 'Ami was completely lacking in guile; equally, I was now sure that Hapai was honest, too. Yet I knew that 'Ami's stories bore little exact resemblance to Hapai's and I suspected that neither account jibed exactly with historical "truth"— things as they really were. I felt that the accounts of both were *based* upon truth. Neither had consciously lied, and the differing details of their stories were a reflection of varied cultural and personal factors. This sort of variation I had now come to believe was inescapable when dealing with accounts of long-past events.

The fact that there was a strong erotic basis to the ancient religion was inescapable. The fact that parents lengthened the clitoris as a mark of beauty was clearly corroborated. But we were wrong in asking our friends such questions as those concerning the number of "sexual-inspection maraes" or the exact nature of the ceremonies conducted there. As for the number of the maraes, Hapai had recounted some sixty odd; 'Ami noted that there was only one for the entire island. Certainly it would have been unreasonable to expect maidens from enemy tribes to assemble together on a single inviolate marae. But it is equally certain that even in Ra'ivavae's heyday there were not enough nubile girls to justify sixty special sexual-inspection maraes. Personally I would venture to say that there was probably one particular "sexual-inspection marae"—or at least one marae used for this as well as for other purposes—in each of the formerly independent districts of the island. The other temples which Hapai recounted probably represented the well-known Polynesian family marae; these may have served occasionally (among other functions) as sites in connection with clitoral lengthening.

The more I pondered the matter the more it seemed to me that the anthropologists are often more to blame than the informants when conflicting information is given. When we ask abstract historical questions—such as "Did your ancestors do so-and-so? Why did they do thus and thus?"—we are expecting the informant to do our work for us, for one simple fact is inescapable: they were not there. Despite the great age of Haramū, who was the teacher of 'Ami and Hapai, it is obvious that he was not there, for the functioning culture of ancient Ra'ivavae had died before he was born. Ra'ivavae had died in the great epidemic of the 1820's. It died with the passing of the warriors and sages, the kings and priests, with the coming of Christianity. What was left, even to old Haramū, were vague accounts of old practices, stray bits of surviving custom now removed from the context which once gave them meaning. Many of these old ways soon were to be labeled by the people of High Island as "heathen, dirty, contemptible." What did survive in a way were the folk tales and folk histories, which were either written down in old books or passed on orally to the few interested youth of the land: to Hapai, and to 'Ami, and to some extent to Tauira'i. I do not include Piahuru, for as a partially educated and self-styled "sophisticate" he had no interest in the past until in his declining years he saw there a source of personal aggrandizement and profit.

It is in these stories that the gems of ethnographic information lay. It was in collecting and translating these stories that Frank Stimson made his greatest ethnological contribution. When he and Seabrook worked with Tauira'i and Hapai, gathering stories, collating and interpreting the facts contained in them in order to gain ethnographic information, they were on solid ground. When they asked the old men "what" and "why" about ancient days, they erred. For Hapai and Tauira'i, and later Piahuru, could only ponder the ancient stories for the facts which would enable them to give an answer. And it is inescapable that as analysts and scholars the High Islander is far more poorly equipped than the stranger.

There may be some who say that Hapai, or Tauira'i, or Piahuru, or 'Ami lied. This shows a lack of understanding. I am willing to admit that Piahuru may be at fault for deliberately concealing information which he had been paid to give, or when he attempted to draw a veil of Christian prudishness over the ways of his ancestors. But Hapai's many errors in dates and facts are probably due to the typical Polynesian lack of segregated time-period sense coupled with the Polynesian storyteller's genius for being specific. The Polynesian does not speak vaguely; the language is innately definite and specific. When the Polynesian speaks to the foreigner, his cultural need to be precise leads him into errors of "fact." He sets a date for the purpose of telling his story, not as an aspect of conscious truth or falsehood. To the Polynesian these specifics are essentially of supreme unimportance. They are told in order to make his story whole. Polynesian life cycles, for example, do not move along by individual years. To the islander, there are periods of infancy, childhood, youth, adulthood, old age—periods which in actual years may differ widely from one individual to another. The exact chronological period is of no importance to him, though it may be for us. Those of us who have lived in the islands have all had the experience of being told by a good friend that a place was only a "short distance" away, only to find that it is many miles away.

Truth is obviously a different thing for the Polynesian than it is for us, particularly for the Western scientific mind. For the Polynesian, "truth" is a concept related not to facts, but to speech. The Tahitian words for "truth" are *parau mau*—"firm speech" or "fixed talk." To the Polynesian this "fixed talk" about the past has two sources: the "talk" of his kinsman (particularly elderly folk) and "books." As do other simple folk, the Polynesian of today is likely to consider the printed or written word as *"parau mau"*—something true merely because it is "fixed" on paper—especially if it is on a paper passed down in his own family.

Though the data of Hapai, 'Ami, and the others may be false in detail, I think that on the whole it has a basis in truth. The only literature these people have today is the oral literature of the past and the mistranslated version of the Bible. In the Bible are no stories of temples devoted to the inspection of the clitoris, of sodomistic exhibitions upon the altars of god, of smearing of sperm upon priestly faces, of the use of the exaggerated female genitalia as a mark of marriage preparation. I have found no trace of any of these concepts in the literature which Stimson had access to when he began to work and which he might have used to prime his informants. My comparative studies, the objects I have seen preserved in museums, my linguistic analyses, all have served to convince me that while such stories are poor in detail, they represent basic truths about the Polynesian past.

Fittingly, we left High Island on a Sunday. It was a day of sad emotions and slapstick comedy, a miniature version of our entire stay here. I was awake at five o'clock and had to rouse Tioti for the first time since our arrival. Pogi was outside cleaning up the front lawn, making things attractive for our last few hours. Tino brought us a chicken as a going-away present, and Uncle Bert gave me a dozen eggs in a beautiful pandanus basket—after first having shrewdly asked me to carry a sack of taro to his son in Papeete and begging an envelope in which to write a letter advising him of the gift.

I went to my last daybreak service and was so impressed with the young chap who led the meeting that I decided to give way to his pleadings and take him to Tahiti with us. We had to sign him up as a member of the crew, since half the island was besieging us for passage and we were not allowed to take anyone not connected with our work. Afterward we were very happy to have done so, for Zenie found that his wife had given birth to a "blue baby." The French physicians in Tahiti had advised her that the only way the baby's life could be saved would be for her to allow them to send the infant to Paris for an operation. The terrified mother refused, and our friend wanted to go to Tahiti and arrange to save his baby's life.

Our final breakfast was a good one—Zenie's own excellent French pancakes, our last Ra'ivavaean coffee, the fresh cheese which the captain had brought to us from Papeete. Immediately following this, Zenie, Ta'oto, and her scamp of a niece washed all the dishes and pans and I packed them in our cases. All was finished and stowed away on board the *Mareva* by the time the church service began. All of us but Jim attended, for he was still recovering from the effects of bareback riding on one of the High Island horses. The pastor favored us with a prayer for our safe voyage to Tahiti.

Following church services we went directly to the house of our landlord, Toāri'i, who had invited us to a farewell feast.

He had done it up in full Polynesian style, and no one could accuse him of meanness. The pig which he had killed for the affair was worth far more than the rent we had paid him for the entire stay! Besides the pork on the nicely laid table were mounds of fish, *popoi*, taro, pancakes (for my special benefit), puddings, bread from the Chinaman—all the varied dishes that the High Islander could conceive of. Our pastor was with us, and the meal—watched over by Toāri'i's entire family, who had prepared it out of affection for us—was both gay and sad. We all took great pains to taste everything. As we finished, Toāri'i spoke on behalf of his whole family. He noted that we had started out as friends, but had finished up by becoming one big family. Particularly notable to him was the fact that there had never been a misunderstanding between us in the course of our stay. Speaking through Alan, I replied as best I could. I noted our affection for Polynesians in general and Toāri'i and his family in particular, and gave our deep appreciation for all they had done for us. Then, following a final round of handshaking and kisses, we made an immediate departure.

The whole village was on the shore to say good-by, and we walked through a gamut of handshakes and farewell Polynesian *hoŋi* as we made our way to the waiting dinghy. Ta'oto, Mama Iē, the Widow-in-brown, and all our other friends had farewell wreaths for Zenie and me. Clearly all were sorry to see us go, and all wanted to know how soon it would be before we would return. As we struggled with our badly overloaded dinghy, with the wind and current against us, Alan's beautiful white hat blew off into the water. Someone retrieved it for him and he clapped it on his head. Water streamed down over his face. Then Jim's hat—decorated with two valuable tropic bird feathers—blew off into the water, and he leaped into the lagoon, clothes and all, to retrieve it, almost swamping the dinghy. After this bit of comedy it took us half an hour to

make the few hundred yards to the ship. Our last glimpse of
the village was that of the overwhelming bulk of the church,
its white walls glistening in the morning sunlight, its bright-
red roof contrasting brilliantly with the green foothills and
violet-gray cliffs behind it. Soon we were off Ra'irua, where we
paid final farewell calls on the gendarme, picked up the mail
for Tahiti, denied the Chinese storekeeper's final request for a
bottle of rum, and put out to sea. For hours we watched the precipitous outline of High Island becoming smaller and then we
were out of sight.

EPILOGUE

WHAT did it all mean, this mélange of data about the new and the old ways of life on Ra'ivavae? As the *Mareva* made her way to Tahiti and then to my next site of study on the island of Mangaia, I had time to ponder the questions I had asked myself before we had arrived at Ra'ivavae. Some answers came easily, some with more difficulty. Some did not emerge until after I had completed my work in the Village of God.

Clearest was the confirmation that ancient Ra'ivavae had been as grand, as erotic, and as fierce as Stimson had depicted. His manuscript was justified. I found no indication of exaggeration or that he had projected his own emotions upon this vanished world. In fact, the stone remains we found on Ra'ivavae and those I previously had studied in museums and was to see later in my travels, together with wooden objects preserved elsewhere in the world, might urge one to say that Stimson's depiction was not as grand as it might have been.

When we had finished the field studies, the whole Ra'ivavaean cultural picture jelled in my mind. From the broken fragments of stone and scattered wooden artifacts I could visualize the originals with startling clarity: misshapen images became the obviously proud bodies of long-pregnant women, a smoothly finished eccentric curve of stone became the superb torso of a young girl in the first proud swellings of motherhood. Only these tangible remains in stone, bone, and wood were evidence of the grandeur that once had been. Nothing was to be found in the behavior of the Ra'ivavaeans today which suggested their fierce and erotic past.

Occasionally Seabrook and I differed with Stimson's detailed translations, but we found no indication of falsified evidence or lack of critical judgment within his sphere of competence.

Despite my confirmation of Stimson's personal integrity, I was somewhat unhappy about his informants' data. I could not share the enthusiasm of Stimson for Hapai. Although A-Tangaroa-i-Mahara was proven to be the first-born descendant of the kings of Mahanatoa, I could not verify Stimson's opinion that he was "the greatest of all the Polynesian sages." The omissions of facts by Piahuru and the unconscious commission of errors of analysis by Tauira'i had not been lies, but their testimony was far from expert. The best explanation of the significance of the data has been given by Hamilton Basso in his essay on Stevenson's experiences with the Polynesians of Samoa:

. . . All their own stories, their myths and legends, had some assumed relation to fact—these were the old times, and these were the old gods, and this was what happened—they do not know what it is to make up a story.

The information given Stimson was correct in its general effect, but incorrect in certain details.

I was satisfied with the progress we had made in the allocated period. Our general objective had been achieved. In thousands of pages of notes, and hundreds of photographs, sketches, and paintings, we had recorded in broad outline how modern Ra'ivavaeans lived and worked and loved. When contrasted with the pre-European picture which Frank Stimson had drawn of life on Ra'ivavae, it helped us to understand what happens to humans under certain social and economic conditions—and why.

My first lesson was clear-cut: I learned that patterns of culture may die without leaving a trace, despite the fact that the people who once molded their existence to such patterns continued to live. Perhaps I should have known this from my schooling, but I confess that such was not the case. Even after my first trip to Ra'ivavae and the initial shock of viewing these puritanic and culturally impoverished remnants of a once exotic civilization, I had harbored the belief that such a rich past could not vanish without a trace. I had hoped to find in some secret spot in the hills or on the *motu*, or in the guise of innocent merriment within the village, a hidden trace of love for beauty, some public acknowledgment of the social function of the display of erotica, some remnant of heroic daring. But my hopes vanished in the light of our systematic acquisition of knowledge of what went on in modern Ra'ivavae.

The civilization of the past was dead; not only functionally dead, but as good as forgotten. All of the old ways of life that were not concerned with bread alone, or with the most elemental kin relationships, were gone.

It was not so much the new ways of the West which had driven out ancient custom as it was that wave of disease which followed the Western arrival. Patterns of culture had died with the death of those who could pass on the ways of the past to those who might carry them into the future. And with the drastic decline in population, with the disappearance of warfare and of the old gods and the old temples and the old foci of all that was colorful and stimulating in life, there passed the conditions which could have been strong enough to provide a link with the past.

There were two important exceptions to this loss. Although most of the ancient behavior patterns were dropped, the attitudes which had been associated with them were not replaced by Western attitudes. Thus, the ancient values are still alive.

This was true, for example, in the acceptance of Christianity. The Western attitudes of the newly accepted patterns were antithetical to those of the old, yet the High Islander adopted those patterns without having any idea of the implications they were to have for him. This fact was of the utmost significance in explaining certain contradictions of behavior in the field of religion and sexual behavior, and to this we will return shortly.

The second exception was that in certain spheres, such as local and introduced diseases, there were no practical Western cultural patterns to take the place of the old. Hence the Ra'ivavaean continues his ancient practice in curing bodily ills.

The effect of geographic environment on human behavior and human affairs offers the best example of the retention of some few ancient patterns. Because of the shallow fringe reef which surrounds the island and the wide lagoon which separates the shore from the economically valuable *motu*, the sewn canoe is still the best solution to intra-island transportation, although the construction of seagoing ships has been halted. Taro continues as the best food crop, but when the system for allocating water was lost and the islanders were unable to keep in workable shape the complex engineering feats required to water the taro patches, they shifted to dry-land taro techniques, despite the inferior flavor.

Even the few old techniques which remain are probably doomed to extinction. We could clearly see that the decline in population had reduced leisure time; the available labor source is barely adequate to provide the day-to-day necessities of life. Brief changes in weather can now bring about long periods of hunger; short storms can cripple the entire island. Changes in the pattern of life, such as the shift from pandanus shacks to limestone houses, could trigger a cycle of events which will make the island even more susceptible to the whims of nature.

Remote Ra'ivavae now has a close relationship to the economic cycles of the Western world. Changes in the price of coffee beans in America or Europe, for example, mean feast or famine to High Islanders. Having tasted the fruits of a cash economy—English cloth, New Zealand tinned beef, flour, sugar, kerosene, paint, watches, and costume jewelry—the Ra'ivavaean will never again be content to return to a diet of fish and taro, or the hammering out of bark-cloth clothing. He has to depend on our Western economy.

Immediately following the crash of the old gods and the ensuing cycle of death, the focus of life had been the daily meal, to the exclusion of all else. But now the islander is seeking some new reward and meaning from life. This reward must be wrought from the geographic resources of the island. During our stay we saw the start of the changes to come. All the available land is planted with coffee, thus the Ra'ivavaean seeks new resources to exploit, such as pearl shell from the lagoon and coconuts from the land on the *motu*, where pandanus are being cut and ironwood trees burned off to make room for new coconut trees. This shift in the ecology of the island will eventually have repercussions, as did the cutting of the protecting windbreak of the ironwood trees which once surrounded the island.

In addition to geographic environmental factors there are social forces at work. Clearly there has been a loss of social complexity on the island, as one would expect with the reduction of population from many thousands to a single hundred in less than a generation. With a reduction in the size of the family which lives in single households, and with the greater opportunity for young men to earn cash on other islands, there is a loss in the social power of older folk.

Too, aggressive democracy prevails on Ra'ivavae. This is due, possibly, to the cessation of war, traditional training ground of leaders, and the acceptance of outside civil and religious administration. There is no opportunity or need to develop new leaders to replace the kings, chiefs, judges, priests, and magicians of the past.

Yet such a loss of leadership has not occurred on the island of Mangaia. In the Village of God, the *Aroŋo Mana,* "those of power," still control the system of land tenure. They adjudicate boundary disputes, redistribute unworked land, and handle the periodic reconstruction of dikes and the water distribution in the taro fields. Mangaia is the only Eastern Polynesian island where the land is locally controlled; Mangaia is the only island to retain an effective pattern of local leadership. In Polynesia, where from the land comes life itself, he who controls the land holds the reins of power. On Ra'ivavae, as elsewhere through Polynesia, when the local people gave away their right to handle their own problems of land tenure, they also gave away the only avenue to leadership which was left. With the training ground for leadership gone there is nothing in the modern conditions of life on Ra'ivavae strong enough to create a link with the past.

But what of the special problem I had set for myself on Ra'ivavae, and from the analysis of which I hoped to derive something of value in understanding the ways of man—the end goal of my life's work? In choosing sex and religion to compare past and present Ra'ivavae, and then comparing Ra'ivavae with general Polynesian patterns, and finally contrasting Polynesian patterns with those of the Western way of life, I had hoped to derive rules about why man does the things that he does.

My first step was to confirm that religious worship in ancient Ra'ivavae had involved ceremonial copulation on the temple altars, and that concern with the genitals had occupied much of the activity of the Polynesians of High Island. I was able to confirm this as a result of data obtained directly from our Ra'ivavaean informants, such as 'Ami and Mama Iē, from archaeological remains from High Island, and from comparitive studies of the Polynesian marae, the Polynesian language, Polynesian ethnology, and objects of Polynesian material culture which remain preserved in museums.

Although I was not able to gather details enough to reconstruct the actual order of events during ceremonies which involved sexual intercourse on the marae, the verification that such copulation had taken place was enough to set apart Ra'ivavae in particular and Polynesia in general from the rest of the world.

There has been temple prostitution in other times and other places in man's history. Priests and priestesses have been available for sexual usage. Indeed, some of the Near-Eastern cults went so far as to include the partaking of bread spread with human sperm in their rites. But rarely, if ever, has there been actual copulation in the temples related to the propitiation of the gods. In certain Hindu cults, now held in disrepute by the majority of adherents to Hinduism and thought to stem back to the pre-Hindu era in India, there is worship which involves the linga and the yoni, male and female parts of generation. The cult's temples, like the Ra'ivavaean marae, held huge reproductions of the male phallus. Carved on the temple walls were the innumerable ways in which man and woman, in couples and in groups, could unite in sexual pleasures, and in the temple proper priests and worshipers alike, regardless of kin relationships and age differences, copulated in the frenzy of worship. As in Polynesia, there was a reason for this kind of behavior. Esoterically, the highest priesthood believed that copulation cemented man to the universal sea of existence, while the common priests and worshipers believed that such couplings ensured fertility and fructification of man and nature alike. It is to those areas in India and Southeast Asia where such practices took place—and to some degree still do—that our most learned ethnologists trace the origin of the Polynesian peoples!

But my concern with the nature of the connection between sex and religion on Ra'ivavae was of a different order than the tracing of possible historical migration routes and locating points of origin. On this voyage we were more interested in answering questions which began with "what" and "why," rather than those merely concerned with "when" and "from where."

Why? Why in ancient Ra'ivavae were there exhibitions of sexual coupling upon the altars of God? Why were huge stone images of man's prime organ of generation and those of woman in her supreme moment first graven and then placed in the temples? Why did people spend hours, weeks, years of activity in attempting to change the shape of God-given organs of joy? Perhaps the dark grandeur of ancient Ra'ivavae reflected a survival of the most ancient past, patterns developed in India or Southeastern Asia which were carried on through the millennia, much as certain Hindu sects continue to carry on similar erotic patterns. Some scholars might be satisfied with this, but I am not convinced that it is the best explanation.

To begin with, it is likely that the Ra'ivavaean intensity upon man's supreme passion represented a local efflorescence of one of the major facets of general Polynesian culture. Just as on the island of Mangaia the warrior-hero had personified the development of an extreme concern with personal combat, so in Ra'ivavae a concern with the erotic eventually became a dominant theme in the culture. The theme was a characteristic of all Polynesian groups. But each group seemed to place overwhelming emphasis on its theme.

Author Robert Dean Frisbie had sensed the sexual factor in modern Polynesian life and had hinted at it in his work; yet Frank Stimson was, I believe, the first scholar to glimpse in full measure the significance of the sexual theme to Eastern Polynesian culture. But Stimson had seen this upon a subjective rather than an objective basis. His long years of association with aged sages, and his decades of experience in translating the Polynesian sagas and tales, had made him feel that the culture had an erotic basis. Because he lacked certain professional training, however, many of his conclusions did not contain the detailed substantiation which scientists require before accepting the work of an "outsider." Because his conclusions pointed to a way of life which could have been practiced in our own culture only by a person with a diseased mind, those who preferred the smug innocuous picture of early Polynesian life were shocked. Thus Stimson's beliefs were little heeded by his own colleagues.

That Eastern Polynesian culture was—and to a somewhat lesser degree still is—immensely oriented to the sexual pleasures has escaped many scholars. This lacuna is partly a result of our immense preoccupation with such special investigations as the classification of stone tools, the preservation of string figures, the comparison of plaiting techniques, and the recording and analysis of kinship terminologies. In part it is a result of older techniques of field research, which involve brief trips to outer islands, with most of one's time spent interrogating a few old informants who are partially imbued with Western mannerisms. Their attitude is best reflected by one of them who said to a great Polynesian anthropologist: "How can we know what was in the mind of the heathen!"

In part, however, the lack of knowledge stems from the early missionaries who zealously eradicated Polynesian public behavior which did not conform to English lower middle class concepts of "respectability." These missionaries, horror-stricken at the mere intimation of what had been going on, were the first to suggest that the physical indications of this darkness be burned, buried, or broken. Their converts, went to even greater lengths to rid themselves of the material and social evidence of "heathen ways." The erotic images were destroyed, although some were hidden in remote caves. The warriors' long hair was cut off, and women's once cropped locks were allowed to grow naturally; the body hair which was once so aesthetically offensive was allowed to grow naturally rather than be plucked out;

dancing was forbidden and golden bodies were covered with shapeless dresses and long trousers; perfumed oil was no longer rubbed into the skin, and the wearing of flowers became "sinful"; extra wives were cast aside and Christian marriage became the requisite rite of passage to responsible adulthood and membership in the only significant nonkinship social group, the *Etarētia*.

Yet the attempts of converts to destroy the erotic work of their ancestors could not conceal evidence from those who would patiently search it out. In the dusty basements and cluttered exhibits of the public and private museums of New Zealand, England, Scandanavia, and many other countries of Europe; in the United States, and in Australia, are to be found the material remains of Polynesian culture—objects recovered from caves and swamps or brought back by explorers and whalers before the missionaries took over. Carved in wood and in stone are indications of the overwhelming Polynesian concern with copulation and with the sexual organs. Objects used in every phase of life, such as door lintels, war clubs, temple plaques, and digging sticks are a depiction of either the erect male member or the spread female organ. The objects vary: an eighteen-foot sacred male phallus; stylized reproductions of the tremendously enlarged clitoris; the portrayal of ecstasy, with the couple in the more usual forms of copulation as well as unique depictions of pennilingus and cunnilingus. And these are not an oceanic version of our stag-party movie films or toilet-wall scribblings. These are, where they survive, the major element in the decor of every aspect of life—on boxes for holding feather ornaments and on boxes for holding the bones of the dead; on spear throwers and on the prows of great canoes; on containers for holding coals of fire and in the wands of the priests. Nor are they unique to one group, for the objects come from all islands; from Easter Island and New Zealand, from Hawaii, the Marquesas, and the Southern Cooks.

And just as culture is a "mirror for man," so is language the mirror of culture. One may also carry out "linguistic archaeology," much as we may dig in the earth for cultural remains. In the language of Polynesia, amid the dialects of Samoa, and those of the far-flung Tuamotus, unmistakable evidence of the Polynesians' fascination with sex survives. As one of the most important early recorders of ethnological data has said, "The predominant theme of conversation from youth to old age is the coition of the sexes." In no other language does one special word, *tīrau*, pithily convey that "a pair of copulating turtles has been seen." Where else in the world are the highest-ranking chiefs known as the *uretu*, the "erect penis"? From lengthy and detailed linguistic analysis, from the study of material remains, from the scraps of data in the journals of early explorers and missionaries, and from a study of modern Polynesian beliefs and behavior, data have been gathered which prove that Stimson's interpretations of the sexual basis of Polynesian life were, if anything, conservative.

Other questions plagued me. Why were not the copulatory pleasures considered "profane," as they are in our own civilization, rather than "sacred," the *noa* rather than the *tapu*? The answer lies in understanding the basis of Polynesian religion and the meaning and function of the ancient marae.

Our modern term "religion" probably is derived in part from the Latin term *religare*, "to bind together." And this binding together, that is, the binding of those of the past and present to those of the future, is a major function of the Polynesian marae.

Closely related to the sexual factor were the innumerable *tara*, the still upright pointed or rounded rods of stone which we had found scattered in the courtyards of the many temples we visited. Although *tara* itself is an erotic pseudonym (for it means literally "any sharp pointed projection"—including the penis or the clitoris), it is more enlightening to discuss it under

its alternate term *tutiki*, "ancestral upright," or "an ancestor."
For *tiki*, the word which Thor Heyerdahl misunderstood as a
"Polynesian God" in the Marquesas and thence was inspired
to his subsequent fabulous adventures, is in fact not only a
term for any "image of a human," but it is the name of the
"first man." It is, indeed, a common and ancient term for the
human phallus, male or female. And it is these *tutiki* which
symbolize the connection between past and present in the
marae—the structure which the Polynesian characterizes as "a
temple consecrated to the two thighs of the Earth-Mother—
ever bringing forth children into this world of light."

These temples, scene of ceremonies which were rich in color,
were the focal point of all life in ancient times. On the pagan
altar the enemies of society were sacrificed to the gods to insure
prosperity and the continuation of life. Here the *tara* or the
tutiki represented the seed of the past being passed to the present via the phallus. This was the ancient Polynesian religion:
the continuation of power from its age-old source via the increase of the family. Hence on Mangaia the warrior copulated
with his wife in the marae in order that the resulting child
might be a warrior, like his father, and his fathers before him.
And so in Ra'ivavae the priests copulated before their congregation, and smeared the life-giving sperm, which connected the
lines of ancestry, upon the most sacred part of the body, the
head.

Why did they encourage public copulation? We will never
know exactly. Perhaps some strong individual persuaded his
fellows to follow this direction, possibly the culture hero, Tage,
to whom 'Ami alluded. Whatever or whoever incited the original approach, it is clear that in permitting public sexual exhibitions the Ra'ivavaeans were tinkering with an explosive
social force which most other cultures keep more rigidly
controlled.

Why did the Ra'ivavaeans publicly emphasize the enlargement of the clitoris? Once again this is a general Polynesian pattern brought to its most exaggerated social form in Ra'ivavae. The original emphasis upon clitoris enlargement stems from general Oceanic practice. Attempts of the family members to enlarge the clitoris of the newborn female child stem from islands as far apart as Ponape in Micronesia to Easter Island in Polynesia.

In Gray's *Anatomy* the clitoris is defined as "an erectile structure, homologous with the penis," and it is noted to be "partially hidden between the anterior ends of the labia minora." Although Kinsey has clearly shown that the clitoris and the labia are the seat of female pleasure, as far as the sexual orgasm is concerned, this fact and the implications for this fact are not known to the average American male. Yet the ancient Polynesian was, and his present-day descendants still are, supremely aware of the erotic supremacy of these organs. This fact was shown in the former art motifs and is still taught to the newly superincised youth.

The difference between Polynesian and American knowledge of the clitoris is striking.

The most authoritative investigators of the sexual practices of the American male find that there are three groupings with respect to knowledge of the clitoris: a rather small number from the upper economic bracket have read marriage manuals or medical books and hence have obtained some idea of the clitoris and its actual function; another relatively small number from the lower economic brackets have some idea of the location or function of the clitoris although they do not recognize its name, referring to it, instead, as the "man in the boat" or the "spur tongue"; and there is the majority of American males who know nothing about the word *clitoris* as such, and know little about the erogenous aspects of the organ, although they may realize that the upper part of the vulva is a useful area in which to fumble during sexual play, and may even connect it with Ernest Hemingway's "island in the great river with the high steep banks."

When first I began my study of Ra'ivavae, I did not understand the factors involved in the Polynesian's regard for the clitoris. I did not believe that an organ of the human body could be markedly enlarged, and I could not comprehend the significance of such enlargement. But now it seems clear that the emphasis upon clitoral treatment of females is as related to the Polynesian concern with sexual pleasures and well-being as is the superincision of the male. The reason for this concern is amply clear in the studies of Kinsey and his associates, and in comparative data from other tribes which practice clitoral manipulation.

My disbelief in the "enlargement" of the clitoris had to be revised after careful research into the anatomy and physiology of the organ, which showed me that the actual "enlargement" was the freeing of the clitoris from its bed in the surrounding tissues of the prepuce, labia minora, and fat, and the developing of erectile powers through habitual handling. This factor is somewhat related to the so-called "increase" in the size of the clitoris of aging American females which is due to shrinkage in the surrounding tissues and fat pads. There are also racial factors which might cause an innate biological difference in size between American and Polynesian women.

The Polynesians treat the clitoris in order to expose it rather than to "enlarge" it. Both the exposure and the treatment involved appear to prepare the women for the pleasures of sex in a biological sense. In the cultural sense they were prepared by being taught what men desired to see and to experience in a woman. To have a large clitoris was to be able to attract a more suitable husband, just as having large breasts or wearing "gay deceivers" is an asset to the American woman. The distinction is that the enlarged clitoris plays a more substantial role in the enjoyment of the sexual act than do large breasts. Clearly the

Ra'ivavaeans knew this, just as they realized the connection between the clito¬is and the penis, when they nicknamed the penis the *tikiroa*, "the long ancestral figure," and the clitoris the *tikipoto*, "the short ancestral figure."

And what happened when such sexual practices were met by stringent bearers of the Christian message? Immediately dis-- carded from the social life were public fornication, the public display of feminine charms, and presumably the practices of enlarging the clitoris. The religious stress upon human procreation and fructification disappeared, as did the pagan images. The Holy Bible took their place as an object of sanctity. All that remained was the superincision of boys and extensive premarital intercourse.

Why do they no longer appeal to God for human increase? The obvious answer is that Christianity drove away war and it is, therefore, no longer necessary to increase the population in order to bring death to one's enemies.

Why did not the Christian pattern of premarital chastity become an overriding rule? The strongest answer is that the stress upon premarital chastity is a Christian ethic not spelled out in the Bible. Instead, it stems from the development of later codes of moral behavior which apply in only some parts of the Christian world. The Ra'ivavaeans, without a resident European missionary to guide them, find virtually nothing prohibiting premarital intercourse in the version of the Bible which is available to them. In their badly translated Bible the strongest sexual prohibition is against adultery, and to this prohibition they give uniform allegiance. They also have given up the varied practices of homosexuality in which they once indulged, for these also are prohibited in the Holy Book. But the new God did not specifically prohibit premarital intercourse in his written word, nor did he prescribe patterns of courting before marriage. Hence, the Polynesians retained their age-old attitudes toward private sexual intercourse.

The most significant of the retained attitudes is the super-incision ceremony for boys. This act, in their version of the Bible, is not prohibited. Indeed, does not Paul himself say that the value of circumcision is "much in every way"? The missionaries to Polynesia apparently never found out that this ceremony triggers off a boy's sexual life. From that moment on he is dedicated to seeking out partners to satisfy his urges. This means that despite the loss of the stimulus of public fornica-tion, the youth seek sexual intercourse almost as much as they once did.

It is clear that where Ra'ivavaeans were extremists in eroti-cism, they are now extremists in their Christian interpretation of sex. The Ra'ivavaean follows a path laid down by the nine-teenth-century missionary with exactitude if not with vigor. He has repatterned his daily, his weekly, and his entire life cycle so that he may go to church several times a week, and he has changed his residence pattern in order that he may live near the church. The percentage of members of the community who attend church, and the knowledge of Biblical stories held by most Ra'ivavaean adults, are reckoned as extraordinary by Westerners. But the Polynesian religion as we saw it on Ra'iva-vae, despite its Christian trappings and schedules, is not the Christianity of our Western heritage. Divorced from European ethics and morals, it is really the old Polynesian religion under a new guise, the Christian pattern. The old gods merely sleep as a new God takes their place in the daily life of the people.

Nowhere does the past and present Polynesian concept of religion vary more distinctly from the Western view than in the relationship between religion and sex and marriage which we have been discussing. No longer is the phallus revered in the temple, no longer does ceremonial copulation or sexual rite form a part of worship, yet to the Polynesian the relationship between sex and marriage remains as distinct as it was two centuries ago. And the meaning of this to those of us of the

West was best explained to me by a remark of Zenie's when we were discussing love and marriage one day. She stated that "in marriage, it is not the sexual love that is important, it is the company."

Polynesians, on the one hand, generally consider sex and sexual enjoyment to be completely distinct from marriage. From puberty both sexes know from several partners the physical joys of sex. Even on Ra'ivavae, the most puritanical of Polynesian islands, there was no realization of the basic ethical or moral concepts of Christian marriage or the Christian family by which one puts one's mate "before all others"; social companionship between the sexes was unknown apart from sexual or economic partnerships.

On the other hand, although the Polynesians have yet to glimpse the fundamental sociological and psychological truths which lay behind Christ's and Paul's concept of the Christian family, they have long since grasped truths which have escaped those of us of the West. These truths stem from the understanding that between the sexes there can be a mutually satisfactory and passionate enjoyment. Sexual gratification is not just the lot of the male. Although there are great variations in sexual compatibility between individuals, a fact which Polynesian youths realize, Ra'ivavaeans know that virtually every male can physically gratify almost every female with whom he has a sexual relationship.

This ability of the Polynesians to satisfy one another stems in part from their knowledge of the sexual organs and the physiological aspects of sex. It may well be such knowledge which insures the great stability of Polynesian marriage. Can we take this knowledge and build upon it, setting aside the Polynesian custom of "shopping around" before marriage and retaining the ideals of our own more suitable courtship patterns, to go further along the road to Christian marriage and the family? May we make use of the binding psychological forces which emotionally tie a woman to the man who first brings her the joys of sex? And is it possible to avoid the diffusion of loyalty and the disruptive forces of jealousy which result from spreading around one's sexual favors? I believe so.

And, finally, what of my ultimate goal of understanding the very bases of human behavior? The work on Ra'ivavae added up to this: the species of social animal we call man has perfected a unique means of meeting his countless individual and group needs—mating, family relationships, social relationships, the exercise of political power, aesthetic outlets, and the like. This means, called culture by the anthropologists, is a series of ready-made answers to the problems of life for a particular group in a particular place and through a particular period of time. These answers provide ready-made paths and roads of behavior which tend to form mutually consistent patterns and are passed along from one member of a group to another, either from older members to younger, or among age mates, by the medium of language. If there was no such phenomenon as language there could be no culture; in fact, the faculty of language is essentially what separates man from the other animals.

Owing to variation between individuals and to the development of both themes and counter-themes within the patterns of culture, stable societies are usually able to meet the challenge of changing geographic and social situations. However, if cultural patterns become so rigid that they cannot be changed by some individuals within the culture, then the group's way of life will be shattered if it comes up against a situation where the ready-made answer does not apply.

The shattering effect of near extermination and the loss of the old ways of life without an adequate substitute for them is what caused the death of ancient Ra'ivavae. The new patterns have not yet been fitted to the local needs and situation. Worse still, there is a clash between the attitudes and value patterns of an earlier period and the new patterns.

I learned, on the one hand, that cultural patterns were far more fragile than I had expected them to be. On the other hand, the fact that cultural attitudes may survive although the cultural patterns which produced them were gone was a revelation to me. The lack of a suitable mechanism to test, accept, and utilize what is good of the changes which history inevitably brings seems to be the death warrant of a culture. And an unwillingness to accept unorthodox individuals sounds the death knell of a society.

As I finished my field work in Polynesia and returned to teaching and research, I could not help but wonder if Western culture in the next decade would find a mechanism for change, without being shattered by new forces arising in the old continents of Africa and Asia and the newly born South American cultures, as did the Ra'ivavae which was destroyed by the forces of Western Europe.

The insights I derived from my work on Ra'ivavae were important to me; I felt that from them and from the Polynesian field work which I was to carry on in the future, in Mangaia and elsewhere, that I would be able to contribute my share of data toward the gradual accumulation of scientific knowledge about the "why" of human behavior. But I must also admit that in addition to scientific rewards there were personal pleasures of field work in Polynesia. These joys were best expressed a generation ago by Nordhoff and Hall with respect to their own work in the islands: "There remains the charm of living among people whose outlook upon life is basically different from our own; of living with a simplicity foreign to anything in one's experience, amid surroundings of a beauty unreal both in actuality and in retrospect."

GEORGE ALLEN & UNWIN LTD

London: 40 Museum Street, W.C.1

Auckland: 24 Wyndham Street
Bombay: 15 Graham Road, Ballard Estate, Bombay 1
Buenos Aires: Escritorio 454-459, Florida 165
Cape Town: 109 Long Street
Calcutta: 17 Chittaranjan Avenue, Calcutta 13
Hong Kong: F1/12 Mirador Mansions, Kowloon
Karachi: Karachi Chambers, McLeod Road
Madras: Mohan Mansion, 38c Mount Road, Madras 6
Mexico: Villalongin 32-10, Piso, Mexico 5, D.F.
New Delhi: 13-14 Ajmeri Gate Extension, New Delhi 1
Sao Paulo: Avenida 9 de Julho 1138-Ap. 51
Singapore: 36c Princep Street, Singapore 7
Sydney, N.S.W.: Bradbury House, 55 York Street
Toronto: 91 Wellington Street West

ULU: THE WORLD'S END

JORGEN BISCH

The lives of the little-known natives of British Borneo are vividly described and superbly illustrated in colour in this book by a well-known Danish travel writer and photographer.

After a journey by junk across the South China Sea on which he shared the life of the Chinese crew, the author visited Sarawak, North Borneo and the Sultanate of Brunei. Here he stayed with former head-hunters in their communal long-houses built on piles, made friends with a female medicine-man and took part in many of the day-to-day activities of these primitive tribes. The author was exceptionally successful in winning the confidence of the natives and was able to participate in their tribal ceremonies.

The climax of his adventures was a voyage by canoe over the rapids to 'Worlds End', in order to discover the pygmy Punans, who have been described as 'the most primitive people in the world', and are known to other natives of Borneo as 'the forest devils' because of their stealthy movements and the deadly accuracy of their poisoned arrows. These natives also the author succeeded in making friends with and photographing.

As a seasoned traveller, Jorgen Bisch writes with authority and sympathy and his book has great freshness and vigour.

Small Royal 8vo. 144 *pages.*

Profusely illustrated in colour and monochrome. 28s. net

WE ENDED IN BALI

SVEN GILLSATER

Taking his cameras with him Sven Gillsater, a famous Swedish photographer set out on a romantic and unforgettable journey through the remoter and still primitive parts of Indonesia. Beginning in Australia he passed through an astonishing variety of island life. There was Melville Island, an aborigine reserve in the Timor Sea; Heron Island, in the Great Barrier Reef, densely populated with sea birds; the deep jungles of Borneo and their fantastic plant life; remote Dayak communities on the Bornean equator; Komodo, the main objective, with its giant lizards, like dragons; and finally Bali, where civilisation is already making rapid inroads upon the traditional behaviour of the people.

This intrepid photographer's adventures are unusual and exciting, and they are recorded with disarming simplicity. His book is lavishly illustrated with his own pictures, in black and white and in colour.

Translated from the Swedish by F. H. LYON

Small Royal 8vo. Illustrated 30s. *net*

CHAVANTE

ROLF BLOMBERG

The Chavante are a tribe of primitive and warlike Indians who inhabit the shores of the Rio das Mortes—the River of the Dead—in the remotest jungles of Mato Grosso in Brazil. Rolf Blomberg's thrilling account of his expedition to these remote peoples is lavishly illustrated, with many photographs in colour. *Small Royal 8vo.* 30s. *net*

LONDON: GEORGE ALLEN & UNWIN LTD